Hood AND Bismarck

DAVID MEARNS AND ROB WHITE

9 8 7 6 5 4 3 2 1

A CIP catalogue record for this book is available
from the British Library.

Designed by DW Design

Printed and bound by The Bath Press

Contents

PREFACE

Saturday, 24 May 1941 was Empire Day. The previous day, in school assemblies throughout the embattled British Empire, imperial ties had been emphasized, especially in the context of the war against Germany and Italy. Britain had no allies in Europe – apart from a number of governments in exile – but she was still the centre of a global political unit on which the sun never set, held together by command of the sea.

At 05.30 a.m. British Summer Time that Saturday, the embodiment of Britain's naval strength, HMS *Hood*, was speeding through the overcast northern waters of the Denmark Strait. *Hood* was accompanied by Britain's newest battleship, HMS *Prince of Wales*. Their target was the latest and most mighty instrument of the upstart German navy, the battleship *Bismarck*, which was accompanied by the cruiser *Prinz Eugen*. The established whale was about to clash with its latest challenging elephant and the outcome must have seemed to many to be in little doubt. Yet just over half an hour later, the shattered remains of *Hood* were sinking to their permanent resting place almost 10,000 feet below on the Atlantic floor and *Prince of Wales* was being forced to beat a hasty retreat. It was the German navy's finest hour and a bitter and memorable blow for the British navy, nation and empire.

Just over seventy-two hours later, nemesis also overtook *Bismarck*. Forced to make a run for German-occupied France because of damage received from *Prince of Wales*, she had then been fatally crippled in her steering by Swordfish torpedo bombers from the aircraft carrier HMS *Ark Royal*. On the morning of 27 May, the British navy closed in for the kill. There was to be no mistake this time. *Bismarck* was overwhelmed by

the gunfire of two battleships and two heavy cruisers. In about forty minutes she was reduced to a wreck, but one that would not sink before many more shells and more torpedoes had been poured into her. The Germans, who refused to strike their colours, were reduced to trying to speed up the demise of their once-fine ship, which eventually slipped beneath the waves at 10.40 a.m. More than 1,400 men had been lost in *Hood* and more than 2,000 in *Bismarck*. Then came the final act in the tragedy. The cruiser HMS *Dorsetshire* (which had inflicted the final damage on the German ship) was reluctantly forced to leave most of the hundreds of German survivors to their fate because of the threat to the would-be rescuers from German U-boats.

Two important symbols had gone: the sleek, modernist maritime embodiment of the new German Reich and the more traditionally elegant mascot of the old British Empire. The former had been overwhelmed by superior naval power, as the Reich as a whole would be four years later; the latter by more subtle forces of strategic overstretch and technological and industrial decline. The empires that clashed in the Denmark Strait on that overcast morning were as doomed as the ships themselves had been. The brazen German Reich was to disappear faster and in a more obvious way, but the eventual collapse of the established British Empire was equally certain.

May 1941 was the last month in which Britain would be fighting an imperial war. On 22 June, Britain would finally choose to which totalitarian nation she would be forced to ally herself. It turned out to be Stalin's USSR rather than Nazi Germany, whose Deputy Führer had flown solo to Britain in a desperate attempt to achieve some kind of compromise peace only days before the *Bismarck* chase. Encouraged by Hess, Hitler saw the British Empire as a positive force in the world – if only it would grant Germany the suzerainty of Europe. Britain could not do this. Yet were the alternatives any more welcome? Stalin was the implacable foe of all imperialism but his own. Roosevelt's USA – upon whose support Britain was already coming to rely – was the foe of formal imperial control everywhere. With allies such as these, victory over Germany could only be won at a crippling price: the end of that very world position for which a united British Empire had gone to war in 1939. *Hood*'s catastrophic demise – and that of her crew, who were drawn from all parts of the empire – marks a major turning point in the history of imperial Britain and of the world.

The drama played out in the Atlantic in May 1941 thus has an historic resonance that continues to give it meaning today, although it also has enough internal drama to make it one of the greatest sagas of the sea in its own right. The story of the *Bismarck* and the *Hood* was made the subject of a classic British feature film, *Sink the Bismarck!* which helped stimulate my own interest in modern naval strategy and operations – an interest that I have been lucky enough to develop academically and professionally. The fate of *Hood*, in particular, has fascinated me. In the early 1990s, when working on an article on the sinking of *Hood* for the US Naval Institute's journal *Naval History*, I tried to get people interested in an expedition to dive on the wreck, but my efforts proved abortive. I was, therefore, especially pleased when Channel 4 asked me to act as historical adviser to the expedition to view the wrecks of *Bismarck* and *Hood* for the purpose of making two new

documentaries, one on each ship, with an additional film about the search for them. I was sure we would learn an enormous amount and I was not disappointed. For the month of July 2001, I accompanied the team in the converted trawler *Northern Horizon*. I stood by spellbound as David Mearns and his remarkably professional group of underwater explorers found both wrecks on sonar and examined them with unprecedented thoroughness using a camera-equipped, remotely-operated vehicle. The thrill of discovery was extraordinary and unforgettable. We found hitherto unseen parts of *Bismarck*, notably her forward superstructure broken off the main hull. We also found all the main pieces into which *Hood* was blown on that dreadful 24 May, as well as a huge amount of smaller debris from the once-mighty battlecruiser.

Much that is new came to light, as is described so ably in these pages by David Mearns and Rob White, a long-standing *Hood* expert and maker of an important TV programme about her a few years ago. Inevitably, our work threw up as many questions as it answered. The input of Bill Jurens, the expedition's technical adviser and a world expert and consultant on battleship design and gunnery, proved extremely valuable in our dialectical development of ideas. We had much to discuss and argue about. The full analysis of the hours of footage we brought back at the end of our month of hard work will take years of equally painstaking study. But what we have found in our preliminary analysis is interesting and significant in its own right, as I hope readers will agree.

Dr Eric Grove
Centre for Security Studies, University of Hull

Once Were
Giants

chapter **one**

MIGHTY HOOD - BIRTH OF A GIANT

Both *Hood* and *Bismarck* were born out of what seemed to those who conceived them a pressing national need – on the one hand to resist, on the other to conquer.

Throughout her twenty-year life, and entirely by chance, *Hood* was unique. She was conceived as a battlecruiser – a class of ship devised to counter the colonial threat of fast enemy cruisers descending on Britain's imperial territories overseas. Admiral Jackie Fisher's concept, when he became First Sea Lord in 1904, was that fast, but relatively lightly armoured big-gun ships – protection was sacrificed for speed – could be relied upon to defend the almost impossibly far-flung outposts of the empire from cruiser attack. The defence of home waters, he decided, could be left to the torpedo-armed destroyer and the 'unsporting' submarine. The birth of the equally revolutionary 'dreadnought' – a slower, more heavily armoured, all big-gun battleship – took attention (and funds) away from this concept, but Fisher was always to regard dreadnoughts as 'old-testament' ships. Fast battlecruisers were his 'new testament'.

The battlecruiser idea was also taken up by the Imperial German Navy. By the middle of the First World War, Germany had six such warships. And now they were building eight more battlecruisers. Most had 14- and 15-inch (35- and 38-cm) guns and were very fast, with a top speed of 30 knots.

Hood, with her planned sisters *Anson, Howe* and *Rodney*, was brought into being as a counterbalance to these new German battlecruisers. However, before much construction work had been done on *Hood*, British naval intelligence concluded that more German naval effort was going into U-boats than into completing capital ships. So *Hood*'s sisters-to-be were cancelled in October 1918, in spite of the fact that almost a million pounds had already been spent on them. *Hood* was completed, but she was the first and last of her line (which would have been called the 'Admiral' class). Nonetheless, she bore one of the most famous names in Royal Naval history – the Hood family had served in the navy with distinction from the eighteenth century on.

Dr Eric Grove, director of the Centre for Security Studies at the University of Hull, says: '*Hood* was a transitional ship, Britain's first attempt at a heavily armoured battlecruiser, where nothing would be sacrificed to speed and the price for that was paid in increased size. During her construction, ideas on armoured protection changed and so the decision was made not to build her three sisters and for *Hood*'s design to be recast more thoroughly. A new class of "Super-*Hood*s" was projected, but these fell victim to the Washington Treaty of 1922, which set limits on capital-ship building among the great powers, and two smaller and slower battleships were built instead.'

ABOVE Hood *fitting out at John Brown's Shipyard, Clydebank.*

But what a ship *Hood* would be. As she took shape on the slipway at John Brown's shipyard in Glasgow, it was clear that a giant was in the making. *Hood* was 860 feet (260 m) long and weighed 46,700 tons full load. She was armed with eight 15-inch (38-cm) and twelve 5 ½-inch (14-cm) calibre guns, as well as torpedo tubes and four 4-inch (10-cm) HA (High Angle) guns. As she fitted out, she dwarfed the destroyers alongside her. But, although she seemed to be a confident statement of Britain's naval might, already the question marks about *Hood*'s capacity to survive were mounting up, especially in the wake of the disastrous Battle of Jutland in 1916, which saw the loss of three battlecruisers: *Invincible, Indefatigable* and *Queen Mary*.

Four major modifications were made to the design of *Hood*'s armour, the last over the magazines and above the slopes of the main deck. This led to the loss of four of the ship's 5½-inch (14-cm) guns to compensate for the extra weight she now had to carry. As late as July 1919 – even after *Hood* was launched – still more was intended for her, but never fitted. But as she entered the water, she seemed as well armoured as she could be given her design requirements: 12 inches (30 cm) narrowing to 6 inches (15 cm) in the great slabs bolted on her sides, and an increase to a foot (30 cm) too on the huge barbettes housing her turrets.

Bill Jurens, a world expert and consultant on battleship design and gunnery, notes: 'For the time, *Hood*'s design was a good balance. The warship designer always has to juggle three major factors: armament (gunpower), speed and protection. He must also take into account issues of range and habitability. If *Hood* was to be kept a reasonable size – and she was a very big ship already – adding something onto her meant

something else had to be removed. It's a zero-sum game for the warship designer – a series of compromises where any increase in one factor means a necessary decrease in the others.'

Dr Eric Grove's research has revealed that a major row also erupted between the Admiralty and the Director of Naval Construction. The Director warned that the above-water inboard torpedo tubes insisted on by the navy would threaten the structural integrity of the ship if they blew up in a battle – sitting as they did above *Hood*'s armour belt and right on her 'strength girder', which effectively held her together.

Dr Grove says: '*Hood*'s designers tried as hard as they could to take the above-water torpedo tubes out of the ship. They thought they had won the argument when the armoured mantlets intended to protect the torpedo warheads had to be removed to release space for extra armour protection elsewhere. But the naval staff still insisted that the after set of tubes be carried to test new sighting equipment. It was agreed, though, that the unprotected torpedoes and their tubes should be removed if the ship ever went to war. Sadly, however, the final extra armour was not fitted. This allowed the torpedo warhead mantlets to be added at a later refit, which converted the after-tubes into war fittings once more – with all the threat to *Hood*'s structure that that implied.'

At her launch in August 1918, Hood entered the water as the largest capital ship in the world. For all of her life, she remained the longest capital ship in existence. But she had put on a good deal of weight to get as far as her launch – and what that meant showed itself as early as her first short journey from the mouth of the Clyde to the naval base at Rosyth. *Hood*'s reputation as 'the largest submarine in the Navy' began here – her stern dug in at speed like a fast motorboat's, repeatedly rendering the whole space of the quarterdeck awash as she ploughed through a Force 8 gale and its attendant 16½-foot waves. Den Finden, who was to serve in the *Hood* for three years, leaving not long before she was lost, can still remember all too well what her seakeeping was like:

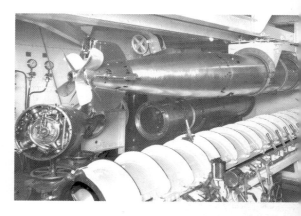

'At times she'd shake like a jelly. I'm not kidding – she'd shake like a jelly. When I went on to the foc'sle the only billet I could get was underneath the hatchway going

Vibration was already a problem too, a characteristic of the ship, as former *Hood* Boy Seaman Frank Pavey recalls all too well:

'At high power she would throb like the devil. I felt sorry for the midshipmen, because their flat was right aft – the very after part of the ship, right above the screws. So they had a massage every time they turned in, I should think!'

Both those problems would stay with *Hood* throughout her life. But for now such problems – as well as that of the armour, the inboard torpedo tubes, and all the other concerns about her construction – faded away as she began her long career as cock o' the walk: the Royal Navy's most famous ship, both at home and abroad.

A FLAGSHIP TO THE MANNER BORN

Hood had been built to impress, and impress she most emphatically did. The first sight of her for the many thousands who were to serve in her during her long career seems to abide with them all. They all remember 'their' 'Mighty *Hood*', and age does not wither that memory.

Of her final ship's company, let the last living survivor be the first to speak. Ted Briggs MBE was just a thirteen-year-old boy when he first saw *Hood*, off his home at Redcar in Yorkshire.

'It was in the mid-1930s. She came up the mouth of the Tees. Local fishermen were charging five shillings a time to row people round her and I badly wanted to go. My mother, being a widow, couldn't afford the money and I remember crying my eyes out that I couldn't afford it. The majesty of her registered – I decided there and then that I wanted to join the navy. I went round to the recruiting office and they patted me gently on the head and said, "Come back when you're fifteen." Seven days after I was fifteen I joined HMS *Ganges,* the training ship!'

The Reverend Ron Paterson, now Chaplain to the HMS *Hood* Association, joined *Hood* as a Boy Seaman First Class. 'The ship was lying just below the Forth Bridge at anchor. It was very rough, very misty and very dull … and this huge thing loomed up. As an Irish boy in the middle of Ireland, I'd never seen a ship in my life before and this huge, mighty *Hood* suddenly appeared out of the gloom and it was a wonderful sight and a great joy to be joining her …'

Den Finden remembers her huge size too: 'We got aboard – we got sent down to the boys' messdeck – and for about two days I was completely lost, until I was found on the seamen's messdeck … and put back on the boys' messdeck!'

And for one young man having doubts about his parents' choice of a career for him in the Royal Navy, the sight of *Hood* at anchor and at work had a distinctly therapeutic effect. A seasick future vice-admiral, Sir Louis Le Bailly CB, first saw her from the ferry

St Helier, returning from Jersey in the 1920s:

'Misery enveloped me … until we reached Weymouth harbour where, for the first time, I saw HMS *Hood* at close quarters. As the *St Helier* tied up, the *Hood*'s brass-funnelled picket boat, driven by a young midshipman seemingly little older than me, cut through our wash to come smartly alongside the harbour steps. I needed no more and never wavered again.'

As Dr Grove says: '*Hood* symbolized the British maritime supremacy upon which the continued survival of the empire depended. As the biggest and fastest capital ship of her day, she represented a qualitative superiority that made up for the unwelcome acceptance of numerical parity with the Americans. America might have as many

capital ships as Britain, but none were anywhere near as good as *Hood*, so Britannia, not Columbia, still ruled the waves. And there were many in the US Navy who would have agreed. She was also by far the best-looking capital ship of her time. She could wow the crowds, both at home and overseas. She had an elegance that American and Japanese ships of the time lacked. There was just nothing like HMS *Hood*. She dominated every harbour she visited.'

ABOVE *Early days: HMS* Hood *departs Plymouth.*

'VENTIS SECUNDIS'

Hood's role as a symbol of Britain's imperial and naval power developed soon after she entered service on 15 May 1920. The era of the flapper, jazz, dancing till dawn and bright young things in Oxford bags might have just been getting underway, but *Hood* had a completely contrasting role marked out for her; that of the ultra-traditional 'showing the flag', the standby of British diplomacy. Firstly though – under her motto '*Ventis secundis*' ('With favourable winds') – she would fulfil another classic imperial task, obeying the immortal command: 'Send a gunboat'.

Under the command of Captain Wilfred Tomkinson – at forty-three, quite young to take command of such a high-profile ship – she set sail on her first mission: to Estonia, to impress the Bolshevik fleet with her brooding power. The Soviet navy would have to wait its turn, however, while she paid a goodwill visit to Scandinavia. In company with HMS *Tiger* and a flotilla of destroyers, she anchored off what is now Oslo on 1 June 1920 – the Glorious First of June, always remembered by the Royal Navy for Lord Howe's victory in the French Revolutionary War in 1794. She was flying the flag of Rear-Admiral Sir Roger Keyes, hero of the audacious First World War raid against Zeebrugge that Tomkinson had also taken part in. Then followed the first of her Royal visits – from the king and queen of Norway, on His Majesty's birthday, 3 June. *Hood* resounded to a Royal Navy speciality – three cheers for their royal visitor.

Hood's next visit was to Kalmar, in Swedish waters, to be greeted by an aircraft sortie weaving around her in airborne salute. In return, the huge ship's saluting guns roared out over the Baltic in respectful tribute to the distinguished visitors who came aboard. More honours followed on 7 June, as the king and crown prince of Sweden stepped onto the ship. Again the crews cheered their visitors, manning the sides to welcome them. Then it was on to Denmark – with 'making smoke' exercises on the way (the bane of the life of a peacetime executive officer who dearly loves to keep his ship smart and clean). At Copenhagen there were more visits, royal and otherwise, including a two-hour inspection by the king and queen of Denmark. It was in Copenhagen that Sir Roger learned that his exercise in gunboat diplomacy was over before it had begun. States neighbouring the new Soviet republic had come to an accommodation with the Bolsheviks, the blockade of Petrograd had been lifted, and the naval threat to Lenin's regime in the Baltic had been brought to an end. *Hood* began the journey home.

A task awaited her there which, at the beginning of July, brought her as near as she would ever come to the enemy she had been designed to fight. At the beginning of August, off Rosyth, *Hood* provided boarding parties to search and take control of three of the older German dreadnoughts as they came in to surrender under the guns of the Home Fleet. The lesson of the rest of the High Seas Fleet's self-destruction at Scapa Flow the previous year had clearly been taken to heart.

After completing torpedo and gunnery exercises off Portland in the autumn of 1920, *Hood* went on her second major cruise. She was to impress Spain with her presence by visiting Vigo, Arosa Bay and Gibraltar. This so-called 'Spring Cruise', scheduled for January 1921, was ill-fated from the start. On its very first day, disaster struck when the large fleet submarine *K5* failed to surface after evolutions in which *Hood* and other ships were involved. Little of *K5* came to the surface, but it was enough to fix a spot for a memorial service to be conducted on the orders of Sir Roger Keyes on the return voyage. This tragedy was a stark reminder to all – and especially to former submarine commander Sir Roger – of the ever-present dangers of a submariner's life. In those early days there was little or no hope of recovery for submarines that suffered such a fate.

It was a sad end to a mainly happy and successful first commission. In March 1921, a complete change of command was to follow with the appointment of a new admiral and captain – a change that many were to feel was very much for the worse.

HOOD UNDER PRESSURE

Judged by normal standards, the two men who now succeeded to the command of HMS *Hood*, Rear-Admiral Sir Walter Cowan and Captain Geoffrey Mackworth, made a bad combination, likely to reinforce each other's worst qualities. Cowan – nicknamed 'Tich' – is remembered as a short-tempered man, irritably bent upon chasing the highest standards for his ship. Along with this temperament went poor communication skills, the product, perhaps, of a shy and reserved nature. Cowan's short fuse had led to his presiding over no less than three mutinies in six years. The most recent of these had also involved his new captain in *Hood*, reportedly for similar reasons – a failure of leadership that led to the crew of the cruiser *Delhi* refusing to stand to when a change of orders sent her back to the Baltic in 1919 instead of returning home. Even in a disciplined service, such changes of plan often require careful presentation in order to get a body of men on side, and Mackworth had not troubled to break the news gently.

Yet these were the two men chosen to take command of the Royal Navy's newest and most powerful warship. It would not be the last time that the Admiralty showed itself singularly ill-adept at dealing with those of senior rank whose personalities made them unsuited to roles that called for a proper range of officer-like qualities. But Cowan was a friend of Lord Beatty, the First Sea Lord. Their association went back to the training ship *Britannia,* where both had been severely punished for bullying another cadet.

The Cowan/Mackworth effect soon made itself apparent aboard *Hood.* An officer of the deck allowed a small boat alongside in Weymouth: he was censured in writing for acting 'against the spirit of the orders of the Captain'. Another was censured for being too lenient in failing to arrest a stoker who came aboard drunk (a procedure which, if followed to the letter, would have left most Royal Navy ships without enough crew at liberty to get their ship to sea). For officers and petty officers, there followed speeches on their duties to their ship, their captain and the navy. *Hood's* log steadily filled with instances of Mackworth's righteous wrath – often, it seemed, for matters scarcely worth the full formal weight of written disapproval.

In this atmosphere, one of *Hood's* first tasks under its new commanders must have been a nightmare for 'Tich'. For, not long after his experiences in the Baltic opposing the new Bolshevik government, Cowan found his ship in Rosyth just as coal and rail strikes were convulsing Scotland. Three battalions of marines and seamen, under the command of midshipmen, were detailed off to Cowdenbeath, following a riot there at Kinlassie Colliery in April 1921. Later, the same parties found themselves detailed off to protect the Forth Bridge from sabotage. Tensions were eased somewhat in traditional naval manner when the sailors put down their rifles to challenge the striking miners to a game of football (presumably without shinpads – bold indeed); and at Lochgelly a dance was arranged, with music courtesy of *Hood's* Royal Marine band.

For all that, to the wrath of Captain Mackworth, the 'Red Tide' even lapped its way into his ship. On commander's rounds, a messdeck was found to be decorated with red bunting. Retribution followed, with Able Seamen Thomas Guthrie and John McKirdy court-martialled for 'mutinous practice'. They were acquitted, but neither Cowan nor Mackworth was ready to leave it at that. Even a 'jaunty' (a master-at-arms, responsible for lower-deck discipline) was tried for concealing a mutinous practice, and Stoker John Hall for incitement to mutiny. Although the verdict was not proven in the case of Master-at-Arms Walter Batten, Hall was sentenced to three years in jail. Clearly, the land fit for heroes was not yet ready for their opinions – at least not in Cowan and Mackworth's *Hood.*

It is to the credit of the ship's company that the atmosphere left by the intemperate behaviour of their commanders did little to dent their morale. Neither did it hinder their performance in the first of the major sporting contests for which the ship was to become so famous.

PLAY UP, PLAY UP AND PLAY THE GAME

In summer 1921 *Hood* was exercising off Gibraltar. The series of evolutions was enlivened when she was against the harbour wall in the Crown Colony for ceremonial duties much favoured by her admiral and much endured by her ship's company. Meanwhile, the strictures of *Hood*'s martinet Captain Mackworth continued while she carried out her duties as flagship of the Atlantic Fleet's Battlecruiser Squadron. The reprimands and exhortations went on as the commission continued into its second year.

The start of 1922 saw *Hood* on her regular cruise in the Mediterranean, with full-blown visits to Gibraltar, France and Spain. The summer cruise, however, was cancelled to allow for a visit to Brazil to mark the first hundred years of that nation's independence from Portugal. It was in Brazil that *Hood* showed in full the sporting prowess that was to mark her out as 'cock o' the fleet'.

In early September 1922, the ships of many nations, including Japan, America and Argentina, came to their moorings off Rio de Janeiro, alongside *Hood* and *Repulse*. What amounted to an international sporting festival was soon organized, featuring events such as regatta and skiff races, athletics and tug-of-war competitions. The *Hood*s excelled at them all. Boxing was a triumph too, until the last bout, which would decide the Rio naval games champion. Then – before touching gloves – the American contender piled into his *Hood* opponent, knocking him down. Four thousand sailors in the stadium made their anger known, and although the fight was declared void, it took some adroit work by 'Tich' to calm things down.

Hood's journey home took her via the West Indies. Mackworth was still hard at it, despite the crew's successful exertions at the Rio games, where they had won three silver cups. Hands had to set to and 'paint ship', despite poor weather in Barbados. Awnings were spread and put away again and again, evolutions were carried out and completed in races with *Repulse*. Back in Devonport by December, *Hood* got ready for another spring cruise. But soon the ship would have a much bigger public relations task on her hands, and under new management.

HOOD – CRUISING THE WORLD

The 1922 Washington Treaty had forced Britain to accept parity in capital ships with the United States. In the wake of that agreement, some global demonstration of the continued naval might of the empire was required. Moreover, the often heroic self-sacrifice of the Commonwealth and Dominions in the First World War seemed to call for some special demonstration by the 'mother country'. By 1923, that idea had taken root in the form of a proposed 40,000-mile cruise. The aim was to demonstrate

Britain's power to the world and to show her support to all key parts of the 'pink on the map' and to some beyond it, including the USA. In company with her 'oppo' *Repulse* – her sister in the Battlecruiser Squadron – and five cruisers, HMS *Hood* slipped out of Plymouth at the end of November 1923. She was under the command of Captain John Im Thurn and the flag of Vice-Admiral Sir Frederick Field.

This was a showing the flag to end all showing the flags. The 'Special Service Squadron' found the Royal Navy's traditional skills in hospitality and presentation were to be tested to the limit, as never before or since. Paintwork gleamed, brass shone, the quarterdeck was scrubbed a dazzling white.

The first stop was Freetown in Sierra Leone. Salutes boomed across the harbour, there were formal visits by and to the governor, and *Hood*'s first shipboard dance was held. For five days, scores and scores of visitors came aboard, eager to see Britannia's latest and greatest fighting ship for themselves.

That visit to Sierra Leone set the pattern for the tour. Christmas at Cape Town in South Africa followed, with a welcoming fly-past as *Hood* entered Table Bay, *Hood* contingent march-pasts on shore, lavish entertainment and sporting contests. Vice-Admiral Field called on the South Africans to build up their own navy; his sailors distinguished themselves by not painting the town red over the holiday. And the flag was shown with a vengeance, with *Hood* arousing keen interest at every South African port she touched. Durban was *Hood*'s port of departure for Zanzibar, just up the East African coast. Here honours were rendered to *Hood* by Sultan Sayyad Khalifa ben Harud's war canoes, with a twenty-one-gun salute the acknowledgement. Then *Hood* crossed the Indian Ocean for a 'rest' – a couple of thousand visitors and time for the crew to draw breath in Ceylon. Singapore was a different story – *Hood* arrived at a sensitive time, with Japanese sensibilities to be calmed as plans for a new Royal Navy base hung in the balance. The sensation that she caused – nearly 30,000 people came to visit in a matter of days – had to be balanced with an awareness of the geopolitical ambitions growing in Japan, as she mistrustfully eyed the European colonial powers in what she saw as her backyard.

Australia next, and the Dominion caught *Hood* fever: in eight weeks the squadron led by her visited Fremantle, Adelaide, Melbourne, Hobart and Sydney. Crowds of sightseers thronged the huge ship: the parades and the parties mounted up in the sweltering heat. From the end of February, for eight weeks, *Hood* was more of a circus than a warship. Two hundred thousand people visited her in Melbourne, and a reported half a million watched her enter Sydney's magnificent harbour. Field went public with assurances that heavy warships like *Hood* would watch the sea routes of the empire for Australia if she would supply herself with cruisers. The Australian government promptly ordered two.

New Zealand took over one of the squadron's five accompanying cruisers when the great ships came into Wellington. During that visit, all engagements were abandoned to give the *Hood*s a chance to clear their party fatigue. But it was back to the grindstone in Auckland, where tens of thousands of would-be visitors stormed the dockyard gates. On the way to Auckland, *Hood* had flown the flag of Admiral Lord Jellicoe, commander at the battle of Jutland in 1916 and now Governor General of the Dominion.

Visits to Fiji, Samoa and Hawaii followed. But then came a sporting setback – in Hawaii *Hood*'s cricket team yielded best to an eleven of basketball players! After the long Pacific crossing to Canada, followed by trips to Victoria and British Columbia, *Hood* docked in Vancouver on 25 June 1923. Here, there was yet more evidence that the constant partying was taking its toll on *Hood*'s crew: the Mounties beat the *Hood*s at football. A brief American breathing space followed this unfamiliar mixture of sporting defeat and unrelenting parties. *Hood* visited San Francisco, where even the chippy anti-British feeling so often evident on the American scene melted away before the mightiness of *Hood*. 'We capitulate!' said the city's mayor, in expansive mood. (His choice of words was interesting – strange as it now may seem, both countries were at that moment secretly updating contingency plans to fight each other.)

Then, at last, towards the end of July, *Hood* turned south to squeeze her huge bulk – just – through the Panama Canal to make a heading for the Atlantic crossing. Now the final stage of this extraordinary tour was at hand. After still more visits, to Jamaica and Canada (the USA's eastern seaboard could not be relied upon to be so welcoming), *Hood* turned her graceful bow east, back into familiar waters: the long swells of the Atlantic.

BELOW *Crowds flock to see Hood in Melbourne.*

She arrived home on 9 September 1924, making her way up the Hamoaze to Devonport. In just under a year, *Hood* had played host to three-quarters of a million visitors and had gone back and forth across the equator six times. Her squadron's successful cruise resulted in decorations for Field and Im Thurn, and a headache for those charged with dispersing the ship's accumulated menagerie, which included a flying squirrel, two pink cockatoos and a ring-tailed opossum. All were destined for zoos, their Special Service was over too.

ROUTINE AND RANK MUTINY

After the feats of entertainment and (literal) showboating that characterized the cruise of the Special Service Squadron – or 'Booze Cruise', as the lower deck had it – *Hood* found herself back in the routine of the peacetime Royal Navy. Back in the Home Fleet, she underwent a refit – the first of many that were never to modernize her quite enough – and set off for the spring cruise, Gibraltar bound. En route, she joined other navies in Lisbon to mark the four hundredth anniversary of the death of the great explorer Vasco da Gama. In May 1925 the commanding duo of 'Tam' Field and Im Thurn left her, and *Hood* began a pattern of gunnery training, home-port visits and cruises. This was the normal routine of the Home Fleet at this time, and was set to continue for the next four years. During that period, the flag of the Third Sea Lord Sir Cyril Fuller was succeeded by that of Rear-Admiral Fredric Dreyer, designer of *Hood*'s gunnery tables (once state-of-the-art, but fated to be outclassed in May 1941). Much was to happen in Britain over those four years from 1925, the most momentous event being the General Strike of May 1926. By 1929, *Hood* was ready for a major refit, which would take two years to complete. But that had hardly been completed when the Royal Navy found itself embroiled in a general strike all of its own.

What took place aboard the *Hood* at Invergordon was an outbreak of mass disobedience of a kind not seen since the great mutinies at Spithead and the Nore during the Napoleonic wars. The causes of the Invergordon mutiny, as so often with such events, were insensitivity compounded by cock-up. And by economics.

The incoming national government, led by Ramsay MacDonald, had inherited a £170,000,000 deficit. Something had to be done, and the Royal Navy's share of that 'something' would mean cuts in pay on the lower deck of as much as twenty-five per cent. Seamen with families were set to lose most of all. At the same time, petrol, beer and income tax were to rise. Warnings about the potential impact of these measures on the *Hood* crew were sent to Rear-Admiral Tomkinson (*Hood*'s first captain, now flying his flag in her), who seems to have failed to recognize the gravity of the situation. Further warnings from the Admiralty were then issued to Admiral Sir Michael Hodges, Commander-in-Chief of the Atlantic Fleet. The latter mailing ended up unnoticed in the admiral's pigeonhole, for by the time it arrived he had been seriously ill in hospital for some days. Tomkinson had taken the Atlantic Fleet to sea and to its nemesis at Invergordon.

Hood arrived at Invergordon on Friday, 11 September 1931. The Budget in which the cuts were announced had been made public the previous day. Tomkinson's chances of heading off the mutiny that was to engulf his career were vanishing fast. But he failed to realize the significance of these draconian pay cuts for his men and their families. By the time *Hood* led the fleet to its Scottish anchorage, a dangerous situation was brewing, and Tomkinson's men were reading their daily newspapers with a growing sense of anger and injustice. A new Admiralty Fleet Order, arriving on the evening of the Saturday, also got pigeonholed for the weekend, while Tomkinson's personal copy was mis-addressed to his old ship *Renown*, which he had left some two months earlier.

It had all the makings of a 'snafu' – the services' in-house label for a fiasco ('Situation Normal, All Fouled Up') – and it duly became one. By late afternoon on Saturday, 12 September, there was talk of a strike in the shore canteen. On Sunday evening, angry speeches were heard there and glasses were smashed. The situation was quietened by a shore patrol, but the mutinous spirit was now well and truly abroad. Despite briefings, based on the Admiralty letter, throughout the fleet the next day, there were more disturbances in the canteen. The officer in charge of the shore patrol was pushed out when he first tried to intervene. Tomkinson signalled the Admiralty about the disturbances, but judged it better to proceed with the exercises planned for the Tuesday. He sent a conciliatory signal to all the ships in the Atlantic Fleet at Invergordon, but it was too late.

Dr Eric Grove comments: 'The Sea Lords of 1931 were out of touch with the contemporary sailor. The ratings these senior officers had known when they had been midshipmen in the Victorian navy had not had the same lifestyle or aspirations. Older ratings now had settled families and commitments like hire-purchase obligations and it was precisely these men who were most hard hit by the Admiralty's reneging on its promise to keep the 1919 rates of pay. It was noteworthy that the depth of concern over the pay cuts was in direct proportion to the number of good-conduct badges on the sailor's uniform. Nothing could have been more corrosive of normal standards of discipline. Invergordon also destroyed confidence in the pound. If the greatest ships of the British Fleet could mutiny, then anything was possible. Britain was forced off the Gold Standard (although that probably had positive economic effects in mitigating the worst effects of the depression).'

The mutiny proper began in the battleship *Rodney* and the cruiser *Dorsetshire*, with hundreds of sailors refusing to report for work. Soon *Hood* had the contagion too. Then the crews of the cruiser *Norfolk* and the battleship *Nelson*, recently arrived, joined in.

This half-mutiny in *Hood* continued the next day. Disturbance flared up again after an anodyne Admiralty statement about 'unrest among a proportion of lower ratings' appeared in the press. Meanwhile, Tomkinson's unceasingly concerned signals to the Admiralty, calling for some concessions to end the disturbances, met with long delays and little in the way of a useful response. Finally, as the shouting rang out in solidarity from ship to ship around the fleet on the afternoon of Wednesday, 16 September 1931, the Admiralty instructed Tomkinson to disperse the ships to home ports with a view to 'necessary alleviations' being made in the pay cuts. *Hood*'s captain addressed his men, assembled on the foc'sle. Having heard Tomkinson promise to look into their grievances, the men dispersed in silence, but later seemed to reject his pleas for a return to good order.

The fleet was due to sail at 9.30 p.m. that night. Four hours were needed to raise steam. Would the men obey orders? It was a moment of crisis. At 6 p.m., engine-room staff reported for lighting boilers. At first, the sailors gathered in large numbers on *Hood*'s foc'sle would not budge. But then, following a signal from Tomkinson that the fleet should sail independently, the old battleship *Warspite* slipped her mooring and made her slow but steady way to sea. Her departure broke the spell. *Hood*'s mutineers slowly returned to their duties, and she sailed out to sea with the rest of the fleet. The Invergordon Mutiny was over.

However, its repercussions were not. After *Hood* and her fellow mutiny ships returned to home ports, Tomkinson was at first congratulated on his handling of the affair by the First Sea Lord 'Tam' Field, himself formerly a *Hood*. But neither Tomkinson nor the mutiny's alleged ringleaders were to escape the consequences of Invergordon. Twenty-seven men were dismissed in November, seven of them *Hood*s.

Three months later it was the turn of their admiral and their captain to be dismissed, along with the captains of six of the other ships involved. Tomkinson was told his appointment would be terminated early, and several of the other captains were also punished. The Admiralty criticized Tomkinson in particular for 'a serious error of judgement in omitting to take any decided action … when dissatisfaction had begun to show itself amongst the men'.

Historically, of course, these reproaches need to be balanced with their Lordships' own delay and indecision, and their failure to fight off such harsh pay cuts in the first place. And the economic utility of those pay cuts may perhaps be judged by the fact that they were much reduced within days of the end of the mutiny.

LEADERSHIP AND RUMOURS OF WAR

After the Invergordon Mutiny, *Hood* – like many other ships in the fleet – had ground to make up. Reputations, once tarnished, take time to regain their lustre, and *Hood*, however mighty she might be, was no exception to that rule. She was fortunate that her new management following the mutiny had the capacities of leadership that she sorely needed.

Rear-Admiral William James had a singular handicap. He was the grandson of the painter Millais, who had left James a heavy legacy by making him his model for the picture *Bubbles* – a curly-headed tot, seated and gazing brightly at the soap bubbles he had just blown into the air above him. Worse, the picture had been used as an advertisement for Pears' Soap, making the image an icon of Victorian sentimentality. That might have been enough to warp any man, especially one aiming at a career in the strictly masculine world of the navy.

However, James was far from warped. As soon as he took up his post on *Hood* in August 1932, he set to work to rebuild his new crew's damaged morale, declaring, 'I am proud to have joined you.' It was a sentiment reinforced by his new commander, who was later to carry on with verve and enthusiasm the mending and healing begun by James and his first captain in *Hood*, Thomas Binney.

Commander Rory O'Conor's reputation in the navy as a leader of men has a legendary quality. He burst onto the *Hood* scene in 1933 with the kind of ideas that would later become common coin for good management, but which, in those days, must have seemed little short of radical to the traditionalists of the Royal Navy. O'Conor believed in building strong links between officers and men and in creating a sense of common purpose. Efficiency could and should be combined with the humane treatment of the men under his command. He ran an 'open-door' policy, and was available always to those who needed his help and advice. And he was nothing if not ambitious for *Hood*. On joining, he told the ship's company that they would win every sporting trophy going, as well as being the smartest and happiest ship afloat. They might have scoffed at the time, but in fact it's fair to say that they went on and did just that. There is little doubt that *Hood*'s high standing in the fleet owed a great deal to O'Conor and his methods. And it was a high standing that was about more than just success, as Ron Paterson, who joined as a Boy Seaman, well remembers:

'She was what they call a happy ship. Everybody did their best, everybody pulled their weight. The officers were superb – they were really all there to help you. They

were what I would call a band of brothers – like Nelson's band of brothers – and they were remarkably good to us junior ratings. Rory O'Conor had a system – everybody joining the ship had to see his "Ten Commandments" – they were more or less the rules for the ship. We boys were all ushered up to the cinema and shown the Ten Commandments, and given a lecture about our conduct on board which all went home and sunk in!'

Those Ten Commandments found their way into O'Conor's classic book about ship management: *Running a Big Ship on Ten Commandments* which carried on his influence well beyond his death in action in the Second World War as captain of the cruiser *Neptune*.

Two years into O'Conor's tenure as *Hood*'s commander, the aggression inherent in fascism that would end in world war erupted. At the beginning of October 1935, Mussolini's Italy invaded Abyssinia – a late-colonial land grab against a weak and near-defenceless adversary. The League of Nations called for economic and military sanctions. *Hood*'s value as a deterrent to the Italian dictator's ambitions was obvious. However, the British government decided to play it safe, and brought the ship home from the Mediterranean at the end of the month. Her next role in the conflict was not to be until the very end of it, when the Emperor Haile Selassie and his daughter, on their way into exile after the fall of Addis Ababa to the Italians, were *Hood*'s guests at Gibraltar.

ABOVE *Ten Commandments man: Commander Rory O'Conor.*

That was in May 1936. By July, another war had broken out: the Spanish Civil War. From the first, the British policy of not intervening while still protecting the national interest (by such means as the sight of HMS *Hood*) posed great difficulties for all involved.

Dr Eric Grove comments: 'The Royal Navy was in a difficult position in the Spanish Civil War. It tended to sympathize with the Nationalists, but it was also anxious to maintain its tradition of safeguarding the rights of those plying the seas on their lawful occasions. Politically, the British government could not grant Nationalist warships belligerent rights, so it was unlawful for the insurgent navy to stop ships on the high seas. There was no better asset than *Hood* to overawe Franco's ships into laying off British merchantmen as they tried to break his blockade of ports still under government control.'

The Germans and the Italians, of course, didn't stop at overawing; flagrant intervention, including submarine sinkings of neutral ships was the order of the day for them. But it was a confrontation with nationalist Spanish warships that got *Hood* involved. In the *Thorpehall* incident on 6 April 1937, a British freighter was fired at off the coast of northern Spain. She was rescued by British destroyers and completed her voyage into the government-held port of Bilbao. On 10 April, *Hood* raced to take up station to remind Franco's nationalists and their Fascist allies to mind their manners.

ACTIVE SERVICE

Hood based herself in St Jean de Luz, close to the Spanish border. From here, she readied herself to offer assistance, should any other British ships be menaced by the Nationalists. It wasn't long before three merchantmen, the *MacGregor*, *Stanbrook* and *Hamsterley*, decided they too would make a run for it to get their cargo of food into Bilbao. Departing St Jean de Luz on 23 April, the three found themselves in international waters off Bilbao the following morning and under the guns of the Francoist cruiser *Almirante Cervera* and the armed trawler *Galerna*. After just over an hour's stand-off, the *Galerna* fired on *MacGregor*, the lead ship of the trio, as she made for the port. For the first time, *Hood* trained her guns on an adversary as the Spanish cruiser turned hers on one of the accompanying British destroyers. But then, suddenly, the three merchantmen crossed the 3-mile (5-km) limit line and made their way in to a rapturous welcome from the people of Bilbao. *Hood* had not needed to fire a single shot – the sheer threatening power of the great battlecruiser had won the day.

Hood's symbolic power continued to impress throughout the conflict, even when the bombers came. It was noted that, whichever Spanish port she happened to be visiting, the air attackers stayed away while *Hood* was there. But her presence was no deterrent to the submarines now sinking any ship, including British ones, thought to be helping the government of Spain. An Italian submarine even tried to sink a Royal Navy warship, HMS *Havock*. Meanwhile, with 'A.B.C.' (the soon-to-be-famous Admiral Cunningham) flying his flag in her, *Hood* gave big-ship cover to the 'Nyon Patrols' – destroyer operations aimed at protecting neutral vessels off Spain during the war. But scant protection came the way of ships such as the Dutch *Hannah* and the British *Endymion*, both of which were sunk by submarines, probably from the Italian navy.

In March 1938, as the tide turned against the elected government of Spain, the

presence of *Hood* still seemed to be enough to fend off the persistent air raids in which hundreds had already died. From April, *Hood* became a mercy ship, helping to move more than a hundred evacuees, including nuns from a convent in Barcelona, out of harm's way. It was *Hood*'s first sight of real war. When the guns next sounded, she would be more than an onlooker.

'HMS HOOD WILL PROCEED...'

In September 1939, it fell to Ted Briggs, by then a young signalman on board his beloved *Hood*, to tell the Home Fleet at Scapa Flow that it was at war with Germany. By an extraordinary trick of fate, the ship that had sparked Briggs' determination to join the Royal Navy had become his first posting. His first signal in a warship could hardly have been more momentous. He recalls:

'Chief Yeoman George Thomas ordered: "Briggs, get a pair of hand-flags and get up to the 15-inch director and show up 46". It was with a strange sort of pride and yet a sinking feeling in my belly that I spelt out to the fleet: "Commence hostilities against Germany."'

Then followed what for many *Hood*s must have felt like their very own phoney war. Already a patrol to hold in the 'pocket battleships' *Graf Spee* and *Deutschland* had been seen to be a waste of time. The patrol had been sent too late: the two raiders had slipped away before the end of August. That set the tone for several months, as a darkened-down *Hood* in blackout conditions was sent on one long and fruitless patrol after another. Apart from a brief encounter with a German JU88 bomber when rescuing the crippled submarine *Spearfish* in the North Sea, *Hood* had little sight of the enemy she had been born to fight. She covered convoys, protected troopships, sailed in and out of harbour after German surface raiders probing into the Atlantic, and even patrolled the Channel in joint operations with the French fleet under the command of Vice-Admiral Gensoul. As she did so, more and more miles of seatime appeared in

Hood's log and she began to show her age. The long refit planned for 1942 began to look increasingly necessary.

The plans for the refit were extensive, as Bill Jurens recalls:

'In 1942, *Hood* was to have her longest refit since 1929, thirteen years before. There had been other, shorter refits in the meantime, but this would have been a big one, lasting three years. Much would have changed. She would have had more armour added, her conning tower removed, aircraft hangars built, and new guns and machinery fitted, and so on. But I doubt whether such a substantial rebuild would have been fully completed, even if *Hood* had survived the Denmark Strait action. It was a *very* ambitious scheme for a vessel of her age, especially given changes in naval strategy, such as the rise of the aircraft carrier. In any case, after 1940 British shipyards were fully occupied with new construction and the repair of war-damaged veterans.'

Dr Eric Grove adds: '*Hood* had become a middle-aged lady by the late 1930s. Her wrinkles were beginning to show under the shining coats of battleship-grey make-up. Yet there were many even older ladies in the fleet more in need of major face lifts than her: the other two *much* more thinly armoured battlecruisers *Renown* and *Repulse*, for example, and the more lightly protected, fast battleships of the "Queen Elizabeth" class. The Lords of the Admiralty were absolutely right in their priorities to put *Hood* last in the queue for rebuilding. She was one of the best all-round ships they had as she was. In the early war years, they fitted her with a new secondary armament of anti-aircraft guns and the latest fire-control radar. That was all that could be done.'

Hood would have to make do. And make do she did, as she joined the Mediterranean war – and Force H.

FORCE H – 'OUR SEA, NOT YOURS'

Led by *Hood* and the aircraft carrier *Ark Royal*, Force H had been brought into being to challenge Italian dictator Benito Mussolini's assertion that the seas of antiquity constituted '*Mare nostrum*' ('Our Sea'). Her role in the Force H strike force, based in Gibraltar, would bring HMS *Hood* her first battle, not with Italian or German ships, but with those of an ally. By the time *Hood* arrived at her new posting, France had fallen. However, much of the French battlefleet lay at anchor at the naval base of Mers-el-Kebir, near Oran in the French colony of Algeria. For the *Kriegsmarine* this fleet could provide the solution to its deficit in warships – the cross the German navy had always had to bear in its conflict with the Royal Navy. The thought of this powerful fleet falling into German hands sent a chill down the spine of the planners in the Admiralty Building in Whitehall. Something had to be done – and Force H, with *Hood* in the van, was the tool with which to do it.

So it was that on the morning of 3 July 1940, Force H arrived off Mers-el-Kebir. The plan was simple – and distasteful. The French navy would be forced to choose whose side they really wanted to be on. The destroyer *Foxhound* delivered a message calling on the French (who, by sad coincidence, were under the command of the pro-British Vice-Admiral Gensoul) to join up with the British, disable their ships as fighting units or sink them where they lay. Despite Force H commander Vice-Admiral Sir James Somerville's pleas for moderation, London had insisted on these harsh terms.

Force H stayed on station as the hours passed and the tension mounted. Slowly, it became clear that none of the British ultimata would be accepted. Finally, with pressure from London building, Somerville knew he could wait no longer. Once again Ted Briggs had to send a momentous signal, one he could hardly believe he was making: 'Flag 5' – 'Open Fire'.

'It was like shooting fish in a barrel, virtually,' Ted recalls. 'You could see the absolute carnage, the shells bursting – it was a very enclosed harbour. The French did manage to open fire with some ships; naturally, they were concentrating on *Hood*. She was straddled a couple of times, the funnels were peppered with shrapnel but that was all – whereas the French, it was carnage, pure and utter.'

Force H's onslaught on the French fleet lasted just over a quarter of an hour. It did not achieve all its objectives: five destroyers and the battlecruiser *Strasbourg* escaped. But four warships, including the battlecruiser *Dunkerque,* had been put out of action. This achievement came at a heavy price: close to 1,300 of Britain's former allies had died. However necessary it may have been (or may not: none of the ships that escaped to France was ever used by the Germans), the attack on Oran remains a black moment in the Royal Navy's history. Some believe that what took place there still has a doleful effect on Anglo–French relations to this day.

With the bitter taste of what it had had to do still lingering, Force H turned its attention towards its true enemy in the Mediterranean – Mussolini's navy, the Regia Marina. Somerville was under pressure to put the Italian navy to the test in '*Mare nostrum*'. The plan was for a combination of pincer movement and diversion: Force H would shield two British convoys bound for Alexandria with sorties from the eastern and western Mediterrranean simultaneously. 'A.B.C.' – Cunningham – would come out of Alexandria, Somerville and Force H out of Gibraltar, to target the Italian air base at Cagliari. The idea was to catch the Italians somewhere in the middle. Or be caught by them. A major force of seventeen ships, including *Hood, Valiant* and *Ark Royal*, left Gibraltar on 8 July 1940. They did not have long to wait for action. From four o'clock in the afternoon on 9 July, four waves of high-altitude bombers assaulted Force H. There were plenty of near misses but no hits. That forced the conclusion that this diversion towards Cagliari was being bought at too high a price, and as darkness fell, Somerville ordered a withdrawal. He was frustrated, but the diversionary tactics had done the trick: the two convoys arrived safely at Alexandria, while 'A.B.C.' had routed the Italian battle fleet off Calabria.

Hood had fought her first major battle. Her next one would be her last.

INVINCIBLE BISMARCK

The story of Bismarck, from her beginnings up to the point at which we left Hood, is perforce a far shorter one – Bismarck had an operational life of just eight days, compared to Hood's twenty years at sea. The German ship was a brand-new, state-of-the-art warship, cut down when she had barely begun to fulfil her function. Yet, despite this imbalance, the two warships have their genesis in similar events and in

LEFT 'Like shooting fish in a barrel' – the attack on Mers-el-Kebir.

the same desire for power and control, expressed in very similar ways. The story of each ship tells us a great deal about the naval thinking that gave birth to her.

On 31 May 1916, the German High Seas Fleet met the British Grand Fleet at the Battle of Jutland. Both sides won – and lost. For the British, the aim of driving the enemy fleet back into port was achieved. For the Germans, better gunnery and ship construction seemed to win the day, on the day. They inflicted a greater toll of casualties in ships and men than they themselves suffered, and in the process blew a large shell hole in the century-old idea of British naval supremacy. But the British failed to deliver the crushing defeat expected of the navy of Nelson and Trafalgar, and the Germans learned that they dare not risk the losses another major encounter might bring (although they did make later sorties into the North Sea).

After the humiliation endured over the next two years – the German Imperial Navy rotting slowly at its moorings in Wilhelmshaven; the mutiny of the seamen that blocked a final suicide sortie against the Royal Navy; the mass impounding of Germany's best warships in Scapa Flow, and their mournful self-destruction; the treaties that had reduced German capital stock to a collection of elderly museum pieces – the head of steam building up in the German naval hierarchy for new construction, even prior to Hitler's election to power, was enormous.

That head of steam began to vent with the '*panzerschiffe*', the armoured ships of the *Deutschland* class, first constructed in 1929.

But these were more heavy cruiser than capital ship, as the *Admiral Graf Spee* was later to demonstrate in her defeat at the hands of far lighter cruisers at the Battle of the River Plate. Ill-adapted, with their low foc'sles, to seakeeping in distant oceans, fast but very lightly armoured, and with an unsatisfactory bridge structure forcing their commanders to fight them from a vulnerable position, these ships did not deserve the appellation of 'pocket battleship' so lightly given them. Against serious opposition they would quickly find themselves in trouble.

Importantly for the international politics of the time, however, the *panzerschiffe* fell within the terms set at Versailles in 1919, which confined Germany's warships to a 10,000-ton maximum. But the naval powers anxiously watching the new *panzerschiffe* rise from the slipways had limits of their own to respect, imposed by one of the first arms-limitation agreements ever reached – the Washington Treaty. Concluded seven years before the first 'Deutschland' was started, this had limited new battleship construction among the great naval powers, and had seen the scrapping of some capital ships. New construction had been forbidden for a decade (apart from the Royal Navy's *Nelson* and *Rodney*) and limits on tonnage and size of armament had been imposed.

The steam vented further with the Third Reich's first grandiose naval project – the construction of the battlecruisers *Scharnhorst* and *Gneisenau*. The Anglo–German

Naval Treaty, the terms of which were agreed in the summer of 1935, cleared away any Versailles-type impediment to the construction of these 31,000-ton ships. However, at this time Hitler's intention was not to use these ships to challenge the Royal Navy, but to counterbalance France's new battlecruisers of the 'Dunkerque' class with their high speed and 11-inch (28-cm) main armament. Accordingly, the German battlecruisers can be seen as onward developments of the *panzerschiffe*, rather than the kind of warship that might be able to complete the business that had been left unfinished after Jutland.

BELOW Panzerschiff Admiral Graf Spee.

But then came Battleship 'F' – and that post-1918 head of steam vented completely.

BATTLESHIP 'F'

It was a dingy, formal appellation for ship that was to become a legend in its own short lifetime. And, like the *panzerschiff*, this great ship began life as a get-out clause – the 1936 London Naval Treaty permitted larger ship construction all round if Japan and Italy refused to sign it. They did refuse, so up went the ante, and the German designers pushed forward their work on the greatest and most powerful battleship they were ever to build – the *Bismarck*.

Dr Eric Grove notes: 'In the end, to achieve the combination of armament, speed and protection required, Battleship 'F''s displacement had to go up to 42,000 tons, but

ABOVE *Battlecruiser Scharnhorst.*

the Germans had got used to a twenty-per-cent cheating margin over treaty limits during the Versailles period. In any case, the international limit was increased to 45,000 tons while the ships were under construction. It suited the Germans to keep up the pretence of 35,000 tons to allow them extra tonnage under the 1935 Agreement, but in 1939 Hitler finally denounced that agreement as Anglo–German relations went into free fall. It is worth making the point that *Bismarck* and *Tirpitz* were built to fight not the British in the Atlantic but the French in the North Sea or the Russians in the Baltic. Perhaps most of all, Hitler saw them as status symbols for the new Reich – one reason he was loath to risk them during the war.'

In the end, 'F' came out with a formidable legend. She had 50,900 tons full-load displacement and eight 15-inch (38-cm) guns, with thirty-four other mountings of lighter and anti-aircraft armament. The armour on her main side belt was a foot (30 cm) thick. She had a top speed of 30 knots. Design work was complete by the autumn of 1935 and, courtesy of the intransigence of the Italians and Japanese, the keel was laid in July 1936.

Bill Jurens comments: '*Bismarck* represented a thoroughly modern and well-thought-out design for the time. A secret American and British analysis of her design, carried out in 1942 using captured blueprints, concluded that she was in many ways the equal or the better of her American and British counterparts, such as the *North Carolina* or the *King George V*.'

The *Bismarck* was launched in the presence of Adolf Hitler on 14 February 1939 by Dorothea von Loewenfeld, granddaughter of the 'Iron Chancellor' Otto von Bismarck. The name was later to prove an ironic choice: the ship named after the man who had first united Germany into a nation-state was to be an instrument of the

ambitions that led to the dismemberment of the German Reich.

Commissioned on 24 August 1940, *Bismarck* could confidently see herself as a distillation of capital-ship power. Wide in the beam, giving her greater stability as a gun platform, a shallow draft (a key consideration with the Kiel Canal to negotiate) and a good distribution of armour, in profile she looked hunched and purposeful – like a heavyweight preparing to land a devastating punch. Like *Hood*, *Bismarck* always impressed, as one of her few survivors, Fourth Gunnery Officer Baron Burkard von Mullenheim-Rechberg remembers:

'At first sight of this gigantic ship, so heavily armed and armoured, I felt sure that she would be able to rise to any challenge, and that it would be a long time before she met her match. A long life was very obviously in store for her … As I began my service in the *Bismarck* I had supreme confidence in this ship. How could it be otherwise?'

Now she was commissioned, *Bismarck*'s work-up began. Under their captain, Ernst Lindemann, her crew had to get her – and themselves – in shape. That meant moving out from the Blohm and Voss yard in Hamburg, up the Kiel Canal and into the Baltic to Gotenhafen (now again called Gdynia). The great ship was as steady as expected in

BELOW *14 February 1939 – the launch of the Bismarck.*

a seaway, smoothly running at speed, well-behaved under low power, with good rudder response. But one thing her captain discovered she could not do well was steer without her rudder by using opposing engines – not even with the rudders amidships. It would prove to be a fatal flaw.

ABOVE LEFT Bismarck *fitting out at Blohm & Voss, Hamburg.*

Bismarck's trials continued from the end of September right into November. Then followed the first firings of her huge 15-inch (38-cm) guns. Again she reacted well, as her proud fourth gunnery officer recalls:

'Boom! The ship seemed to be abruptly jarred sideways, a few loose objects came adrift, a few light bulbs shattered, but that was all … Of course, the concussion had already been felt throughout the ship. Her steadiness in the water showed the *Bismarck* to be an ideal gun platform.'

With *Bismarck* back at Blohm and Voss in Hamburg for final completion, her crew were able to celebrate Christmas on shore, many with their families. A blessing indeed, as, for most of the ship's company, this would be their last Christmas. But once they were all back on board in the New Year, there was frustration for Captain Lindemann: the Kiel Canal was blocked by a sunken ship and heavy ice. *Bismarck* could not get back on trials until March. So in the meantime, training and battle practice went on in the confined waters of Hamburg harbour, with the men 'shaking down' into their ship and making it their home.

Bismarck then returned to Gotenhafen. Now the pace quickened, with hydrophone trials (listening out for other ships with underwater echo-sounding), practice on the guns and battery firing day and night. *Prinz Eugen* – soon to be *Bismarck*'s companion in short-lived victory – came on station with her for more exercises. The *Arado* seaplane air crews were trained, exercises were conducted with U-boats and refuelling at sea and searchlight drills were carried out. *Bismarck* and her crew were nearing readiness.

They would need all those skills, and more. *Rheinübung* (Exercise Rhine) was approaching.

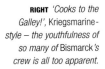

RIGHT *'Cooks to the Galley!', Kriegsmarine-style – the youthfulness of so many of* Bismarck*'s crew is all too apparent.*

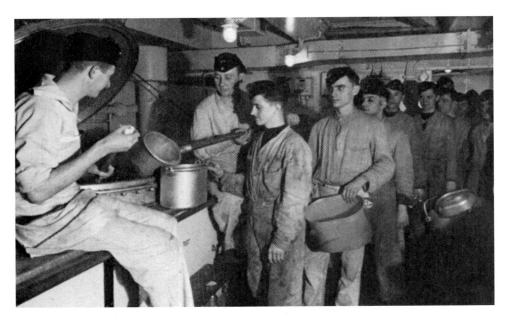

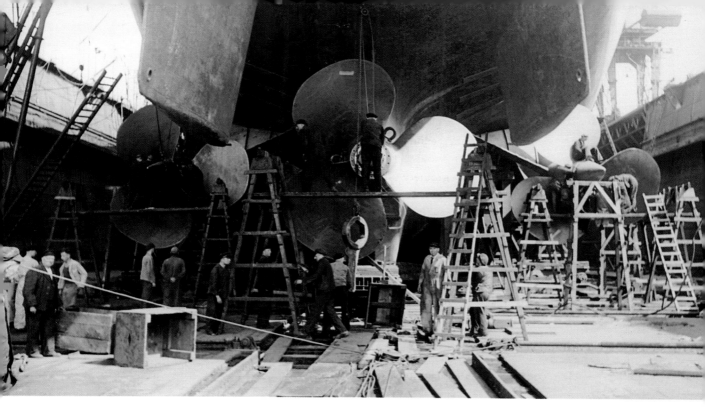

ABOVE *Achilles heel –* Bismarck*'s rudders and propellers.*

LEFT Bismarck *returns to Hamburg, Christmas 1940.*

Six **Years** in the **Making**

chapter **two**

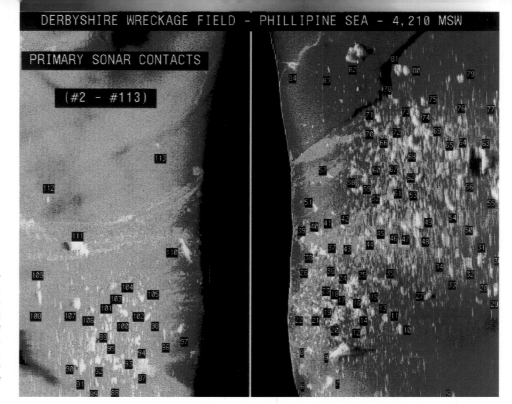

DERBYSHIRE WRECKAGE FIELD - PHILLIPINE SEA - 4,210 MSW

PRIMARY SONAR CONTACTS

(#2 - #113)

THE BIRTH OF AN IDEA

It is interesting how an idea like this one – to mount an expedition to locate and film one of the world's most famous warships, now lying 3,000 metres beneath an extremely inhospitable stretch of water known as the Denmark Strait – gets started. I certainly had no great plan when I first broached the idea at a party in early March 1995. In fact, my naïve announcement that 'I would like to find the wreck of HMS *Hood*' was a somewhat cheeky reply to a completely reasonable question put to me by my co-author, Rob White. If Rob hadn't asked me what I would like to find next, I seriously doubt whether we would have ever embarked on this journey together.

The cause of our celebration and the reason for this gathering on a typically cold and wet, early spring evening in London was the transmission of a television documentary on the loss of the MV *Derbyshire*. The *Derbyshire* is a British combination (oil/bulk/ore) carrier that sank without trace in 1980 with the loss of forty-four lives. The vessel's disappearance still represents the largest single shipping casualty in British maritime history. While working for Oceaneering Technologies – an American company that specializes in deepwater aircraft and shipwreck investigations – I had directed the search for *Derbyshire*. We had found it in 1994 lying shattered at a depth of 4,210 metres off the coast of Japan.

The successful location of *Derbyshire* was a triumph on many fronts. Firstly, the search was funded by the International Transport Workers Federation, a trade union that included seamen of all nationalities. (Many such seamen were being killed at alarming rates through the loss of bulk carriers like Derbyshire.) The ITF's funding of the Derbyshire search was significant, in that it was the first time a seafarer's union had taken matters into their own hands and actively investigated why its members were dying in suspect ships while the rest of the industry turned a blind eye to this appalling loss of life. Second, the search for the Derbyshire was an underdog project that was hugely successful despite

'Derbyshire' search team finds wreckage of vessel

By Andrew Guest, Industrial Correspondent

having being dismissed by some experts (notably Dr Robert Ballard of *Titanic* fame, who was reported to believe that a *Derbyshire* search would be unfeasible and financially prohibitive). Finally, Rob White had arranged for a television reporter to accompany the search and this had led to the production of an award-winning documentary that was being shown as part of the Channel 4 series *Dispatches*.

Although based in America, I was in London at the time of the broadcast. I had been invited to view the *Dispatches* programme with Rob and the ITN production team at their headquarters on Gray's Inn Road. Everyone involved in the project was in expectant mood, hoping the documentary would be well received, and, more importantly, that it would force the government to reopen the formal inquiry into *Derbyshire*'s loss. Looking to kill some time before the programme, I decided to visit the Guildhall Library in central London to conduct some basic research using their Lloyd's Marine Collection. My work in recent years had focused increasingly on shipwreck investigations and, as I needed to familiarize myself with public sources of maritime information, the Guildhall Library was a good place to start.

I had no particular ship in mind when I entered the library. I just wanted to learn how to use the collection in case I had a future need for information. As I sat down at a computer terminal in the reading room, I realized I would need the name of a ship to start my practice research. Then it popped into my head – HMS *Hood*. The only reason the *Hood* was on my mind was because of a brief conversation I had had with a friend and colleague, Don Dean, the previous month about important shipwrecks worth finding. We both agreed that, as *Bismarck* had been found by Ballard and his team years before, it seemed appropriate that *Hood* should be located and filmed in order to tell the other half of the story. At the time, my knowledge of *Hood* was limited to the battle she fought against *Bismarck*, and I knew very little about her glorious life as Flagship of the Royal Navy and how important a symbol she was to the British public.

My research directed me to microfilms of *The Times*, which reported in bold headlines, two days after the battle, the loss of *Hood* and the continued pursuit of

Bismarck by British naval forces. The reports were riveting – they related the deep sense of grief and shock at the loss of the ship ('the heaviest blow the navy has received in the war') and her crew ('the finest officers and men in the fleet'). The Admiralty's official statement also pointed to the likely cause of *Hood*'s loss, saying she 'received an unlucky hit in a magazine and blew up'. Two days later, on 28 May 1941, in even larger headlines, the sinking of *Bismarck* after a 1,750-mile chase was announced. This was followed by the full story of the relentless pursuit, told in a detailed statement by the Admiralty. The *Hood* had been well avenged, admiration for the British Navy had been restored and the scales were more than evened.

I was fascinated by the news reports, but what intrigued me most was a secondary article which commented on the design of *Hood*, supposedly improved after the lessons of the First World War to make her invulnerable to the danger of a lucky shell penetrating directly into a magazine. The writer surmised: 'Her loss therefore immediately raises the technical question of whether a miscalculation was made, while probably leaving no evidence to assist in answering it.' This article drew an immediate and sharp rebuke in a subsequent letter to the editor, which argued that a lucky hit or technical miscalculation were not the reasons for *Hood*'s sudden annihilation. Rather, claimed the writer, it was 'because she had to fight a ship twenty-two years more modern than herself'.

In this difference of opinions I saw a unique opportunity to prove how it was possible to locate virtually any ship on the seabed and solve the mystery of why it sank. If I could do this with *Hood* – a famous and beloved ship lost in a swirl of questions more than a half a century ago – it would give further proof to the shipping industry that it was feasible to investigate shipwreck casualties to determine their cause and to use those lessons to prevent similar losses. Armed with improved technology in the form of sonars, robotics, lights and cameras, we no longer had to wait fifteen years before lessons could be learned from losses such as that of *Derbyshire* – lessons that could save lives today.

So, when later that evening at the end of the *Dispatches* documentary, Rob asked me what I would like to find next, my immediate reply was HMS *Hood*. Rob's reaction was palpable. His eyes widened and his mouth opened but not a word came out. I had no true sense at the time of why he was so stunned by my answer, but my enthusiasm for the idea of finding *Hood* would grow immensely less than two months later when I met Ted Briggs for the first time.

MEETING TED BRIGGS

As soon as the idea of locating *Hood* was out in the open we began to make progress on making it happen. The following day I was back in the Guildhall Library continuing the preliminary research and Rob was working the phones and his naval contacts to find out what authority(s) would need to be consulted for their approval to dive on the wreck if we were successful in locating it. The popular view, and in my opinion the correct one, is that the wreck of HMS *Hood* is a war grave, and thus express permission would be needed to visit her. Wrecked British military vessels such as *Hood* remain the property of the Crown. Legal authority over the wreck therefore rests with the Ministry of Defence. It is only right that moral authority – arguably the highest authority – rests with the survivors and the direct relatives of those killed. Without their support, it was clear the project would never get off the ground, so the first port of call for Rob was Ted Briggs, the sole living survivor of *Hood*'s sinking and president of the HMS *Hood* Association.

Within days of my return to America, Rob phoned to report that he had been in touch with Ted and that we had been cordially invited to the *Hood* Association annual reunion dinner, which was held in Portsmouth each year on the weekend nearest to the date of the sinking. At the dinner we would be given the opportunity to present our plan to the association membership for their consideration and approval. Scarcely

BELOW *Rob White (*centre*) with* Hood *veterans outside the* Hood *Church in Boldre, Hampshire after the 1995 commemoration service.*

a week had gone by since I mentioned *Hood* to Rob and already he had organized a meeting that would likely determine the fate of the project. I was worried about the short time we had to put together a credible plan, but realized that the opportunity was too good not to accept. I began making plans to be back in London two months later.

The Seatrade Awards Ceremony – a prestigious event that recognizes improved standards throughout the maritime industry – provided the perfect reason for my quick return to London. Oceaneering had been short-listed in the Safety-At-Sea category for our work in locating *Derbyshire* and I was invited to accept our award. My schedule also allowed time for a visit to the Public Records Office (PRO) in Kew, where the most important naval archives are held. It was vital to unearth more clues to the sinking position of *Hood* so that I could be confident of locating the wreck. Sparse or imprecise navigation clues would mean that a very large area would have to be searched, which in turn would mean that the search expedition would be time-consuming and thus very costly. The side-scan sonar system we had used to locate *Derbyshire* and other deepwater wrecks was the most efficient in the world at the time, but there was a limit to how large an area would be an acceptable risk. I put the upper end of this limit at about 600 square nautical miles – roughly four times the area covered in locating *Titanic*. Fortunately, the Official Boards of Inquiry and other records kept at the PRO contained enough navigation clues to suggest that the ultimate search box would be within this limit and that our meeting with Ted and the *Hood* Association the following day would not be in vain.

The *Hood* Association hold their annual reunion dinner in the Royal Sailors Home Club on Queen Street in Portsmouth. This would be their nineteenth reunion dinner since the association was formed in 1975, but I had been forewarned that the number of people attending was slowly dwindling due to the advanced age of the membership – most were approaching their eighties. I had little idea what to expect of the evening, and thought the best strategy would be to remain low-key. Upon arriving in the banqueting hall and finding my seat I could see that remaining low-key would be impossible – I was seated directly in the centre of the head table with Ted Briggs to my right and John R. Williams (J.R.), the association's chairman, to my left. Rob White was slightly less in the firing line than me, but he too was seated at the head table. I didn't feel we merited the attention, but it was clear that the association's executive committee considered us honoured guests – and an honour it was.

Ted and J.R. are obviously close friends, but their personalities are very different. Ted is quite shy and soft-spoken and he is utterly polite. Over our dinner of roast beef with Yorkshire pudding, he listened to my plans and my reasons for locating *Hood*. While Ted seemed open to the idea, he never gave a clear indication of his feelings one way or the other. J.R., on the other hand, is a far more gregarious character. He is always looking for the chance to tell a joke or get in some type of pointed remark to, or about, his ex-shipmates. J.R. was M.C. for the dinner and his humour kept the evening rolling along. It did not take long to recognize that the core group of members who actually served on *Hood* enjoyed a special relationship. They were nearly all ordinary ratings (non-officers), so when they got together as a group there was none of the usual deference to rank. It was as though they were young men again, idly killing time on the deck of a ship telling stories and constantly teasing each other. J.R. would instigate the banter while Ted would stand to the side and roll his eyes heavenward.

After dinner, Rob White was asked to say a few words about our proposal to locate *Hood* and film her for the making of a major television documentary. The core of our idea was to tell the human story of *Hood* through the experiences of those who sailed on her, and to find out what actually happened to *Hood* on that tragic morning in the Denmark Strait by visually investigating the wreck. The expedition, with its focus on technology and underwater adventure, would be a way to get a new generation interested in the story of *Hood* and, hopefully, to keep her memory alive. We hoped to reach a broad audience that included children and young adults who were accustomed to watching underwater films but had no knowledge of *Hood*'s history or the importance of her battle with *Bismarck*. The draw for viewers would be the excitement of the expedition and crystal-clear pictures of the wreck on the seabed, but the hook would be the emotional testimony from her former crew assembled in that hall. They represented the last opportunity for others to hear first-hand why *Hood* was so special and what made her one of the Royal Navy's greatest ships. We also committed ourselves to the placing of a memorial plaque on the wreck on behalf of the association, widows and other relatives.

The following day a commemoration service was held in Boldre's Church of St John the Baptist. The church is known as the '*Hood* church', because it contains the memorial of Admiral Holland, who lived in Boldre and was lost on *Hood*. The day was bright and sunny and the small village church was overflowing – not a single seat was spare and the outer aisles were full of people standing. After the service there was a lovely atmosphere outside the church as the *Hood* veterans stood proudly by their ensign with their medals and decorations gleaming in the late-morning sun. Colin Vass, a superb model-maker and *Hood* Association member, had brought his two large models of *Hood* and *Bismarck*, which attracted lots of admiring attention and technical discussion. Seeing the models, I could truly appreciate for the first time how beautiful and graceful both ships were. Beautiful and graceful – an odd way to describe warships built to be feared as machines of destructive power, but these are the words most often used by those who experienced the ships first-hand and now I could understand why.

Later, in the churchyard, we started to get the first indications of positive support regarding the expedition. A number of the *Hood* veterans had agreed to give

interviews and were speaking on camera with Rob about their experiences. One story that stuck in my mind was told by a bearded gentleman who described how he 'went swimming three times in his naval career', meaning that he had had three ships sunk from under his feet. You would expect some measure of horror in his story, but he was quite jolly about it all, even saying he enjoyed one 'swim', as it was in the Mediterranean during summertime. Ted was gracious as ever, posing for photographs next to the model of *Hood* and pointing to where he was stationed on the compass platform during the action with *Bismarck*. He was still reserved about his feelings and it would take some time before he was completely comfortable with the idea of having someone visit his old ship. Finally, it was left to J.R., chairman of the *Hood* Association and a senior figure among his shipmates in every way, to announce that he thought our idea was a fitting way to pay tribute to the *Hood* and to those who died serving on her. Other members standing alongside agreed readily, and with that we had a small, but extremely significant measure of support for our plan.

It was left to Rob to build on this initial verbal support as I headed back to America. Rob had got on very well with Ted and his wife Claire, having conducted a longer interview with Ted back at his home. Rob's passion for *Hood* and the project was infectious. Because of his father's own distinguished naval service, which regretfully did not include HMS *Hood* (the one ship he had desperately wanted to serve on) Rob deeply respected the Royal Navy and wanted the documentary to be a celebration of *Hood*'s long service as its flagship. Whatever reservations Ted may have initially had about the project soon disappeared under the force of Rob's persuasion, for by the end of the following month we had the association's formal pledge of support in a letter signed by both Ted Briggs and J.R. Williams.

THE RESEARCH BEGINS

The preliminary research I had conducted in the PRO in Kew put the area where *Hood* sank in the Denmark Strait at about 63° 20' North and 31° 50' West (this was the position reported by HMS *Norfolk* at 6.15 a.m. on 24 May in her initial wireless transmission to the fleet, but I was to locate and derive several other positions in the course of subsequent research). If accurate, this position would place the wreck in approximately 2,800 metres of water. Although 2,800 metres could not be considered shallow, it posed no worry to me, because our equipment at Oceaneering Technologies was capable of working in depths of up to 6,000 metres. We had already located and filmed the wrecks of *Lucona* and *Derbyshire* in more than 4,000 metres. If I had any concerns, they centred on the extreme northern latitude of the area and the unknown character of the seabed.

Admiral Lütjens chose the Denmark Strait for the breakout of *Bismarck* and *Prinz Eugen* in part because he felt this route – along the ice border with fog, snow and hail making visibility very poor – would be most favourable for a breakthrough unobserved by air reconnaissance. Lütjens' advantage – foiled only by the efficiency of *Suffolk*'s radar – would, I feared, become our disadvantage. The search area would be in a position not far south of the Arctic Circle, right along the edge of the Greenland drift ice. At best, our working window would be limited to two to three months in the height of summer, when there was no danger of icebergs and when the wind and sea conditions were calmest. At worst, the seabed could be strewn with large boulders carried off into the sea by icebergs broken off from glaciers. These boulders, commonly referred to as glacial erratics, could complicate the side-scan search by appearing to look just like shipwreck debris – a problem I had encountered before during a shipwreck investigation off the coast of Norway.

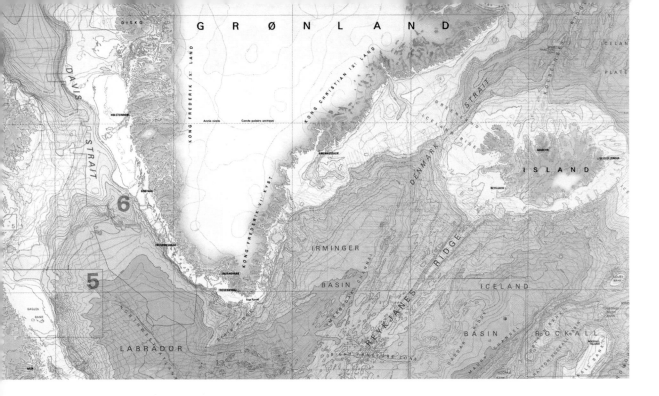

On top of the possible complication of glacial erratics, I had little knowledge of the geology of the search area, as it was so remote and thus relatively unstudied. The nearest major feature was the Reykjanes Ridge, a 2,000-metre high ridge which extends southwest from Iceland to the Mid-Atlantic Ridge and acts as a zone of divergence between two tectonic plates. Fortunately, *Hood* sank to the west of the ridge axis along the margin it shares with a feature named the Irminger Basin (after the Danish Admiral Carl L. Irminger, who conducted hydrographic studies in the area in 1854). Unlike the rocky and rugged terrain of the ridge, I could expect the seabed in the basin to be generally flat and far friendlier to our proposed search efforts. The further west *Hood* actually was when she sank, therefore, the better.

As my research was limited to the odd spare day during visits to London, it was difficult to make much progress in the summer of 1995. That situation was to change, however, when I accepted a position at the UK-based Blue Water Recoveries (BWR) Limited as their survey and research director. At the time, BWR was a newly formed marine-operations firm that specialized in the location of lost merchant cargo vessels and the salvage of their non-ferrous cargoes – mainly copper and tin – on behalf of the original cargo owners. In essence, I had already been working for BWR for much of that summer, as they had commissioned Oceaneering to search for a number of cargo ships in the North Atlantic and Mediterranean and I had been responsible for looking after their project. The career change was an exciting one for me, and I was looking forward to moving to the southeast of England. But the bonus was being given responsibility for developing BWR's fledgling research department, which would involve spending considerable time in the PRO and other UK archives.

The first benefit of working with BWR was the experience I gained in the location of cargo ships sunk mostly during the First and Second World Wars. On behalf of their clients, BWR had established an ambitious plan to locate seventeen shipwrecks over a period of about two years. This plan was unprecedented in its scope, particularly as the average depth of the wrecks targeted was 3,400 metres and two wrecks, if found in 5,800 metres, would represent the deepest ever located. It is difficult enough to go out and find one deepwater shipwreck at a time – the approach followed by most practitioners of the trade – but to attempt to locate seventeen more or less in succession would be a monumental challenge.

At the end of BWR's first season of search operations in 1995, the scorecard read: eight searches completed, four wrecks found and positively identified, and three other wrecks located. Given the short period of time the company had to organize the research and search operations, the result – a fifty per cent success rate – was quite a good one for historic ships.

One of my primary goals after joining BWR was to increase their wreck-location success rate. I began by analysing the 1995 search results to see how they could help predict the navigational errors intrinsic to positions reported during the two World Wars. The concept was simple: when a wreck was found and positively identified you could compare its actual geodetic position on the seabed with the position reported at the time of sinking to determine the error in the reported position. This error could be computed for all types of ships reporting sinking positions, whether friendly or enemy (i.e. mayday reports from the cargo ships themselves, rescue ships, observing ships, attacking submarines and even aircraft). The concept obviously assumes that the wreck falls straight to the seabed without gliding horizontally an appreciable distance, which is not always true. However, for the sake of this analysis, the additional error from this assumption is relatively small – generally less than 500 metres and at most 1 kilometre.

Ships during the world wars all used the same basic method for navigating the seas. They would take daily sextant readings when the stars or sun were visible to determine their observed position, and then, by a method called dead-reckoning, use their logged speed and course to compute a track or estimated position based on the original observed position. As the ship steamed on, errors in the dead-reckoned track would accumulate and the navigation accuracy would degrade until another sextant reading or observed position could be taken. Generally speaking, the absolute best a trained navigator could do in perfect conditions using a sextant was to obtain an observed position that was accurate to 0.5 nautical miles. Positions based on dead-reckoning were considerably less accurate, because of a multitude of factors. Errors could range from a few miles to tens of miles, and in extreme cases hundreds of miles.

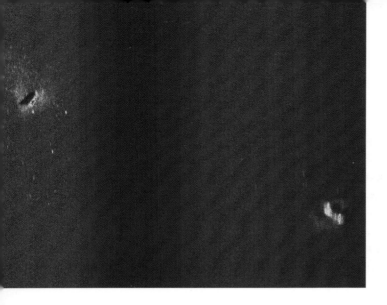

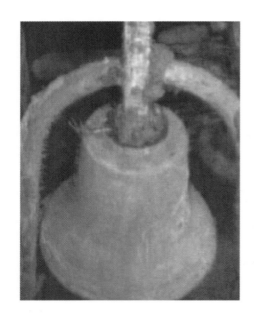

ABOVE *A side-scan sonar image of the deepest shipwreck ever found. The wreck, a Second World War blockade-runner, which broke in two after being scuttled, was found by BWR in 5,762 metres of water.*

ABOVE *An ROV photograph of the ship's bell that confirmed we had found the correct shipwreck.*

My objective in making this study was to establish patterns of different ships' errors that could be applied in future searches. For example, would a British destroyer's navigation be more accurate than that of a German submarine, as might be expected? Would a Second-World-War German submarine's readings be more accurate than those of a First-World-War one? (Surprisingly, we found that German submarine navigation was more accurate during the First World War.)

My first chance to use this data came in 1996 when I was organizing BWR's second season of search operations. I was able to determine two fundamental aspects of each search box: the size of the overall search box and the location of the high-probability zone. The general approach is 'plan for the worst, but hope for the best'. This entails making the search box large enough to account for the worst case of position error – thus ensuring the wreck is ultimately found – but starting the search in the area where the wreck is most likely to be, in the hope that it will be found quickly. In theory, the approach is simple, but in practice it can be complicated, especially when many differing loss clues are involved. In these instances, it is not uncommon to rely on specialized computer programmes to guide your decision making.

The plan in 1996 was to search for eleven wrecks – two of which the team had tried and failed to locate during the 1995 season – in the Mediterranean, North Atlantic and South Atlantic. Oceaneering were again contracted to provide their unique deep-sea, side-scan sonar (Ocean Explorer 6000) and remotely-operated vehicle (Magellan 725 ROV), while my role changed from poacher to gamekeeper. E-mail communications via Inmarsat satellites had improved to the point that high-quality visual images could be sent back from the search ship, allowing me to direct the searches from shore in near real-time. This was a huge benefit, as it allowed me to continue BWR's intensive research programme in the archives while always remaining informed of the progress of the search ship at sea.

By the time our second search season ended it was early 1997 and the new scorecard read: eleven searches completed; eight wrecks found and positively identified; and twenty-two other wrecks located. BWR's success rate had improved to seventy-three per cent, which was a terrific result from any perspective, and we had made some significant gains in our understanding of inherent navigational error and how to apply that error to improve our search results. The navigation-error data computed from each successful search was added to our growing database, enabling us to further refine our search strategies. We also devised a manual method for re-navigating the tracks of ships to correct for surface current and leeway, which paid off handsomely. In one exhilarating three-week period, we found three important wrecks on the trot – all on the first search line. Each wreck was found deeper than 5,000 metres, including the two in 5,800 metres which established a new standard for the deepest wrecks ever found.

My confidence in our ability to locate *Hood* could not have been any higher. I still had some research to do before a final search plan could be formulated, but this was just a matter of finding the time to focus on *Hood* in the archives. More importantly, we needed to find a sponsor who shared our vision for celebrating *Hood*'s long service as the Royal Navy's famous flagship.

A PILGRIMAGE TO HOOD

When Rob and I began to look for a sponsor to fund our *Hood* project, we aimed to find an individual or corporate sponsor who was keen to back the project to the full, including the search expedition to locate *Hood*. This was a costly proposal – I put its price tag at £800,000. We had no illusions about the difficulty we faced in acquiring this sum, especially as neither Rob nor I were skilled in the art of fund-raising. In the end a sponsor was found, but it took nearly two years before the pilgrimage to *Hood* was made. The journey was undertaken on a completely different kind of ship to the one we had originally expected, and there would be no search sonar to accompany the voyage.

Our proposal to potential sponsors centred on the principle that the expedition to find *Hood* was broadly viewed as a good thing to do, in terms of enhancing her memory, and it was to be a project of great respect and sensitivity. These broad themes had struck a chord in the initial meetings and correspondence we had in early 1996, giving us great encouragement. The key first meeting was with the Ministry of Defence (MOD), who, as owners of *Hood* and *de facto* protectors of her war-grave status, had the power to end our dreams immediately if they so wished.

This was definitely an 'all-hands-on-deck' affair, so our 'big gun' – Ted Briggs himself – had been kind enough to travel up from the coast to be with Rob and me.

There was a very tentative start to the meeting, as the three naval representatives present hardly uttered a word. Then, slowly but surely, the ice was broken and I was certain we had their approval by the end of the encounter when they asked whether it would be possible for us to take a white ensign down to the wreck.

The subject of touching the wreck was obviously a very sensitive one, and I felt we had to draw a firm line on it. The topic was raised in our earliest discussions because the idea of bringing one object up to the surface to be part of an exhibition or museum display had been mooted. Much later on, a naval architect in America had proposed the recovery of some steel plate in an attempt to link the loss of *Hood* with that of *Titanic*. This was an even more controversial idea (see page 53). My strong feeling from the outset was that we should not touch the wreck, and that any proposal to do so would attract needless controversy and undermine our precious base of support. Furthermore, recovering an object for display would require special MOD approval, which we were unlikely to obtain. I saw little point in recovering any parts of the wreck, particularly as the National Maritime Museum in Greenwich already had an amazing *Hood* artefact on display for people to view – a wooden transom from a life boat, which washed up on shore years later. 'Look, but don't touch' summed up my feelings, and it was to become a central plank of our proposal.

Acting on the MOD's suggestion that we solicit support from veterans' organizations, Rob quickly obtained strong pledges of support from the Royal British Legion and the Royal Naval Association. In his letter to Rob, the Assistant Secretary of the Royal British Legion, R.D. Hanscomb, wrote of our proposal: 'A visit to the site where HMS *Hood* lies would seem entirely appropriate. The Legion does believe that it is important that we all remember the consequences of war and it is for that reason that we encourage services at war graves in this country and abroad.' Shortly thereafter we were bolstered by an official letter of approval from the MOD, which stipulated that we must adhere to the principle of 'look, but don't touch'.

BELOW *This transom is one of only two items that were found after* Hood*'s sinking and are now on permanent display in UK museums.*

The first glimmer of hope we had in our long hunt for a backer came from America. The US-based Discovery Channel was commissioning a series on battleships and wanted our story of *Hood* to be made as one of their factual documentaries. This was the great news that we had all been waiting for, except that there was one major disappointment: Discovery would fund the making of the documentary, but they could not fund the expedition to find *Hood*. The costs were far too high for the one-hour programme they had in mind, and the story of *Hood* – while a subject of huge popular interest in the UK – would not resonate as much with an American audience.

It was the type of situation that one could only be philosophical about. There would be no search for *Hood*, but there would be a serious documentary made about her life, and all the HMS *Hood* Association veterans, including Ted Briggs, would get a chance to tell their stories. This had been our ultimate objective all along – to make a film to keep *Hood*'s memory alive – so we had to accept this disappointment in exchange for a greater good. The proposal accepted by Discovery also included a trip out to the site of *Hood*'s sinking, so that some of the association's members could take part in a memorial service and pay their final respects to their fallen shipmates. Ted Briggs, if he wanted to make this long, emotional journey back to the place where his life was nearly ended, would be on board.

Thinking big, Rob started making direct requests to various naval staffs on the extremely slight chance that they would be willing to provide a ship to take our party out to where *Hood* lies. I thought Rob's 'slight chance' was more of a wing and a prayer, and so I looked into hiring a transport vessel from Reykjavik, the nearest port, some 250 nautical miles east of the sinking site. For obvious reasons, such as conflicting schedules and the cost of fuel, Rob's requests were all turned down, with one remarkable exception. It turned out that the Royal Danish Navy regularly patrolled this part of the Denmark Strait and, schedules permitting, it was possible that they would have a frigate prepared to combine our trip with one of their patrols. What a stroke of luck! I remember thinking it was too good to be true, but then the offer became even better. Rob was told that the Danes are forever grateful for what Great Britain did in the war to defeat Nazi Germany, and that they consider Ted Briggs a naval hero. They would provide their frigate the HDMS *Triton* for the journey and all stops would be pulled out to make it a very special occasion. They would treat our party as VIP guests.

The trip out to *Hood* was scheduled for March 1997. Three *Hood* veterans had agreed to come: Reverend Ron Paterson MBE (*Hood* 1933–1936), Dennis 'Den' Finden (1938–1941) and Dick Turner (stoker, 1936–1939). They would also be accompanied by Joanna Warrand, vice-president of the *Hood* Association and daughter of the squadron navigating officer who had stepped aside to let Ted off the compass platform as *Hood* was sinking. Unfortunately, Ted had become so anxious about the trip that his blood pressure suddenly rose and his doctor ruled him out. It was a disappointment to everyone, especially Ted, but it was the right decision. Ted had already been at risk once in the Denmark Strait and nobody wanted a repeat performance.

However, it was clear from the accounts brought back by the team that joined HDMS *Triton* that Ted would have greatly appreciated the hospitality enjoyed by his friends from the association. All ten of the party – which included Rob, a camera team and two officers representing the Royal Navy – were made very welcome from the

RIGHT *The service of commemoration for* HMS Hood *aboard* HDMS Triton: Bismarck *is also remembered.*

FAR RIGHT *The Reverend Ron Paterson leads the service on* Triton*'s flight deck.*

moment they joined *Triton* late on Wednesday, 12 March. No sooner had our team come on board than a reception was held for them, with diplomatic representatives, Icelandic media and the ship's officers all attending. The wide bridge of *Triton* became a splendid buffet, well stocked with the excellent food enjoyed by the ship's company. During the party, one of the technicians came forward to present a model of the *Hood* to the *Hood* veterans, who received this unexpected gift with gratitude.

The next day *Triton* sailed at 9 a.m. She arrived at the area of *Hood*'s sinking the following morning at 1 a.m. The entire ship's company, apart from the watchkeepers, attended the service of commemoration that was held later that day on *Triton*'s flight deck. At the end of the service, they all came forward one by one to place a red rose on the waters above the spot where *Hood* lies. A three-gun salute followed.

All of these (and many other) acts of kindness and respect had been suggested and arranged by Captain Svend E. Madsen. The filming facilities on board – from sea level in *Triton*'s RIB (rigid inflatable boat) and in the air from their Lynx helicopter – were both lavish and efficient. The following day, in brilliant sunlight and on a very calm sea, the ship made a visit to the edge of the ice pack off Greenland. Then *Triton* turned back to Iceland. As a final touch, after one more special reception, with the presentation of handsome gifts, the veterans were piped over the side as they left the ship. We could not have had more wholehearted help; our documentary now had its beating heart in all that we had been able to film aboard *Triton*.

The documentary was finished and aired in the US in late 1997. Because it was to be tailored for an American audience more familiar with *Bismarck* than *Hood*, the US producers decided to change Rob's working title from *The Mighty Hood* to *Sunk By The Bismarck* (one could just imagine Winston Churchill turning in his grave over that one). Otherwise, it was an excellent programme that covered *Hood*'s full history, from cradle to grave, and showed why she was such an important symbol to the British public and naval service. The scenes of the memorial service on the deck of the *Triton* were very poignant, and they showed the importance of giving veterans an opportunity to say goodbye to their former shipmates. Regretfully, no main UK television stations could be enticed to broadcast it, so the documentary never reached a wide British audience – perhaps the title was the problem!

By the end of 1997, I had just about given up hope of finding a sponsor to back the expedition. Rob and I had every reason to be proud of our efforts to get the documentary made, and we could be satisfied that our original objective had been fulfilled. An entire year had passed without a single mention of *Hood*, when out of the blue I was contacted by an American reporter who had seen a repeat of *Sunk By The Bismarck* and wanted to write an article about the story of *Hood*'s sinking. His angle was to play up the brittle-steel connection between *Hood* and *Titanic*, largely because the movie entitled *Titanic* had become such a huge hit in America that any article with a connection to the wreck of *Titanic* would be widely published. I was not an advocate of the brittle-steel theory, and – knowing that the brittle-steel theorists would want to recover some steel from *Hood* for testing – I countered that the *Hood* wreck was a war grave and should never be touched. To my surprise, the resulting article was reprinted in *The Times* and the *Daily Mail* in the UK, touching off a storm of controversy, just as I expected it would. Although I came out strongly against touching or disturbing *Hood*, the connection the article made with *Titanic* and brittle steel was enough to raise concerns. The intense reaction many people had to the mere suggestion of touching the wreck proved my initial gut feelings that the British public would not stand for *Hood* being treated the way *Titanic* has been.

Hood's name and the idea of the expedition had worked its way into the press again, but I took no encouragement from this. It had reached the point where I was calling for a 'knight in shining armour' to come to our aid. Unbeknown to me, the knight was named Sarah Marris and she had a block-buster idea.

THE BREAKTHROUGH

The idea of a *Hood* expedition had lain dormant for almost another two years, and any small hope I clung to had long faded, when in the space of a single phone conversation an idea was suggested that transformed my thinking about the entire project and infused me with a burst of reviving energy. I had been speaking with Sarah Marris, a newly recruited commissioning editor for Channel 4, who had shown an interest in the *Hood* project, but felt that the risk of not finding the wreck was too high. To reduce the risk of a total failure, Sarah suggested that the project aim at filming the wreck of the German battleship *Bismarck* as well as finding *Hood*. This way, both sides of the battle could be told in two documentaries. It was an audacious and

BELOW Hood *veteran Dick Turner.*

ABOVE Hood *veteran Den Finden.*

brilliant idea – it had been staring me in the face for all those years, but it was Sarah who realized it in a single moment of clarity. I saw immediately how this new plan would be more exciting to potential sponsors, including Channel 4, but would also be less risky – truly the best of both worlds.

Bismarck, which had already been found, would be easy to re-locate, even though Ballard had kept the precise position secret. I was confident of being able to trace Ballard's steps and in the ability of a wide-swathe, side-scan sonar to cut the search time down to a minimum. *Bismarck* was considerably deeper than *Hood* – 4,800 metres compared to 2,800 metres – but this would not pose a problem for the 6,000-metre rated equipment I planned to use. The video footage Ballard's team had taken of *Bismarck* had been filmed from a towed sled at high altitude with 1980s-vintage black-and-white cameras. Using the latest, most advanced high-resolution colour cameras and powerful, high-temperature lights, we could bring back the first broadcast-quality video of the wreck and probe in places the towed sled could not. *Bismarck* was also closer to obvious mobilization ports such as Cobh in Ireland, which meant the additional transiting time would not be too great. In short, although the addition of *Bismarck* would heighten the challenge, it was a challenge that BWR had successfully faced in the past and we were ready for it.

The sixtieth anniversary of the battle between *Hood* and *Bismarck* was coming up the following year and this gave even more impetus to undertaking the expedition in 2001. The *Hood* veterans whom I had first met in May 1995 would be six years older by then, and even the youngest (like Ted Briggs, who was seventy-eight), could only keep the memory of *Hood* alive for so much longer. I presumed the same would be true of the *Bismarck* veterans, who had also formed an association, the Kameradschaft Schlachtschiff *Bismarck* (Comradeship Battleship *Bismarck*). The idea of finding and filming both wrecks seemed to be the perfect backdrop to a series of documentaries that would recreate the most important battle of the Atlantic of the Second World War and tell the ships' radically different stories through the testimony of those who had served on them.

To get this new idea off the ground, I would have to complete the archival research and navigation analysis on both *Hood* and *Bismarck*, make contact with the Kameradschaft *Bismarck* to seek their approval, and obtain the German government's permission to visit *Bismarck*, which is a war grave to more than 2,100 men. Sarah, along with Julian Ware – Executive Producer of ITN Factual – was standing by to champion the idea of the *Hood/Bismarck* expedition inside Channel 4, subject to me completing the navigation analysis and search planning for both wrecks. Although it would be an unprecedented move by a UK broadcaster to commission such an ambitious and costly project, Channel 4 had recently decided to fund such 'big-event' programmes, and seemed poised to seriously consider our project. The domain of big-budget underwater expeditions had so far been ruled by American broadcasters, but it was clear that Channel 4 were determined to make their mark, particularly as the subject had such important national significance.

I returned from the Christmas holiday break and immediately wrote to Julian to tell him that there was a ninety-five-per-cent chance of finding both wrecks. I reckoned that, at worst, it would take three search lines to re-locate *Bismarck*, and at best one line, but either way I was absolutely sure we would find her. *Hood* was a different proposition altogether, because our search would be the first ever attempted. I still had some fine-tuning of the search plan to do, but I estimated the maximum search box to be 600 square nautical miles. It would take at least eight days to cover such an area, unless we found the wreck sooner in the high-probability box, which I felt we had a very good chance of doing. I drew up a formal proposal for the expedition for Sarah and her colleagues at Channel 4 to review.

Within six weeks the green light I had waited six years for finally came. Channel 4 was one hundred per cent onboard. With ITN Factual's help, they had conceived a multi-faceted approach to the expedition that included a website with live video streaming, live broadcasts from the expedition vessel and a total of three documentaries. Key to the ultimate decision was a meeting we had with Channel 4's Director of Programming, Tim Gardam. In the opening minutes of the meeting, Tim revealed that his family had relatives on *Bismarck* and HMS *Rodney* – effectively both sides of the final battle. I had experienced this many, many times before – mostly with *Hood*. People I met were often proud to tell of the direct connection they had with these honourable ships. Possibly for this reason, Tim intuitively understood what we wanted to achieve and the sensitivity the project required.

One of the first people I called was Ted Briggs. Ted had patiently tolerated the ups and downs of our efforts over the past six years, and I had lost touch with him when the project was in limbo. I wanted to give him the good news, but I also wanted to sound him out about participating in the project if he was up to it. Perhaps this would be a second chance for Ted to realize his own personal dream of making that important pilgrimage to *Hood*.

There were dozens of people to call afterwards: ship owners; camera and lighting manufacturers; weather forecasters; the Kameradschaft *Bismarck*; government ministries; sonar, ROV and submarine operators; navigation suppliers; communication specialists and so on. The list seemed endless, but precise planning is half the battle in a project like this one, especially when the weather window is so narrow.

'Exercise **Rhein**'
Execution
and Denial

chapter **three**

PRELUDE

'The *Kriegsmarine* is to carry out commerce warfare, and it will be aimed primarily against England.'

Seekriegsleitung Directive No. 1 for the Conduct of the War, 31 August 1939.

Clearly, the role of the German navy in the Second World War would turn largely on its ability to destroy merchant shipping. It would aim to starve Britain to death, in very much the same way that Germany herself had nearly starved to death under Allied blockade in the last months of the First World War. The High Command of the German navy – the Seekriegsleitung – accordingly planned for its big ships a war of skulking and attrition, with helpless merchantmen being pounded into blazing wrecks by the guns of the *Kriegsmarine*'s cruisers, while the battleships warded off escorting British ships. The moment the balance of forces went against this licensed slaughter – the moment a serious challenge appeared – the German ships were to cut and run and hide. They were definitely not there to pick a fight with anything their own size.

It was an inglorious but effective concept, which reflected with pitiless accuracy the reality of the balance of forces: the Royal Navy had far more capital ships than the Germans, old though many of them might be, and the profits of attrition were accordingly all on the British side. The German plan may not have been heroic, but it was certainly realistic. Anyone joining the *Kriegsmarine* hoping to end the unfinished business of Jutland would be disappointed.

Directive No. 1 led straight to the framing of the orders that ended with the destruction of the *Bismarck*. '*Rheinübung*' ('Exercise Rhine') followed through the cold logic of the German naval high command to the letter – in theory. '*Rhein*' was put together by the naval staff in the wake of the commerce-raiding 'Exercise Berlin', which the German navy had counted as a significant success. During 'Berlin', the battlecruisers *Scharnhorst* and *Gneisenau*, under the command of Admiral Günther Lütjens, had left Kiel on 22 January 1941 and headed into the Atlantic to cause havoc among the convoys. Their key problem – as always for

THE GERMAN FLEET!

BEST WISHES FROM— MICKEY GLENN. 22-5-40

ABOVE *One Hood's view of his ship's wartime mission.*

'EXERCISE RHEIN' EXECUTION AND DENIAL

German warships operating on the high seas, rather than the confined waters of the Baltic or the North Sea – was how to break out undetected from German home ports, in order to keep the key advantage of surprise. All routes involved going round the north of Britain, but they all had the same disadvantage: they squeezed the ships into narrow corridors in which they might be found by the British. Because of its distance from key ports and airfields, and the high chance of poor visibility, Lütjens chose the northernmost route, the Denmark Strait. The strait lay just off the edge of the ice pack between Iceland and Greenland. The escape was a complete success, despite a near-meeting with an insufficiently inquisitive warship, and on 4 February Lütjens found himself and his two ships heading into the wide Atlantic, ready to hunt down their prey.

In a sixty-day voyage of destruction, *Scharnhorst* and *Gneisenau* set about the shipping bringing desperately-needed supplies across the Atlantic. Their first target was the merchantman *Kantara,* transporting aircraft and a mixed cargo. She was sunk on the morning of 22 February – it had taken Lütjens that long to acquire a target, with his careful withdrawals, as prescribed, from any hint of a ship that might be able to give him a serious fight. The *Kantara*'s crew were picked up, and *Gneisenau* moved on to her next target, the *Trelawny.* Meanwhile, *Scharnhorst* was reporting her first kill – the tanker *Lustrous.* So it was to continue for a month. Lütjens successfully evaded the British forces sent out to hunt him down. He managed to sink a total of twenty-two ships, destroying 116,000 tons of British shipping. Lütjens' targets were all picked off ship by ship; escorting battleships held him off the massed convoys. As he made his way back into Brest on 22 March, his commander-in-chief, Grand-Admiral Erich Raeder, was in no doubt about the significance of what 'Exercise Berlin' had achieved:

'On completion of the first occasion in German naval history in which a squadron of our battleships has operated successfully in the wide spaces of the Atlantic, I congratulate you and your subordinates on the fine resolution you have shown and the fine results you have achieved … I hope before long to be able to put an even stronger force under your command for a similar operation on the high seas.'

Raeder's wish was to come true within less than a month, with fateful results for Lütjens and all who sailed with him.

ABOVE *Vice-Admiral Günther Lütjens.*

MANOEUVRE

As with so many strategic and tactical decisions in war, launching '*Rheinübung*' was as much a matter of balancing political and institutional needs as it was a case of taking the war to the enemy. Typically, too, along the way the first intentions were tossed and turned by the fortunes of war, so that '*Rhein*' ended up a very different operation from the one first conceived by the German naval staff. Those changes may, as much as anything else, have contributed to the disaster that overwhelmed the German navy's – and the world's – most powerful battleship. However, once the exercise was underway, its momentum seemed to carry all along with it. Meanwhile, the original aim of the exercise – the delivery of maximum force to the optimum point – began to be lost from sight.

Hitler had once said: 'On land I am a hero. At sea I am a coward.' And he was right to be a coward as he surveyed the naval forces at his disposal. He had begun the war well before the *Kriegsmarine* was ready. Its devastating achievements against its enemies are all the more remarkable for that. And by 2 April 1941, with the U-boats in the Atlantic under pressure, the staff were preparing '*Rheinübung*'. This time, the force sent out would be far heavier than that for 'Exercise Berlin'. It would consist of the freshly blooded *Gneisenau* (Lütjens' flagship in 'Berlin'), the recently completed heavy cruiser *Prinz Eugen* and the brand-new battleship *Bismarck*.

Again Lütjens would lead. But for 'Rhein' his task was even more complex than before. In attempting to reconcile their ambitious plans for surface warfare against the convoys with their dread of losing their newest and most powerful ship, the orders given to Lütjens by various elements of the German naval leadership left him with a maze of intentions to negotiate that might try the patience of even this most methodical and analytical of men.

Lütjens was to lead attacks on escorted convoys – but preserve his own combat capability. He was empowered to engage other battleships – but this should not be his primary objective, rather he should let the other ships in his command attack the merchantmen. He should fight other battleships – but not to defeat them, just to tie them down. Finally, unavoidable combat should be conducted as forcefully as possible – but, as Lütjens' commander-in-chief reminded him at their last meeting, 'It would be a mistake to risk a heavy engagement for limited and perhaps uncertain results.'

Dr Eric Grove comments: '"Exercise Rhine" suffered from a number of contradictions, all of which stemmed from Germany's position as the inferior naval power. German surface ships were being expected to operate in an ocean that was still commanded by the enemy. Any damage to the raiders might doom them. Friendly bases were not easily available. Therefore risk had to be limited and engagements accepted only when absolutely necessary. The extent to which this allowed the fleet commander to press action was left to him. Raeder thought Lütjens could be trusted to know what to do, and perhaps no one knew Raeder's mind better than the fleet commander did, but not even the brightest and most subtle admiral could overcome orders that gave objectives that were fundamentally incompatible. No wonder that, when *Hood* and *Prince of Wales* hove into sight on 24 May, Lütjens did not, apparently, know quite what to do.'

To add to the teething troubles of 'Rheinübung', the plans suddenly lost a third of their viability. *Gneisenau*, in dock undergoing repairs in the tactically advantageous port of Brest on the Atlantic coast, was severely damaged in an heroic attack by an RAF Beaufort torpedo bomber. The aircraft crashed almost immediately after releasing its torpedo, but the blow she and her crew had delivered told: *Gneisenau*, after this and further attacks, would eventually be *hors de combat* for six whole months. Then there were further delays. Although the 'Rheinübung' departure had originally been planned for 28 April, this date suddenly had to be changed after *Prinz Eugen* detonated a mine near Kiel. She would need a thorough check before she could go to sea. More delays came after 15 May, when Lütjens decreed that a repeatedly faulty crane should be completely overhauled before putting to sea.

All these hold-ups gave time for more reflection. Lütjens even proposed a delay so that the 'Rhein' task force could be doubled in size, allowing it to be joined by *Scharnhorst*, on finishing her engine repairs, and *Tirpitz*, *Bismarck*'s nearly completed sister. But Grand-Admiral Raeder would brook no further postponement – with good reason, says Dr Eric Grove:

'Raeder had to do something. Time was of the essence. The next month would see a whole new war on land and in the air in the east, one that might tie up the navy's strength in the Baltic for a long time. The USA, already a near belligerent on Britain's side, might enter the war at any time, with an immediate effect on the German navy's scope for Atlantic operations. The operation had to go ahead as soon as possible with the available forces. And *Bismarck* gave the Germans a means of neutralizing even the most powerful convoy escort. She could protect an accompanying cruiser, allowing her to make short work of the defenceless merchantmen with gunfire and torpedoes. Whole convoys might be massacred at one blow – with immeasurable effects on morale in battered Britain. The Royal Navy would be seen to have been stretched beyond breaking point. Then might Churchill not at last be overthrown and Britain forced to sue for peace, perhaps before the opening of the planned Eastern Front against the USSR? That way, a war on two fronts might be avoided. It was worth the gamble.'

The delays at least gave time for *Bismarck* to be anointed by a visit from the Führer. On 1 May, Hitler himself came onboard the ship whose launch he had smilingly attended just two years before. He seems to have been somewhat dumbfounded by the sight of her, despite evincing a keen interest in the gunnery-control system. He remained mainly silent in response to two presentations from Lütjens, only raising one issue: the heavy numerical superiority of the British. A prescient remark indeed; as prescient as his clear foreboding that *Bismarck* was too valuable to risk. Fearing cancellation born of those forebodings, the *Kriegsmarine* took care not to give their Führer a firm sailing date – indeed that only came through to him when the operation was already under way. A coward at sea Hitler may have been, but on this occasion history shows that his innate fear of this operation was well and truly justified.

However, despite all the problems, anxieties and delays, 'Rheinübung' was finally on. *Bismarck* slipped away from the outer roads of her Gotenhafen base in the early hours of 19 May 1941. *Götterdämmerung* awaited her.

ESCAPE

But it was a *Götterdämmerung* that would be preceded by a Valhalla for more than 1,400 men of the Royal Navy. As *Bismarck* made her way eastwards out of the Baltic Sea into the 'Great Belt' off the coast of Denmark – in fact a relatively narrow waterway, despite its strange name – the Royal Navy's Home Fleet was already uneasily aware of the threat she posed. The German 'Fleet in Being' – just the presence, the existence of the few capital ships the Nazis could boast – tied up the Royal Navy's warships and placed a constant and unyielding pressure on all the resources it possessed.

On Tuesday, 20 May 1941, the tip of that pressure point was on Admiral Sir John Tovey, Commander-in-Chief of the Home Fleet. His new battleship, *King George V*, was at anchor with *Hood* and the rest of the fleet in the often desolate, sometimes strangely beautiful base in Scapa Flow in the Orkney Islands. Thanks to an early intelligence report, Tovey knew that the Germans were out. The question was, what would Lütjens do next? Tovey had a limited number of ships to cover a vast area of stormy and unfriendly sea. Visibility could vanish almost to zero, icebergs could be mistaken for warships, and even the narrow Denmark Strait – one likely exit into the Atlantic – offered the Germans at least 40 nautical miles of searoom.

BELOW Bismarck *prepares for Exercise* Rhein.

The Mighty Hood – *at home in Scapa Flow.*

The *Bismarck* group had five options and two realistic choices in their bid to break out to the Atlantic. They could make for the Pentland Firth, between the Orkneys and Scotland: virtually impossible because of the certainty of detection and air attack. They could go just a touch further north, between the Orkney Islands and the Shetlands: the same problem applied. They could go between the Faeroe Islands and Shetlands: still problematic. Or, more realistically, they could save fuel by dashing between Iceland and the Faeroes. Or finally, they could go north round Iceland and down through the Denmark Strait along the pack ice of Greenland, giving a wide berth to the British minefields probing out from the northwest of Iceland.

For a methodical and prudent man like Lütjens, the Denmark Strait must have always seemed very attractive – not least because of his successful dash into the Atlantic through it with *Scharnhorst* and *Gneisenau* not long before. But Tovey still had to cover all the options. He made his main dispositions. The three-funnelled heavy cruisers *Norfolk* and *Suffolk* would cover the Denmark Strait; the cruisers *Manchester* and *Birmingham* the Iceland–Faeroes gap; and air patrols would be set in place from Greenland to Orkney. Tovey divided his 'heavies' into two groups: the battlecruiser HMS *Hood* and the barely ready battleship *Prince of Wales* under the flag of Vice-Admiral Lancelot Holland; and *Wales'* sister *King George V* with the thin-skinned battlecruiser *Repulse* under his own command. Each group had its weaknesses, but would have to do.

Dr Eric Grove comments: 'This made two fast forces effectively "one and a half" capital ships strong for each exit. It was the logical deployment pattern. *Hood* with *KGV* and *Prince of Wales* with *Repulse* would have produced two highly unbalanced groups and Holland would have had to shift his flag to *Prince of Wales*, a highly disruptive event when he had a fully operational flagship already, and one into which he had only just moved. Tovey was too sensible to even consider it.'

But where on earth had *Bismarck* and *Prinz Eugen* got to?

By 21 May, Tovey knew the German task force had been in the Kattegat, the waterway between Denmark and Sweden. Her passage had been reported by the Swedish cruiser *Gotland* – a report swiftly passed on through friendly contacts in the Norwegian government-in-exile in Stockholm. That evening, the Norwegian resistance in Kristiansand, at the gateway into the North Sea, reported the passage of the German ships. But then the weather came to Tovey's aid. It was too good, too clear, for Lütjens to risk running out in the open sea between the Shetlands and Norway. He therefore decided to put into a fjord near Bergen in Norway to lie up and wait for the visibility to shut down before his task force came under the threat of British air reconnaissance. During this period of marking time *Prinz Eugen* was refuelled, but *Bismarck*, strangely, was not.

Now the British had a stroke of luck. At noon, two photo-reconnaissance Spitfires, unarmed to save weight and fly high, had been despatched from Wick airfield just south of John o'Groats to try to catch *Bismarck* on camera. The sunny, clear conditions were perfect for photo reconnaissance. So it is that Flying Officer Michael Suckling finds his place in history. Close to the point where his fuel state would compel him to turn for home, Suckling broke through the clouds over Grimstadfjord near Bergen at 25,000 feet to see the shape of a very large warship below him. It was 1.15 p.m. Click-click-click went the shutter on his camera. Blissfully unaware, *Bismarck* and *Prinz Eugen* had been rumbled.

However, it took a *Keystone Cops*-type episode to get this information to London and those who needed it in good time. Once Suckling had touched down in Wick and

BELOW Bismarck *nearing Grimstadfjord.*

the photos had been assessed, there was only one plane that could get the pictures to where they were needed – his own. Back into the Spitfire went the Flying Officer, but before he could reach London, 650 miles away his fuel gauge was heading towards empty. With great initiative, Suckling landed near his home town of Nottingham in the middle of the night, woke up a friend who owned a garage nearby, requisitioned a car and petrol and drove through the blackout to London to deliver his vital pictures first thing in the morning.

So now the Admiralty knew where its threat lay – or at least, where it had lain. The next question to vex Tovey, given the inevitable time-lag in receiving and processing information in those pre-satellite days, was: had *Bismarck* and *Prinz Eugen* set forth again? Grimstadfjord was obviously just a port of call. And now the weather began to play Lütjens' game. Rain and mist, the raiders' friends, had settled over the northern seas. As a precaution, Tovey ordered Holland to sea with *Hood* and *Prince of Wales* and a screen of accompanying destroyers. They were to patrol in a position which would enable them quickly to reach both the key escape routes for Lütjens: between Iceland and the Faeroes, and between Greenland and Iceland. Just before midnight on Wednesday, 21 May 1941, the mighty *Hood* set sail once more from the waters she had known so well in peace and in war. She would never return.

ABOVE *No hiding place: Bismarck caught on camera in Grimstadfjord.*

Was *Bismarck* out and on her way? Or was she still in her fjord, after receiving orders from a justifiably nervous Führer to hold off on the operation? Or was she even on her way back, Hitler having let his premonitions get the better of his grand admiral's plans? A plan to bomb *Bismarck* in Grimstadfjord had flopped: only a couple of the eighteen aircraft that had set out from Wick found the target area, where they bombed blind and ineffectively. With the weather blocking all coastal-command operations, Tovey too was blindfolded, having to guess his way, bouncing from one potential underinformed decision to

'EXERCISE RHEIN' EXECUTION AND DENIAL

another. He really needed someone who could fly blind to Norway and get him the answers he so desperately needed.

He got him. At Hatston air base, just across Scapa Flow, was a remarkable man – an ex-observer and navigator from the 'seat-of-the-pants' days when aerial navigation was almost as much a matter of art form and instinct as it was of training and maps. Commander Geoffrey Rotherham was flying a desk by 1941, helping to run an air station that was more about instruction than actual warfare. But when asked if he would find out what Tovey needed to know, he did not hesitate. He had an equally ready and able pilot: Lieutenant Noel Goddard, himself more used to towing targets than finding them.

The aircraft Rotherham and Goddard used was hardly cutting edge – it was an American Maryland, a bomber demoted to a twin-engined target towtruck. But this scratch combination worked wonders. Through sheer navigational skill, and the occasional foray to 100 feet to check out the sea beneath them, Rotherham made a dead accurate landfall through heavy cloud cover just where he intended on the Norwegian coast. The Maryland lumbered towards Grimstadfjord, found it and a neighbouring fjord empty, checked out Bergen (to a fury of anti-aircraft fire), flew over another empty fjord and turned for home, radioing in the vital information as they went. But, as the aircraft's radio operator John Armstrong recalls, their message almost didn't get through:

'We were briefed to use an HF frequency, a coastal-command frequency, and a coastal-command call sign. But we set the radio up for that frequency, and called and called and called, but no joy – so I took a chance and shifted to a medium frequency, onto our target-towing frequency at Hatston, and lo and behold we called them and he came up first time. It was sheer luck there was anybody on the end of it!'

Bismarck and *Prinz Eugen* had vanished. They were on the way into battle – into their confrontation with *Prince of Wales* and *Hood*. Tovey adjusted his dispositions, called in the aircraft carrier *Victorious* to join him along with four cruisers and six destroyers, and then joined his staff for an eve-of-battle supper.

While the British were enjoying the benefits of accurate intelligence, the *Luftwaffe* and the German naval-intelligence system were delivering duff gen in large quantities to Lütjens and his task force. A full day after *Hood* and her consorts had sailed, Group North – the command team responsible for *'Rheinübung'* in northern waters – blithely informed Lütjens that they were reconfirming that his breakout had not been detected. No ship movements from Scapa Flow had been sighted, they told him, and no operational detachment of British forces towards him had occurred either. It was a kind of Grand Slam of misinformation. Effectively, according to Group North's sunny view of the matter, none of the information from the *Gotland* had been passed on, nor had the sightings by the many other vessels from neutral or hostile nations that had witnessed *Bismarck* and *Prinz Eugen* making for the North Sea. Had Kapitänleutnant von Mullenheim-Rechberg been privy at the time to these upbeat assessments, they would doubtless have stupefied him. 'It did seem to me,' he says, 'that there had been far too many opportunities for our formation to be sighted and, when I thought about what this might do to our mission, I felt that a shadow had fallen over it. I doubt that I was the only one in the ship who had such thoughts, yet none of my younger shipmates, at any rate, said anything about it. What good would it have done? Nothing could be changed. The only thing to do was hope for the best.'

But *'Rheinübung'* was doomed. The fact was that one of the operation's key advantages – which had so sustained 'Exercise Berlin' – had been lost. Surprise was gone, and the pursuit was on.

PURSUIT

For Ted Briggs and his shipmates in HMS *Hood*, the problem was deciding whether or not this pursuit was just another wild-goose chase – of which they'd had at least their fair share – or the real thing at last. Despatched to one of their least-favourite standby locations, the bleak Hvalfjord in Iceland, Ted's first reaction was probably typical of his fellow watchkeepers: '"Oh God, another cold, late night," I thought.' Then, at 10.30 p.m. on Thursday 22 May 1941, Briggs carried a signal to *Hood*'s compass platform that would resolve those doubts and change his life completely. It read: *'Bismarck* and consort sailed. Proceed to cover area southwest of Iceland.'

ABOVE *Ted Briggs as a young signalman.*

Back in Scapa Flow, as the C-in-C Home Fleet sat down to dine, one of his junior ratings, far out in the inhospitable waters off Iceland, was ready to eat too – but at the same time, not ready at all. '"Perhaps this is it?" I wondered,' recalls Briggs. '"Perhaps this is the big one?" The feeling that I was hungry, yet did not want to eat, nagged at my stomach. Looking around me, I could see my mates yawning nervously and trying to appear unconcerned. We all knew it was an act.'

As *Hood* and *Prince of Wales* and their consorts thundered through the night, the weather still favoured their enemies. It was foggy and thick – just the kind of conditions that the German navy's senior meteorologist, Dr Heinz Externbrink, had commended to Fleet Commander Lütjens as perfect breakout weather. The scientist had urged the commander to maximize the potential of this raider's dream by making all speed possible to get through the Denmark Strait under the blessing of this cover. As Externbrink said personally to Mullenheim-Rechberg:

'You've no idea how many times I've suggested that to Lütjens. I've warned him repeatedly that if we don't do so, we'll have to count on unpleasantly good visibility in the Denmark Strait. But he won't budge. He simply rejects the idea without giving any reasons.'

This is one of the clearest examples in '*Rheinübung*' of Lütjens' refusal to listen to advice, or to explain his thinking so that it was well understood among his officers. It is hard to fathom how, as fleet commander, he thought this conduct appropriate to his task. At the worst, it meant that if he were lost to his command – and that could happen as much from a chance fall down a companion ladder as from enemy action – *no one* would be in a position to fully understand his thinking, and to carry on his concept of '*Rheinübung*'. Lütjens was like a man who gambles with his loved ones' inheritance by leaving his will unwritten.

On the morning of 23 May, their engines pounding, *Bismarck* and *Prinz Eugen* drew into the Denmark Strait. Could this be the home run that would unleash their terrible destructive power on the 'Tommies' convoys, the lifeblood of their last unconquered enemy, Great Britain? As the mysterious pack ice slid by on the two ships' starboard side, the chances of escape grew by the hour. But in the evening, the Germans' luck broke. *Suffolk* and *Norfolk,* the heavy cruiser pickets posted by Tovey, made contact. *Norfolk*, with its

ABOVE *The breakout begins:* Bismarck *and* Prinz Eugen *in the Denmark Strait.*

distinctive tri-funnel design, emerged as a target from the murk. For the first time, *Bismarck*'s huge guns roared out in anger, straddling the fragile cruiser with shell splashes, but only pock-marking her with splinters before she scurried away in a pall of her own smoke, laid down to confuse the gunners aboard her formidable attacker.

However, *Suffolk*, with her better radar equipment, still held the two German ships in the spider's web glowing on her screen. From now until her death, with only a day and a few hours' grace excepting, *Bismarck* would struggle in vain to escape the Royal Navy's radar net.

Getting **Ready**

chapter **four**

WHEN TO GO

If you are going to make a voyage, one of the first things you need to do is decide when to go. In our case, picking the wrong month to be in the Denmark Strait could spell disaster for the expedition. For that matter, the outer reaches of the Bay of Biscay, where *Bismarck* is located, also have the reputation of being particularly unkind to ships. Transiting these bodies of water in rough weather is one thing, but we were planning to be either stationary or moving ahead slowly at just 2 knots most of the time, with as much as 10,000 metres of cable streaming off the back of the survey ship. It is not a position you want to be in when a full-blown gale hits – a frequent occurrence in both locations.

I decided to commission a climatological assessment of both sites to help identify the best weather window in which to work, and also to predict the amount of weather down time we could face on an average and worst-case basis. Our enemies are wind and waves, so I set our limits at approximately 25 knots and 2.5 metres high, respectively. If the conditions exceeded these limits we would be forced to suspend operations, because the pitching and rolling on the survey ship would place dangerous dynamic loads on the cables we would be using. The two independent studies I

GETTING READY

commissioned both agreed that July was the best month, with the chance of a gale (winds in excess of 34 knots or Beaufort Force 8) being one in ten at the *Hood* site and one in twenty at the *Bismarck* site. We would not have to worry about Atlantic hurricanes, as they die out before reaching either location. Because of the abnormal weather patterns that have plagued the world in recent years, I stayed on the conservative side and decided to use a weather-down time figure of twenty per cent.

In order to be ready to commence operations in July, we would need to spend the whole of June testing and transporting equipment and preparing it for mobilization on a survey ship. That left me about three months in which to find a ship, people and all the equipment we would need. The schedule was tight, but achievable as long as there were not too many setbacks or complicating circumstances. However, I was not alone in the desire to take full advantage of the best weather window. Each year, everyone in the underwater industry engages in a seasonal race to snap up precious resources for their own projects. Ships are at that top of the list of resources – I needed to find one straight away.

THE SHIP

It didn't take long for me to set my sights on the ship I thought would be perfect for the expedition. The MV *Northern Horizon* was originally built as a deep-sea freezer trawler for fishing in Arctic waters, but had been converted into a deep seismic-survey vessel. She had all the qualities I was looking for: a large, working back-deck, several internal lab spaces and excellent cargo storage. She also had the right type of propulsion for slow-speed towing or station-keeping, and sufficient accommodation for our anticipated crew of more than twenty people. Importantly, the *Northern Horizon* had a reputation as a good sea-boat. An additional bonus was that MARR Vessel Management, who run the ship from her base in Hull, understood the type of project we were going to use her for, having previously supplied vessels for some of Robert Ballard's deepwater projects. Before I joined them, Blue Water Recoveries (BWR) had nearly used the *Northern Horizon* for their 1995 survey season. Although they had ended up using a different vessel, everything I had heard about the *Northern Horizon* was positive.

Two days after our 'green-light meeting', I was in Hull inspecting every nook and cranny of the *Northern Horizon*. She was all that I hoped she would be and I left Hull satisfied that I had found the right ship. Unfortunately, another company shared my sentiments exactly and, within days of my visit, walked into MARR's offices unexpectedly and signed a charter contract for the vessel for the entire summer season. Suddenly the schedule I thought was achievable began to look impossible.

The loss of the *Northern Horizon* was a serious blow. I needed to find a replacement vessel fast or our schedule – and the entire expedition – would be in jeopardy. The pressure stemmed from the narrow weather window in which we could work. For instance, a delay of two months waiting for the right ship to become available would mean working in September, when the weather down time could be forty per cent or more. This was too great a risk for Channel 4 to bear, considering the gamble they had already decided to take on the project.

Six very anxious weeks passed. I could only find one other vessel that was available for our schedule. She was not ideal, being smaller than the *Northern Horizon* and generally less suitable, but I thought she could still do the job. Unfortunately, she had been working in South America – I would need to fly to Brazil to inspect her before she sailed back to Europe. But just a few days before I was due to go, a last-chance gambit I had played for the *Northern Horizon* came good. I had left a standing offer with MARR to pay for the charter contract to be broken if the other company saw the prospect for a gap in their own survey schedule. Luck was finally on my side – a hole had opened up in the other company's schedule and John Cannon, the managing director of MARR, called to say the vessel was available again for our preferred period. As suddenly as I had lost her six weeks earlier, the *Northern Horizon* was mine again. This time not a minute was wasted and we fixed a contract to take delivery of the vessel in Cobh in Ireland on 27 June for the start of mobilization. We had made it by the skin of our teeth.

THE TECHNOLOGY

Given our challenge to find both wrecks as quickly as possible, especially considering the large search area required for *Hood*, I had no doubt that the right tool to use was a wide-swathe, low-frequency, side-scan sonar. Unfortunately, there are only a handful of such systems in existence in the world, and even fewer can be hired commercially. I had just three to choose from. The best option was Oceaneering's Ocean Explorer 6000 system. There is little doubt that I had a natural bias towards this system, as I was responsible for overseeing its acquisition and development in 1990 for Eastport International prior to the *Lucona* search, but I still feel it is the best deep-sea-imaging sonar in the world today. Its prowess in wreck-finding is due to its unique combination of a low-frequency (33/36-kilohertz) sonar to search at very high coverage rates and a higher-frequency (120-kilohertz) sonar for classifying targets once they are detected. Used correctly, Ocean Explorer 6000 can cover from 50 to 80 square nautical miles in a single day, producing beautifully clear sonar images that allow a skilled interpreter to distinguish between man-made objects and surrounding

geology. I already had seven years' experience with this sonar, during which time more than forty wrecks had been located. I therefore looked on the Ocean Explorer 6000 as a trusted ally that would not let me down. The system had sat idle since it had successfully located *Liberty Bell 7* (a tiny Gus Grissom Mercury space capsule which was recovered from more than 4,800 metres of water off the coast of the Bahamas) in July 1999, and was in need of an overhaul. Luckily, Oceaneering were keen to get back in the water with BWR and were working feverishly to meet our mobilization schedule.

Once the wrecks had been found, our aim was to make the highest-quality possible film of them. For this we needed an underwater-filming platform that could reach down to *Bismarck*'s lair at 4,800 metres. Our first choice was the pair of Russian manned submersibles known as *MIR 1* and *MIR 2*, which had established an impressive track record filming such deep wrecks as *Titanic*, *I-52* and *Komsomolets*. The great advantage of the *MIR* subs was their size and mobility and the way they could dive and work in tandem, with one sub providing backlighting while the other filmed. I had never dived in a deep submersible, but I knew from friends what a special experience it was working in a pressure sphere just feet away from your subject. However, for all their advantages, using the *MIR* subs would create some considerable difficulties for the expedition. The most significant problem was that the search and filming would have to be split into two phases, because the *MIR* support vessel, the *Akademik Keldysh*, could not be used to support the wide-swathe sonar search needed to find both wrecks. Although it was possible to conduct the expedition in two phases, it would be costly and it would place huge pressures on everybody's schedule.

While I was trying to resolve the difficulties of the two-phase approach I was alarmed to learn that someone else coveted the *MIR* submersibles as much as we did.

In fact, they coveted them far more than we did, and swooped in to hire them for most of the forthcoming summer season, apparently taking options on them for several years ahead as well. Like the *Northern Horizon* earlier, the *MIR*s were suddenly lost to us, but in this case there was no chance of getting them back. They were going to work for an American film-production company backed by James Cameron, the Oscar-winning director of the blockbuster film *Titanic*. Ironically, the *MIR*s' first dives were to be made on *Bismarck*! I had little time to contemplate how the two expeditions could work on the same wreck without running into each other; I needed a replacement for the *MIR* subs and there was only one viable option available.

The Magellan 725 remotely-operated vehicle (ROV), Oceaneering's trusty companion to the Ocean Explorer 6000 Sonar, was the one deep-sea tool that somehow escaped this season's race for equipment. However, it would be unfair to depict Magellan as somehow being a bridesmaid rather than a bride. Since her debut in 1991, she had probably racked up more 'bottom' time (time spent on the seabed) in ultra-deep water than any other comparable ROV or manned submersible, with the majority of that time working around wrecks. Her conquests include *Lucona*, *Derbyshire*, USS *John Barry*, *Titanic*, an Italian DC9 airplane, the *Liberty Bell 7* space capsule and the numerous cargo vessels found by BWR.

Magellan was one of the few deep-sea ROVs that worked off a small-diameter, 17-millimetre steel cable rather than the thicker Kevlar-strengthened type of cable favoured by the rest of the industry. The power that could be sent through this small-diameter cable effectively limited Magellan to a 25-horsepower motor to power her thrusters and hydraulic controls, whereas other ROVs had anywhere from 80 to 150 horsepower at their disposal. What Magellan lost in power, however, she saved in size and weight, which made it possible for her to use the same cable-handling deck gear and deployment crane as the Ocean Explorer 6000. This common use of heavy deck equipment meant both systems could be operated from the same ship. Whereas all deep-sea search and recovery projects had previously been done in two distinct phases – search first and recovery second – from 1991, they could be accomplished in a single phase from one ship. This was the secret of the success of the Explorer–Magellan combined system.

Once the decision had been made to use Magellan, we needed to equip the vehicle with the best-quality lights and cameras we could find. Our basic aim was to have the flexibility of taking wide-frame, long-range shots during the initial ROV reconnaissance and then be able to zoom in to get close-up images of fine detail, such as the fracture edges of steel plating. The lighting set-up, particularly for the long-range shots, would be crucial. Good lighting is arguably the single most important factor in achieving high-quality video images underwater. We chose to use high-

OPPOSITE *The Magellan 725 ROV would be the 'eyes' of our expedition if we were successful in finding* Bismarck *and* Hood.

efficiency HMI light sources, because they produce a near-daylight colour temperature (5,600° K) which penetrates much further in seawater than conventional underwater lights. A total of four 400-watt HMI light heads would be mounted on Magellan, in addition to the vehicle's two standard 500-watt halogen light heads. The final modification was to mount the HMI lights on a long, tilt-controlled bar in order to get as much separation from the cameras as possible. This minimizes 'backscatter', which can get into the lenses and interfere with the picture quality.

The cameras we selected would need to be equally impressive if we were to take full advantage of our powerful lighting set-up. We wanted our video to be as good as anything seen on broadcast television in the UK, and we wanted to have plenty of back-up in case of problems. Our primary video camera was to be based on the latest Sony camera module, which had only just been released. We bought the first two modules sold in the US and had them integrated into a titanium pressure-housing fitted with a special three-part glass lens to correct for the distortion you get when filming underwater. The camera was capable of producing 850 lines of resolution and it used three separate chips to pick up red, blue and green for superior colour sensitivity. Insite Tritech, the San Diego-based manufacturer, called this new camera Atlas.

In addition to a spare Atlas, we also brought along its celestial cousins: Scorpio (a digital-still camera that could shoot a 3.4 mega-pixel picture), Orion (a colour, zoom-focus video camera), Gemini (a wide-angle, low-light video camera) and Mercury (a standard, black-and-white video camera). With four cameras operating at the same time on Magellan there would be little risk of missing anything important.

RIGHT *The four HMI lights are mounted in pairs on either end of the long bar away from the two cameras mounted in the centre. Two additional cameras are mounted on a pan & tilt mechanism lower down.*

For navigating the *Northern Horizon* up and down search-track lines, or keeping her stationary in dynamic-positioning (DP) mode, we decided to use the SkyFIX differential global-positioning system (DGPS) owned and operated by Thales Geosolutions. Stand-alone GPS is currently accurate to about 15 metres, but can be improved to 2 metres or better by the use of differential-correction information transmitted to satellite receivers on the ship. Every second our computers would give updated and corrected positions for the ship, displayed on remote screens set up in strategic locations throughout the vessel. The most important display was the one on the bridge, which would be used to guide the captain and bridge officers steering along track lines. In DP mode, the DGPS signals would be received automatically and used to control the ship's thrusters, keeping her in positions accurate to plus or minus 1 metre. The *Northern Horizon*'s DP system was one of her best features, but to really make it work for us we needed the 2-metre accuracy of DGPS.

The final piece of technology we decided to take was in many ways the most exciting, but also by far the most worrying. It was a unique, marine-based, satellite-communication system that would allow us to send back live video from the ship to ITN's headquarters in London via France. Known as SeaCast, and developed by France Telecom, the system could be used to turn the *Northern Horizon* into a virtual television field reporter, beaming back live reports and underwater video from the ship as news was breaking on board. Rob White would be writing daily reports for Channel 4's expedition website and at some point we would try to transmit live video streaming from Magellan direct to the site. This would be a UK internet first – underwater video footage from thousands of metres deep in the North Atlantic would be seen live on the internet.

The tricky part of the whole process was for SeaCast's very narrow transmitting beam to stay locked onto the receiving satellite even though the ship might be rolling and pitching about on the high seas. Inside SeaCast's dome was a gyro-stabilized platform that actively compensated for the movements of the ship in every conceivable direction. If the beam lost its lock, the transmission would end and the result would be dead air and a very embarrassed presenter at *Channel 4 News* in London. SeaCast had been used twice before to cover yacht races, but it had never been used from the high northern latitudes of the *Hood* site. From this remote location, the France Telecom satellite lies in a geo-stationary orbit at only 16° above the horizon, and it was calculated that 10° movements of the ship would be enough to break the transmission path. The naval architects reckoned that when the waves were higher than 2.5 metres we would not be able to transmit, but then we probably would not be diving with the ROV in such conditions either. We were clearly pushing SeaCast to the edge of its capacity, but it was a gamble worth taking.

RIGHT *Ted Briggs (centre) seated between myself and Jim Mercer (right), whose father was on board* Hood *for a short time while she was in Scapa Flow.*

THE OPERATIONS TEAM

I am a firm believer that people, not technology, make things happen at sea. So while you cannot attempt an expedition such as this one without the right technology, it is more important to have the right crew to make that technology work. With this in mind, my objective was to assemble a handpicked group of individuals who could work together as a team. I wanted them to be smart and highly motivated.

At the top of my list was Jim Mercer. He is an extremely capable electronics engineer who spent eleven years with the Royal Navy before starting a very active, nineteen-year career in the offshore industry. For the past five years, he had been working for BWR. I value Jim for his calm demeanour and good judgement as much as for his technical ability (he can troubleshoot and repair any piece of equipment on a ship). Jim has an excellent way with people that allows him to solve problems without conflict. At BWR, we know him as 'Mustard', which is his real middle name. It's very appropriate, as Jim really is 'the mustard'! It did not surprise me when, after a week on the *Northern Horizon*, Jim acquired another nickname: 'the unsung hero'. (By a strange coincidence, Jim's father had actually spent some time on board *Hood* at her Scapa Flow base in the Orkneys, just before she sailed on her final voyage.)

In addition to being my second-in-command, Jim's primary responsibility during the expedition would be to take digital-still photographs of the wrecks using a new camera that we installed on Magellan. A tall and retiring engineer named Will Handley was appointed to work alongside Jim during the filming of the wrecks. Will has carved out a niche for himself in the industry as a broadcast-camera specialist. His experience includes building his own cameras and being responsible for the broadcast and high-definition cameras at the Woods Hole Oceanographic Institute (WHOI), where he worked for a number of years. Will, who prefers to be inside a camera rather than in front of one, would operate the three-chip Atlas cameras while filming the wrecks.

To balance the team working inside the main operations centre, we had one of Thales' best young senior surveyors, Chris Jones. Chris is a graduate geographer who climbs mountains as a hobby when not offshore. He ran the entire DGPS navigation spread and was on call at all times to keep the navigation displays up to date and to answer my frequent questions about the position of sonar targets. My job was to look after the operation of our sonar-imaging processing system, so I relied heavily on Chris to take my interpretations of the sonar traces and transform them into his navigation system. Jim, Will, Chris and myself would run the navigation, sonar-processing, video and still-camera operation, and direct the vessel positioning whenever the sonar or ROV was in the water. I anticipated long days for all of us!

To operate the Ocean Explorer and Magellan systems, Oceaneering provided a team of eight technicians. The team would be split into two shifts, each working twelve hours per day to give round-the-clock coverage. Ron Schmidt, a very experienced and talented electronics technician who had played a major role in building the Magellan ROV, headed this team. Ron would be assisted by Andy Sherrell, who would supervise the opposite shift and look after the Ocean Explorer sonar. Ron is a veteran of deep-sea search and investigation projects, having piloted Magellan on almost every dive it had made over the past ten years. He is a quiet guy who leads by experience and enjoys the full respect of his team. I knew much less about Andy, but his handling of some tricky repairs to the Ocean Explorer sonar would later impress me very much. The remainder of the team was loaded with experience in all the various disciplines and skills needed for a project of this complexity. I was glad to see the familiar faces of Troy Launay, Dave Warford and Richard Dailey, with whom I had worked in the past. This trio are as capable as they come in our industry and they are truly colourful characters whose presence would make the long hours ahead of us more enjoyable.

LEFT Bill Jurens (left) and Dr Eric Grove study our model of Bismarck in preparation for their forensic investigation.

Captaining the *Northern Horizon* for this trip was Keith Herron, a straight-talking ex-trawler skipper from the fishing port of Grimsby. Like all the officers in *Northern Horizon*, Keith had successfully transferred his nautical skills to the offshore industry when the UK fishing industry went into permanent decline. Keith was joined on the bridge by Chief Officer Joe Wilcock, Second Officer Sid Brown and DP Operator George Holmes, all trained to operate the vessel's dynamic-positioning (DP) system. Krzyzstof Kubiziak, the Polish chief engineer, looked after the vessel's engines and machinery with three of his compatriots.

We also needed to recruit experts who knew all about the construction and history of *Hood* and *Bismarck*. I don't think we could have found a more suitable pair than Dr Eric Grove and Bill Jurens. Eric is a leading British historian who works as a defence analyst, lecturer and academic, specializing in modern naval history. As a lecturer at Dartmouth and Greenwich Royal Naval Colleges, he is used to challenging conventional wisdom with new ideas. Presently, he is the director of the Centre for Security Studies at the University of Hull. Eric had previously written about *Hood*'s sinking, and had even tried to gather support for this type of expedition many years before, so he was naturally delighted to be part of the investigation team. His enthusiasm for the Royal Navy, HMS *Hood* and many other subjects was limitless. Also, Eric was especially pleased to be sailing on the *Northern Horizon* because her home port is Hull, the city he is proud to call his home.

Bill Jurens, our expert in warship design and construction, is from Winnipeg, Canada, where he teaches technical drafting. Bill is probably best known for his seminal article 'The Loss of HMS *Hood* – A Re-Examination', which was published in 1987 in *Warship International*, a journal he helps to edit. Bill's article was the first complete, post-war technical analysis of the loss of *Hood* and it helped me greatly in formulating an investigation plan for the expedition. Bill's background in big-gun ballistics and marine forensics – using scientific methods to understand ship losses – made him the ideal candidate to partner Eric in studying both wrecks.

Like Eric, Bill had previously thought about investigating *Hood*. When writing his article, shortly after *Titanic* was discovered (which must have opened his eyes to the possibility of deep-sea forensic investigation), Bill even speculated about the role that he would find himself playing fourteen years later. He wrote in the epilogue: 'Until relatively recently, this paper might have been considered definitive. But today, there is still more work that might be done. We live in a marvellous age – an age where men have once more set foot upon the *Titanic*. It is therefore entirely possible that before the end of the century, curious – and we hope considerate – men will gaze upon the shape of "Mighty *Hood*" again. No one can know with certainty what they might find. But only then, if ever, will it be possible to write the final chapter in the checkered life, and spectacular death, of HMS *Hood*.'

FINAL APPROVALS AND SUPPORT

Because of the changes in the expedition plan – primarily the addition of filming on *Bismarck* – it was imperative that another set of approvals was sought. As with *Hood*, our first contact was with the *Bismarck* survivors' association (Kameradschaft Schlachtschiff *Bismarck*). A retired German naval officer called Dieter Heitmann is the association's president. More than ten years before our expedition, Heitmann's former service had asked him to take on this role, because the membership was getting too old to keep the association running. Dieter readily admits that he was not, initially, enthralled by this new posting. However, once he got to know the members – particularly the core group that lived near him in Hamburg – he warmed to them and their stories and now he is truly the glue that holds the association together.

After several telephone discussions and an exchange of letters, it was agreed that I would travel to Hamburg to meet with Dieter and four of the more active *Bismarck* survivors. (Of the reported 2,246 men who were on *Bismarck* when she sank, only 115 survived and were rescued. Of those still alive, about thirty-four are members of the association, but only fifteen to twenty are mobile enough to attend their annual reunion meetings.) I would be accompanied by Dick Bower (another producer at ITN, who was developing the project while Rob White was unavailable). We arranged to meet Dieter at a country hotel on the outskirts of Hamburg, where we could present our proposal to the veterans. Dieter was already favourably disposed to the idea of our expedition, but it was important that the survivors were equally happy with our

LEFT *Dieter Heitmann (*right*) joins me at the site of the* Bismarck *memorial on the grounds of the* Bismarck *family estate in Hamburg, Germany.*

RIGHT Bismarck *survivors (*from left to right*: Hans Stiegler, Rudi Romer, and Heinz Steeg) join Dieter Heitmann and myself at our first meeting to discuss the expedition.*

plans. With Dieter translating, I outlined how we would re-find and film *Bismarck* for the making of a new documentary. I wanted to stress that the same level of commitment would be given to *Bismarck* as to *Hood*, and that our approach would be sensitive and would respect the wreck's war-grave status. Hans Stiegler, who had brought his wife along, spoke openly about his experiences on *Bismarck* and as a prisoner of war (POW) in England. Heinz Steeg, who at eighty-five was the oldest veteran present, also recounted his last moments in *Bismarck* as she sank and his surprisingly fond memories of England and Canada, where he spent more than six years as a POW before being released in 1947.

The meeting lasted about three hours. When all their questions had been answered, the four men agreed that we should be allowed to pay tribute to their former shipmates on behalf of the Kameradschaft Schlachtschiff *Bismarck*. The following day we met at Heinz Steeg's apartment to see his personal mementos from the war. Heinz proudly showed us his memorial to *Bismarck* and his wall covered in ship badges, including those of most of the British ships involved in the two battles – *Hood*, *Rodney*, *King George V*, *Dorsetshire* and *Maori* – given to him by British friends he had met at various naval reunions. Heinz was moved by our interest in *Bismarck* and her German crew. For him, the attention was a welcome reminder of the role they all played so long ago and a friendly way to share his memories. Despite his age and poor mobility, Heinz was willing to come on the expedition with us to represent the Kameradschaft Schlachtschiff *Bismarck*, even if it meant spending forty days at sea! Heinz's remarkable commitment was to be matched later on by that of Ted Briggs. Both men clearly felt a strong duty to represent their respective associations.

The last remaining hurdle for the project was to obtain the final official approval of both the German and British governments. Dieter Heitmann kindly gave me the contact details for the German Foreign Office, whose staff consider such inquiries on behalf of themselves and the Ministry of Finance, which still owns *Bismarck*. My request to film the wreck, backed up by letters of support, was handled with typical German efficiency and was granted within a couple of weeks.

Although the British MOD had indicated their approval in 1996, we thought it was right to update them on our current plans. Diving on maritime war graves happened to be a hot subject in the UK, as the government were in the process of re-assessing their role in protecting such sites from disturbance under the Protection of Military Remains Act of 1986 (PMRA). The flashpoint had been instigated by the disturbance, including outright salvage, of the wrecks of HMS *Prince of Wales* and HMS *Repulse*, which lay in depths reachable by divers. When we met the MOD staff responsible for war graves we hoped to assure them that our 'look, but don't touch' policy would be strictly followed and that there would be no disturbance of *Hood*. For the sake of good measure, Rob White had acquired updated letters of support from both the Royal British Legion and the Royal Naval Association, and so there was ample proof of the wide naval support we enjoyed. I felt very sure we would get the MOD's go-ahead, but I wasn't taking it for granted. So I was relieved to see their approval in writing when the letter finally arrived on the day of Channel 4's first public announcement of the expedition.

MEMORIALS FOR FALLEN COMRADES

One of the commitments I made to both the *Hood* and *Bismarck* associations was to place a memorial plaque on the wreck sites on their behalf. In my mind, this simple promise was one of the fundamental reasons for visiting the wrecks. Ideally, I wanted the plaques to honour every single man who died serving on the two ships. The wrecks were unmarked mass war graves – this was our chance to mark them properly.

In early 1996, at my request, Ted Briggs had suggested that an appropriate inscription for a memorial plaque to place on *Hood* might be: 'In memory of our shipmates, husbands, fathers, brothers and all relatives from the HMS *Hood* Association'. He had also sent me the Book of Remembrance that listed all the names of those who died on *Hood*. Thumbing through the book's many pages, I began to truly appreciate for the first time the sheer scale of life lost in that single moment. There would be no possible way to list every name on a plaque – it would be far too big and heavy to deploy to the seabed by ROV.

ABOVE *A collection of British ship badges given to Heinz Steeg by British veterans he has met at naval reunions.*

IHNEN
ZUR
EHR

UNS.
ZUR
MAHNUNG

2371 MANN
BLIEBEN MIT
IHREM SCHIFF
AUF SEE

ABOVE The memorial to Bismarck's crew in Hamburg.

BELOW Ted and I unveil the Hood memorial plaque, identical to one made for Bismarck.

As the expedition's start date approached, I turned my attention back to the plaques and settled on a way to list all the names. The solution was to create a document that listed each man's name, rank, official number and service detachment, and have it copied onto a compact disk that could be incorporated directly onto the plaque. This digital 'Roll of Honour' would be embedded in a clear, acrylic material specially made to resist deep-sea pressures. Fortunately, my neighbour, Sally Hersh, was a professional sculptor. She was pleased to take on the commission of designing and casting the bronze plaques. Frank Allen of the HMS *Hood* Association and Malte Gaack of the Kameradschaft Schlachtschiff *Bismarck* – two of the new breed of younger members hoping to keep their associations flourishing – provided the detailed lists of all the names and related information. A tremendous amount of thought and attention went into every aspect of making the plaques, and it showed when they were completed. They were beautiful monuments and would be fitting memorials to the 3,546 men (see note on page 221) listed on the two rolls of honour.

MOBILIZATION IN COBH

The reason for choosing the Irish town of Cobh as the mobilization port was its proximity to *Bismarck*'s sinking position. Cobh is just 385 nautical miles northeast from the wreck, making it the nearest major port. It is even closer to *Bismarck* than Brest, where the ship was running to for safety and fuel when she was caught and sunk. I wanted to keep transit time to a minimum in case we had a serious problem on our first dives and needed outside help or spare parts to be flown in. Until I was sure that all our equipment was working, I didn't want to be too far from a friendly port.

Half the secret of a successful mobilization in a foreign port is good planning. The other half consists of a combination of a good team, a good agent and good luck. Planning is all about getting everything and everybody to the mob port on time. So I had good reason to be pleased when I arrived in Cobh on 26 June to find the *Northern Horizon* sitting snug in her berth, all the major players present and the first of Oceaneering's containers arriving on the quayside having cleared customs after its long journey across the Atlantic. Pascal Cahalane, the ship's agent who had been working with me for two months to organize the mobilization, was also on hand, trying to line up more trucks to get Oceaneering's eight containers moved even more quickly. Privately, I was very satisfied with our situation the day before mobilization was due to begin in earnest, but Pascal clearly wasn't and he was trying hard to do more – the first sign of a good agent.

Wednesday, 27 June 2001 was mobilization start day for Expedition *Hood/Bismarck*. A day I had dreamed of for the past six years, and spent the previous six months planning down to the last detail, was now finally upon me. Mobilizations are like moving house, except that they last for a week instead of one day and the contents weigh well over 100 tons. It can be a time of extreme pressure and stress, but I couldn't have felt better. I was delighted that the expedition was actually happening, and that the mobilization had begun so smoothly.

I expected the mobilization to take four days, barring any serious problems or complications. In that time we would transform the back deck of the *Northern Horizon* into a small city of containers, winches, cranes and subsea vehicles. The ship's three internal laboratory spaces would become high-tech operations centres bristling with computers, monitors and video recorders. All these different working spaces would be wired to each other by almost a mile of cable, giving seamless communication between equipment and people. Preparations were also being made to get the vessel ready for being at sea for up to forty days. Fuel, food and water were delivered promptly during the week. Unfortunately, we had no such luck with removing the ship's garbage, which had originated in England – the port authorities ordered it to remain on board because of the foot-and-mouth-disease crisis in the UK.

The first priorities of the mobilization were to carry out the heavy welding of the equipment onto the main deck, and to get the SeaCast container and antenna dish secured as high up on the ship as possible to keep the transmitting beam clear of obstructions. To elevate the SeaCast container, I had the simple idea of welding an empty container to an open space on the ship's bridge deck and then welding the SeaCast container on top of it. This would put the antenna above the bridge and central-mast platform, but also some 15 metres above the water line. On paper, this idea looked as though it would work perfectly, but it had to be carefully checked by a naval architect, as the weight of the container so high up on the ship would dramatically alter her stability. The architect gave the plan his blessing, with the proviso that the two containers be braced on all sides with extra steel plate and welding.

The welding and structural work on the ship dominated the first three days of the mobilization. Because of the extra welding work and the scale of the expedition itself,

BELOW *A gang of dockyard workers welds one of the winches to the ship's deck.*

the ship was absolutely teeming with workers. At one point, I could account for fifty-eight people working on board, not including the film-makers, who were doing their best to capture the action without being caught in the middle of it. I had the dockyard working overtime to finish the welding, for only once all the deck equipment was secured in place could Oceaneering turn the power on to all their gear. This was a key milestone, because it was the first chance to check that sensitive electronic equipment was working and had survived the long transit. At 6 p.m. on day three (Friday) the power was switched on and I was relieved to learn that there were no failures.

Two hours later, the *Northern Horizon* slipped away from her berth to make a second attempt to calibrate the SeaCast gyrocompass by making three revolutions in the harbour. The first calibration attempt the previous night had failed – a score of two out of ten was attained when a nine or ten was required. This result must have been anticipated, because the SeaCast inventor and top technical guru was already on the way to Cobh, having flown from France earlier in the day. To me, the SeaCast container was a complete black box. It seemed foreign in every way, from the thick cloud of Gitanes smoke that billowed out of its open door to the ominous mutterings in unrecognizable French by the technician, Jean-Louis. I couldn't involve myself in the technical details of the problem, so when an eight was scored on the second test and the result was pronounced 'good enough', I had no intention of questioning it.

The ITN Factual film team who were to document the expedition arrived in the late afternoon on Friday, bringing two van-loads of equipment and one very special guest – Ted Briggs. Ted had come to Cobh to have a good look at the spread that would try to find his ship and to wish us well. I showed Ted around the deck and explained how the equipment worked, stopping here and there to introduce him to members of the team. For many of the people he stopped to talk with, you could see how Ted's visit brought a human dimension to the expedition. These were all seasoned wreck-hunters who knew *Bismarck* and *Hood* were important wrecks, but it was Ted's presence on board that gave life to the story of their battle and made the wrecks more than just inanimate objects on the seabed. Ted especially wanted to meet the captain, and when Keith came down from the bridge to greet our guest on the main deck the two men formed an immediate bond. Perhaps it was because they had both spent more than thirty-five years of their life at sea that they felt such mutual respect. Keith was a hardened Arctic trawlerman, a veteran of the Icelandic cod wars, and watching him soften under Ted's gentle charm was a sight to behold.

When Saturday started well with a successful deck test of the Ocean Explorer 6000 sonar, I was still hopeful of being ready to leave on schedule that night. All that was necessary to complete the equipment commissioning was wet tests of both the sonar and the Magellan ROV. Then a departure time could be fixed. However, at noon these hopes were dashed when the ship's generator providing power to the Oceaneering spread suddenly shut down. The *Northern Horizon* has five generators in total, but the one that failed was the only one capable of providing the required 60-Hertz electrical power to Oceaneering's containers. The problem was isolated to an automatic voltage regulator (AVR) that had been fitted especially for our project to increase the generator's output voltage from 415 to 480 volts. Instead of a steady voltage of 480 volts, it was fluctuating rhythmically from 460 to 500 volts – a dangerous situation for Oceaneering's sensitive electronics. This 'black-box' AVR was the latest in computer-controlled technology, and it looked incongruous bolted to the side of the 1960s generator. As the ship's engineers worked feverishly to understand and retune the AVR, our departure that night began to look in doubt.

Meanwhile, the newly arrived film team and two experts had signed on to the vessel and were getting acquainted with the ship that was to be their home for the next month or more. Many had never been to sea before, so there were the usual concerns about meal times, sharing cabins and seasickness. We would have a large team of people on board, occupying very cramped spaces and it was important to get them orientated as soon as possible. In addition to the ship's marine crew of thirteen, there was the BWR/Oceaneering operations team of twelve, the film team of eight and the two experts, making the total complement thirty-five.

The troublesome generator and AVR were still having periodic fits of instability. We decided to fly in some experts from the UK with a replacement unit. For the second time in less than three days a technical expert was urgently being flown in to our rescue.

Sunday morning – day five of the mobilization – began with dry and sunny weather. Despite our continuing problems, I was intent on getting underway today, as I feared a psychological letdown if we found ourselves mired in Cobh at the start of a new week. Ron Schmidt and his team had resorted to using their crane's generator to continue making progress, first successfully wet-testing the sonar and then getting the Magellan ROV into the water to run her through her paces. The two AVR experts arrived in the early afternoon and immediately disappeared into the bowels of the ship to tackle the ailing regulator. When they finally came up for air several hours later, their conclusion was that the generator was fine and so was the original AVR. The system had simply not been set up properly in the first place, because, when it had been installed many weeks earlier, the technicians had not had a 480-volt device against which to test it. For good measure, our experts replaced the original AVR anyway and then stood by to monitor the voltage while the new regulator was burned in.

By 8.35 p.m. Magellan had been through two wet tests to iron all the kinks out and was now back on board being secured for transit. With the new AVR installed, the ship's generator had been solid as a rock, and so Oceaneering's equipment was put back on line. Everything was set for departure in the next hour. However, the ship's superintendent engineer, Steve Spivey, still wanted to install a rental deck generator that he had had trucked down from Dublin as a worst-case contingency. I felt that, since the AVR problem had been solved, this additional piece of equipment would just make the deck even more cluttered than it already was. Unlike me, however, Steve was absolutely determined to get the generator on board, so I let him get on with it. After much tugging with hand winches it was snugly fitted in, taking over the only available free space.

We were finally ready to go. Keith ordered a pilot for departure at 11 p.m. and we bid farewell to those who had waited to see us off. Ted had left a few hours earlier and I had promised to call him before anyone else when I had news about *Hood*. At the appointed time, the *Northern Horizon* slipped her lines and began to make her way slowly out of Cork harbour. The sea was calm and it was a beautiful evening. Everyone gathered along the port railing to look at the town of Cobh, which was full of lights twinkling at us as we passed by. Our voyage to unlock the secrets of a history hidden for sixty years had begun.

Battle and
Disaster

chapter **five**

THE COMBATANTS

The two squadrons were now approaching each other at a combined speed of almost 60 miles an hour, each side racing through the night to get into the best position for the battle that was now inevitable. For Holland in *Hood*, that meant presenting the smallest possible target to the Germans until the last moment, then swinging round to bring all eight of his – and *Prince of Wales'* ten – big guns to bear. For Lütjens, the

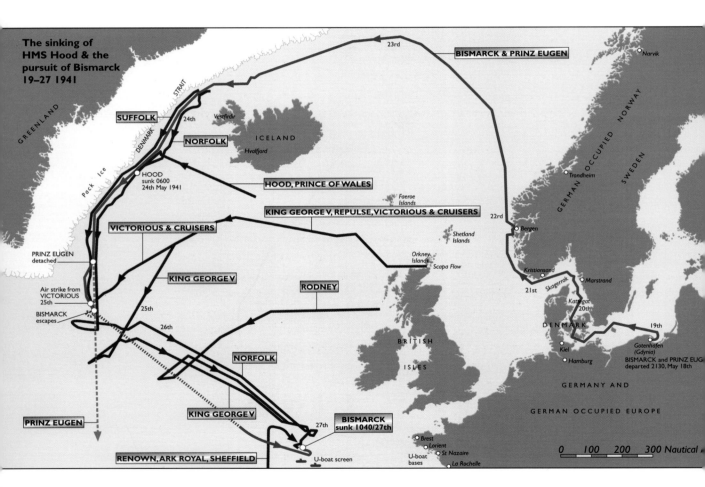

The sinking of HMS Hood & the pursuit of Bismarck 19–27 1941

key aim for *Bismarck* and *Prinz Eugen* had to be to sweep the British aside as fast as he could, and continue into the wide spaces of the Atlantic – so tantalizingly near now – and begin to destroy the convoys. His orders were clear on one point at least: he must avoid like-with-like combat if he possibly could. Indeed, at this stage, Lütjens was totally unaware that such a combat was looming. Holland had played his hand well, and his adversary did not even know that he was up against two capital ships.

How well matched would the enemies be when the moment came to open fire? Bill Jurens has studied the two prime antagonists' technical capacities in detail:

'In age, range, gun-hitting power, weight of armour and thickness of side protection, *Bismarck* definitely had the edge over *Hood*. But their speeds were well matched – in fact *Hood* had begun life with a 2-knot advantage over the younger ship. By 1941 that would have worn away a little though. An interesting point is that in deck armour – where it has long been held that *Hood* was at a disadvantage – the British ship had a slight edge on average: varying from location to location it was nearly half an inch (1.2 cm) thicker, at about 5 inches (13 cm) in total, although arranged in weaker layers. Overall, though, in a one-on-one engagement, we can say that *Bismarck* had a distinct advantage over *Hood*. But that's far from saying that *Hood* was a pushover.'

The moment of crisis was fast approaching now. As if to demonstrate the surprising inadequacy of German radar, *Bismarck*'s forward array had been knocked out by the concussion of her own guns. Lütjens shifted *Prinz Eugen* into the van, so her electronic eyes could guide him.

Holland meanwhile, a gunnery specialist himself, was intent upon closing the range as fast as possible. He knew that his flagship was the oldest of the four combatants, and he knew that he had to maximize her advantages while minimizing her disadvantages. Tactics such as this lie at the heart of naval warfare – the famous command 'engage the enemy more closely' is all very well, but you must do it as much as possible on your own terms. And so far Holland's plans had worked well. For all that, he has been accused in many post-battle analyses of not taking the right line of approach. He is criticized for being at a slight angle rather than head-on, so he presented more of a target to *Bismarck*, while at the same time not being able to bring his two after turrets to bear on the enemy. (Ordered to act in close concert with the flagship, *Prince of Wales*, of course, suffered the same handicap.) Looking at Holland's tactics as a whole, however, Dr Eric Grove is not so censorious:

'Holland has come in for some very unfair criticism for his approach to *Bismarck*, usually informed by twenty-twenty hindsight. He had two problems: covering all potential German movements when shadowing was uncertain, and not scaring the Germans into turning back before bringing them to action. This meant keeping as many options as possible open for as long as possible and not giving his position away. These two things he did superbly well and he succeeded in taking the Germans totally by surprise, forcing them to fight. He then acted as contemporary doctrine dictated, closing the enemy as quickly as possible to come to a decisive gun range where initially superior German rangefinding would be less of an advantage. Holland's tragedy seems to have been not that he turned towards the enemy end on, but that he turned to open his broadside and take up a more parallel course a bit too early. When the action opened, he quickly found himself under disturbingly accurate fire from *Bismarck*'s first salvoes – so it was very understandable he would want to develop his own fire soonest. By then, he had already closed to a range where the enemy's shells, on a flatter trajectory, would be more likely to strike his side armour rather than his deck armour. Unfortunately though, *Bismarck*'s shells seem to have found a chink in *Hood*'s side protection – which, though stronger than the deck armour, had vulnerabilities at the range at which Holland chose to turn. Something similar could have happened whatever tactics he had used.'

Despite his presence with the squadron's senior staff on *Hood*'s compass platform – one of the highest command points from which Holland could fight his ship – these finer points of tactics were far from Ted Briggs' thoughts just then. As the great battle ensign, hoisted on his admiral's order, whipped and cracked at the mast high in the Arctic night above him, more personal issues crowded Ted's mind:

'At least I had a grandstand view and would not die unknowingly in darkness … I'm not, and never have been, a religious zealot, nor a churchman, but my last thoughts in these moments of inaction were of the peaceful little chapel under the flag deck. It reminded me of Nelson's own prayer, "May the great God, whom I worship … " and I offered up a pitiful silent prayer of my own for personal courage and stamina and for a British victory. I suppose it was rather like keeping your fingers crossed!'

On board *Bismarck*, similar thoughts were doubtless running through the minds of many of her crew: at their action stations in the huge gun turrets, on the bridge with their admiral just like Ted, deep in the thundering engine-room spaces, quiet in the sick bay standing by for the first casualties. But at this stage, the Germans did not even know that they were about to have to break one of the cardinal rules of '*Rheinübung*' and engage their enemy's capital ships. That all changed in a flash of fire from *Hood*

and *Prince of Wales* at 5.53 a.m. on Saturday, 24 May 1941. It is a moment that is etched on Burkard von Mullenheim-Rechberg's memory:

'The range, I figured, was less than 16 miles. There were flashes like lightning out there! Still approaching nearly bow-on, the enemy had opened fire. *Donnerwetter*! Those flashes couldn't be coming from a cruiser's medium-calibre guns.'

Indeed they were not, and the German fleet commander soon knew it. In those moments, he must have realized that '*Rheinübung*' was going terribly wrong. He had lost the advantage of secrecy and now he had to do what he had been enjoined not to do, except in extreme circumstances: engage in a set-piece battle with a foe of equal, or even superior, strength. At that point Lütjens actually thought matters were worse than they were – that he was about to engage a fully worked-up *King George V*, from the Royal Navy's newest battleship class, rather than her inexperienced and technically incomplete sister *Prince of Wales*. It is clear that he was 'given furiously to think' – so much so that he seems to have delayed the order to return fire while he wrestled with this unplanned-for contingency. Indeed his captain, Ernst Lindemann, is said to have muttered as the British shells hurtled towards him, 'I will not let my ship be shot out from under me!' Minutes passed and still the salvoes came. Then, at last, Lütjens' order came: 'Open fire!'

BATTLECRUISER CATACLYSM

The choice (and it was a choice, for Lütjens could have turned away and tried to give his pursuers the slip) had been made. The Germans had been helped by the initial direction from the British flagship that fire should be concentrated on the lead ship, which, because of the earlier change of position, was the lesser threat, *Prinz Eugen*. That change, and her similarity in silhouette to *Bismarck*, were vital factors in what happened next. Once the British realized their mistake, they had less time in which to correct their gunnery 'range and line' to get on the target they really wanted. Given the known accuracy of German gunnery, that was a loss of opportunity for which the British would pay dearly; especially as *Prince of Wales* was wrestling with her unprepared state from the moment battle was joined, and *Hood*'s fire control was no match for *Bismarck*'s.

BELOW Bismarck *in action in the Battle of the Denmark Strait.*

Dr Eric Grove notes: '*Hood* is often criticized for her armour protection, but her antiquated gunfire-control system was probably a greater weakness. She had a First-World-War-type arrangement of fixed-control positions with the director crew only in the moving towers, not the control officers. Newer ships had all the gun-control personnel together in trainable director-control towers, all pointing at the same target. In addition, her fire-control computer was the last of the Dreyer type, a fundamentally flawed system that the Admiralty had abandoned after the First World War. The poor computer made it difficult to maintain accurate firing if the rate of change of range was itself changing rapidly and the separation of the control officers from the laying and shooting of the guns made confusion of targets more likely. The addition of radar ranging could only be of marginal help in such circumstances, especially as the equipment was unreliable and unfamiliar. To add to all this, *Hood's* highest optical rangefinder was mounted relatively low down on top of the conning tower and was not useful at the longest ranges. *Bismarck* had defective radar but superb optical rangefinders, one on the foretop, and the latest fire-control computers and director arrangements. This was a major advantage.'

It was an advantage the *Bismarck* used to devastating effect. After six salvoes from *Hood*, the German battleship returned fire and 'straddled' *Hood* – one salvo over and beyond her, one salvo falling short – very rapidly. Split the difference in a straddle, allow your fire controllers to adjust for the constantly shifting range, speed, wind and deflection and you are on your target. A shell packed with high explosive is about to do its worst to your enemy. And it did, as Ted Briggs remembers:

'The whole ship shook. We were thrown off our feet, and then the squadron Gunnery Officer Commander Gregson went out on the starboard wing of the bridge, looked aft, and came back with a rather slightly fixed grin on his face and said, "She's been hit at the base of the mainmast and there's a fire on the 4-inch (10-cm) ready-use ammunition lockers." … By that time there'd been another one which couldn't have exploded, but a shell I think went through the spotting top … and there were bodies falling down on the wing-sail bridge. Bill Dundas, the midshipman, went out on the wing and there was one … We knew every officer in the ship, naturally, but there was one young lieutenant, no face, no hands – the only way you could tell he was a lieutenant was by the two stripes.'

Dr Eric Grove again: 'It's possible that the shell which started the ammunition fire came from *Prinz Eugen*. One of her 8-inch (20-cm) shells would have exploded on the upper deck as this one did, whereas a 15-inch (38-cm) armour-piercing round from *Bismarck* would most likely have penetrated deeper inside *Hood*. Alternatively, as Bill Jurens has suggested, such a very lucky shell from *Bismarck* might have gone through the foretop, wrecking it and causing the terrible casualties described by Ted by sheer kinetic energy, and then exploding by the mainmast. If so, the dice really were falling the Germans' way that morning.'

Then Holland made his fateful decision. He ordered his force to turn to port so that at last all the guns on both *Hood* and *Prince of Wales* could bear on the enemy and fire broadsides. This came at a price – exposing more of his two ships to shell hits and armour penetration. But was *Hood* hitting back at *Bismarck*, or still firing at *Prinz Eugen*? The question vexes historians to this day. Ted's memory, from the bridge on the day, is clear: *Hood*'s forward turrets fired six salvoes at *Bismarck after* Holland ordered a shift of target. But Eric Grove believes that the order from the bridge probably could not have been carried out by *Hood*'s damaged fire-control system:

'Sadly, I fear it is most doubtful that *Hood* fired anywhere near *Bismarck*. The decisive evidence is from Skipwith, *Prince of Wales*' spotting officer, who had his eyes fixed on *Bismarck* throughout and never saw anything else but his own shells landing. What probably happened is that a mixture of the initial mistake in identification by *Hood*, the separation of control officers and director ratings in the fire-control positions, and the putting out of action and/or contact of the main spotting top by a hit conspired to make effective switching targets from *Prinz Eugen* impossible in the time available.'

We shall never know for sure. But we do know that the 'time available' was bitterly short. As the fire raged on the boat deck of *Hood,* with the 4-inch (10-cm) ammunition exploding and the agonized cries of the wounded rising up to the bridge through the voice pipes, Holland ordered another turn to port. But just as *Hood* began to turn, the great and beautiful ship staggered under another terrible blow. This one was terminal.

'I didn't hear any explosion at all,' Ted Briggs remembers. 'All I saw was a gigantic sheet of flame which shot round the bridge … again we were thrown off our feet … We picked ourselves up and she started to list over to starboard and at the same time I heard the quartermaster report on the voice pipe, "Steering gear gone, sir", and the captain said, "Change over to emergency conning". As he was saying that, she righted herself and she started going over to port – she'd gone I suppose about 40 degrees, something like that – we realized she just wasn't coming back. There was no order given to abandon ship. It wasn't necessary …'

THE MIGHTY FALLEN

As death came to claim *Hood*, *Bismarck*'s men could scarcely believe the evidence of their own eyes. The mighty *Hood* – Number One threat in their war games – had simply shattered into thousands of fragments under the fire of their guns. 'Sie blastet

AUF!' ('She's blowing UP!') yelled First Gunnery Officer Adalbert Schneider over the intercom. The incredible had happened. But the way *Hood* disintegrated was bizarre – the great cloud of smoke and flame over her didn't roar up and then straight down, as explosions should, but burned on, as First Lieutenant's Runner James Gordon in *Prince of Wales* clearly recalls:

'Suddenly this flame shot out of the ship … The flame shot up, but instead of like normally when you get explosions, it dies off – this one didn't. It carried on blazing as if it had been fed by all the cordite in the magazines … There was a noise like high-pressure air, or steam … and it looked as if it was burning out the whole guts of the ship.'

His captain, John Leach, concurred. He was to describe the fire as 'like a blow-lamp'. His drawing of what he saw, presented to the second inquiry into *Hood*'s demise, (see page 194) graphically makes the point.

That all-consuming, lightning-like fire roared on, along with countless other explosions, burning out the ship in seconds. During those few seconds, Ted Briggs found himself coming out through the starboard door of the compass platform to find the cold, grey waters of the Denmark Strait coming up to meet him. As Navigating Officer Commander John Warrand stood back to let him through, 'with a funny little smile on his face … that I'll never forget', Ted took one last glance back into the compass platform, and witnessed a sight at once chilling and pathetic. Vice-Admiral Holland was making no effort to save himself – he sat immobile in his admiral's chair as *Hood*'s deck canted steeply to port. 'He was just slumped in the chair,' Ted recalls, 'completely and utterly dejected by the look of it.' As he walked on the side of the bridge superstructure that had once stood upright and proud, the waters of the Strait suddenly carried Ted away. Now, greedily, the ocean sucked him down.

The sudden shattering death of *Hood* left *Prince of Wales* exposed alone to the full fury of *Bismarck* and *Prinz Eugen*. The British ship was an easy target for the stereoscopic sights of the battleship to fix – as ordered, she had remained in close company with her shattered flagship. Once again *Bismarck*'s guns bellowed out, and *Prince of Wales* had to swerve around the wreckage of *Hood* to clear away. Then the battleship too took a 15-inch shell, right through her bridge. This one did not even explode, but its concussive effect killed everyone on the bridge apart from the captain and two others. Then came three more shells: another 15-inch round from *Bismarck* and two 8-inch rounds from *Prinz Eugen* smashed into *Prince of Wales* below the waterline. Captain John Leach, still feeling the aftershock of the hit that had almost killed him too, knew *Prince of Wales* had had enough. She was no match for her enemies in her present condition, with her guns constantly malfunctioning, despite the heroic efforts of civilian workers still on board. He turned away to fight another

day. As he did so, as if to confirm his decision, his after turret jammed, rendering all four of its guns useless. He put down smoke and withdrew from his attackers before they destroyed him and his new ship.

Now Ted too was fighting for his life, slipping down into the dark waters of the Strait, falling deeper and deeper despite all his efforts. He had not been able to inflate his life jacket – it was *under* his Burberry waterproof – and he found himself inexorably drawn down with his ship. Then suddenly a mighty rushing pressure from below pushed him back to the surface. He drew in great lungfuls of air as the rough waters crashed and broke about him, and the thunder of battle continued out to the horizon. Then Ted saw a sight that he would never forget: the graceful bows of his beloved ship standing vertical in the water, the two forward 'A' and 'B' 15-inch turrets still visible. A huge hissing filled his ears as the red-hot metal sank back into the sea.

BATTLE AND DISASTER

'B turret was just going under … that was about 50 yards away. I panicked and I turned and swam as fast as I could away from her. There were lots of 3-foot square Carly rafts … I managed to get on one of those. I turned and looked and by that time she'd gone, but there was a fire on the water where she'd been. Now the water was about 4 inches thick with oil, and again I panicked and turned and swam as fast as I could, paddled the raft as fast as I could away from her, and when I looked round again the fire had gone out … It was then that I saw the other two men. They were over on the other side. They were the only others. There was no one else in sight. Not a soul …'

The three survivors watched as *Prince of Wales* withdrew. They even saw the distinctive three-funnel silhouette of one of the shadowing cruisers on the horizon. Then they were alone on the implacable sea, 240 miles from land.

Needle in
a **Haystack?**

chapter **six**

WHERE TO LOOK

People searching for anything lost in the sea often describe the task as being 'like trying to find a needle in a haystack'. This, of course, suggests that finding the needle is nigh-on impossible, or that if it were to be found, it would be through such blind luck that the finder should take no credit for his or her skill and perseverance. But is this well-worn truism losing its force when it comes to undersea search, as remarkable discoveries of lost objects become increasingly common? If the needle and the haystack are still the measure, how is it that we can now consistently locate relatively tiny objects, such as an aircraft cargo door lost in 4,300 metres of water? Or the *Liberty Bell 7* space capsule, which plunged from outer space in 1967 and sank to a depth of 4,800 metres? Or indeed a 'black-box' flight recorder no bigger than a lunchbox? The reality is that technological advance, in combination with our better understanding of all the factors involved, means that essentially any man-made object lost in the sea, regardless of depth, *can* be found through the application of a scientific and systematic search plan.

So, has it become possible to locate the needle? In undersea search the answer is now, undeniably, yes – as long as you look in the right haystack. Look in the wrong one and no amount of technological wizardry will save you from failure. And this is what presents today's wreck-hunters with their major challenge.

In terms of our expedition, the wrecks of *Bismarck* and *Hood* were certainly no needles. Both were massive warships that sank in a manner that would make it even easier to find them on the seabed. *Bismarck* had been heavily shelled by the British, and as she turned turtle on the surface all the debris on her decks would have fallen to the seabed, creating a very large debris field. Ballard's earlier expedition had already shown this. *Hood*'s demise was even more cataclysmic, and her telltale debris field would also present a large target during a side-scan sonar search. Our expedition's success effectively hinged on the decision of where to look.

Because *Bismarck* had already been located, I could safely assume that the reported sinking positions were fairly accurate. Ballard had kept the precise coordinates of *Bismarck* a secret because he didn't want 'treasure-seekers and souvenir-hunters turning this war memorial into a scavenger's carnival'. I agreed wholeheartedly with Ballard's view, even though it meant that we would have to re-locate *Bismarck* ourselves without the benefit of his knowledge. But knowing that the reported sinking positions were good gave us a major head start, made even better by some inadvertent clues I picked up along the way.

It would be far more difficult to decide where to look for *Hood*. Our search would be the first ever attempt to find the wreck, so there was no way of really knowing the accuracy of the reported loss clues and sinking positions. Each piece of information would have to be analysed on its own merits to judge its accuracy, which led to many questions. Is the source credible? Is it a primary source? Is the information independent? Was the information reported correctly? Can the information be corroborated? It is the unknown elements of searches that weigh most heavily on your mind, because, if they are not handled correctly, they can lead you into disastrous error. There would be a good deal of uncertainty with *Hood*, and I knew the haystack would be big – very big. I just had to be sure I looked in the right one.

HOOD'S SINKING POSITION

The final result of all my delving into archives for reports of *Hood*'s sinking position was a mixture of good news and bad news. The good news was that, hidden away in the thousands of pages of documents I eventually pored over in the Public Records Office in London, there were up to ten independent clues to the position. The bad news, as you might expect, was that the locations differed considerably – some by as much as 32 nautical miles.

Clearly, some of these positions had to be wrong. My first task was to identify the incorrect ones and eliminate them from consideration. In total there were three suspect positions, two of them sightings of the battle and its aftermath made by British aircraft flying overhead. Generally, aircraft positions are not all that accurate, so I was not surprised to find these two out of agreement with the positions reported by surface ships.

One of the British planes, a Lockheed Hudson patrol aircraft piloted by Flying Officer Pinhorn, observed the entire battle and the moment when *Hood* exploded at 5.59 a.m. on Saturday, 24 May 1941. Pinhorn's log read: 'One ship on southeast quarter suffered large explosion which must have been caused by a direct hit, as guns on northwest quarter had fired shortly before it. The violent explosion, followed by slowly dying fire, lasted approximately one minute.' Pinhorn also saw the destroyers *Electra* and *Echo* arrive at 7.40 a.m. to begin their search for survivors through the spreading oil patches. His reported positions appeared to be accurate in a relative sense, comparing one position to the next, but not in an absolute sense, as they were out by roughly 23 nautical miles to the northwest. While I couldn't use Pinhorn's positions, the times he reported were very important in corroborating other sources' versions of events.

The second British aircraft, piloted by Flight Lieutenant R. J. Vaughan, was a Sunderland flying boat which had been scrambled from its moorings when *Bismarck* and *Prinz Eugen* were initially sighted by HMS *Suffolk*. Circling above the stunning sea battle raging below the Sunderland, Vaughan was close enough to observe the fall of salvoes from both sides and to draw anti-aircraft fire from the *Prinz Eugen*. Vaughan wrote a detailed report of the action, including a seemingly precise track chart for all the ships involved and a sinking position for *Hood*. Unfortunately, Vaughan's positions were way out – by more than 30 nautical miles to the southwest – as was his misidentification of *Prinz Eugen* as the pocket-battleship *Admiral Scheer*.

The third sinking position I treated as suspect was the one reported by the German fleet commander Admiral Günther Lütjens in a wireless transmission he made at 7.05 a.m. to Group North: 'Have sunk battleship Qu. 73 AD.' I immediately recognized Qu. 73 AD as the code that was adopted by the German navy during the Second World War to secretly report their positions at sea. I had come across it many times before in U-boat war diaries and had learned the procedure for converting the data given into longitude and latitude. It was a grid system that divided the oceans into large squares bearing two alpha references. These large squares were further sub-divided into medium-sized squares that measured 54 nautical miles on each side, which were then further divided into smaller-sized squares measuring 6 nautical miles on each side. Therefore, Qu. 73 AD stood for Quadrant AD, which was located in the Denmark Strait, and medium square 73. Unfortunately, the two digits that would normally follow 73 to identify the smaller square, and so offer a more precise sinking position, were missing. For some unknown reason – perhaps simply because he had more pressing things to worry about – Lütjens did not report the full grid reference. This meant that *Hood*, if Lütjen's position was taken literally, could have sunk anywhere in a square that measured 54 by 54 nautical miles – an area half the size of Wales. Some printed sources have subsequently reported Lütjens' position as 63° 10′N, 32° 00′W, which is the exact centre of the grid square 73 AD, but that is still a very imprecise position. I had no choice but to ignore it.

That left seven clues or outright sinking positions from five different sources, which in the business of undersea search is practically a bonanza of information. Generally, you are fortunate to find two or three sinking positions, and the most I had ever had to work with in all my previous searches was four. With each new clue unearthed from the archives my confidence that I could find *Hood* grew.

Initially, my greatest fear had been that the reported sinking positions would be wildly inaccurate because of a combination of reasons. For one, the day of the battle was overcast and cloudy, which meant that none of the ships involved could take a sextant reading from the sun, or the stars the night before. Therefore, their dead-reckoning plot (calculated by working out their latitude and longitude using the ship's course and speed since the last celestial fix) had gone a long time without correction. Also, the relative high speed of the pursuit and the numerous changes of course required would introduce a wide margin of error into the positions. And, of course, the overwhelming pressure of the action could well have caused the navigators to make mistakes. For these reasons, the significance of having several independent sources more or less corroborating each other cannot be overstated. While it is entirely possible for one ship to be wrong in reporting its position, it is extremely unlikely that five ships navigating independently will all be wrong.

When *Hood* was lost at 6 a.m. on 24 May, the *Prince of Wales* was in close company with her flagship, sailing just 741 metres astern of *Hood*. *Prince of Wales* was so close, in fact, that she was forced to alter course to avoid *Hood*'s wreckage, and presumably to give her crew the opportunity to record and transmit a very accurate sinking position to guide ships for the rescue of survivors. But then something about the *Prince of Wales*' log struck me as odd. Its exceptionally neat penmanship just didn't fit with the horror her crew must have felt when they saw 'the mighty *Hood*' destroyed so suddenly, only minutes after one of *Bismarck*'s shells had killed fourteen from their own ship's company. Unfortunately, despite this orderly and *detailed log, no sinking position was recorded.*

Prince of Wales did, however, transmit an enemy-sighting report at 5.37 a.m. when she first spotted 'a large vessel'. At the same time, she gave her own position as 63° 20'N, 31° 28'W. This was the clue I needed to derive a sinking position for *Hood* based on *Prince of Wales*' navigation. It was simply a matter of plotting a dead-reckoning track for *Prince of Wales* based upon her known courses and speed up to the time of *Hood*'s sinking. Steaming at 28 knots for twenty-three minutes, the *Prince of Wales* had travelled 11 nautical miles further west (actually 284°T, or True) by the time *Hood* was lost. With that information, I was able to calculate the first sinking position.

BELOW *A small section of the* Prince of Wales' *ship log for 24 May 1941, listing all the crew killed by a shell from* Bismarck. *Note the remarkably neat penmanship.*

	Currents experienced			RETURN OF DEATHS			ANCHOR BEARINGS	
DATE OF DEATH	NAME OF DECEASED	SEX	AGE	RANK OR OCCUPATION	LAST PLACE OF ABODE	CAUSE OF DEATH	NATIONALITY
May 24. 1941	Norman Johnstone	Male	17 years	Boy Sig. D/JX 162832	H.M.S 'Prince of Wales'	Enemy action.	Scottish.
May 24. 1941	Edward James Hunt	Male	22 years	Act. Ldg. Sig. D/JX 141718	H.M.S 'Prince of Wales'	Enemy Action.	English
May 24. 1941	Walter Graham Andrews	Male	20 years	Act. Ldg. Sig. D/JX 147668	H.M.S 'Prince of Wales'	Enemy Action	Welsh.
May 24. 1941	Mervyn Richard Tucker	Male	21 years	Ldg. Sea. D/JX 113167	H.M.S 'Prince of Wales'	Enemy Action	English.
May 24. 1941	Thornton Smith.	Male	21 years	Ord. Sea D/JX 197804	H.M.S 'Prince of Wales'	Enemy Action	English
May 24. 1941	Thomas Ronald Slater	Male	20 years	Able Sea D/JX 152140	H.M.S 'Prince of Wales'	Enemy Action	English
May 24. 1941	Leslie Waddocks Deeds	Male	21 years	Able Sea. D/SSX 28435	H.M.S 'Prince of Wales'	Enemy Action	English
May 24. 1941	Harry Hallam	Male	33 years	Able Sea D/J 112521	H.M.S 'Prince of Wales'	Enemy Action	English
May 24. 1941	Arthur Molyneux Harper	Male	28 years	Able Sea R.F P/JX 190690	H.M.S 'Prince of Wales'	Enemy Action	English
May 24. 1941	Edward Patrick Diamond	Male	21 years	Ord. Sea D/JX 206256	H.M.S 'Prince of Wales'	Enemy Action	English.
May 24 1941	Dreyer		16	17 years Midshipman R.N.	H.M.S 'Prince of Wales'	Enemy Action	English
May 24 1941	John Bret Ince	Male	18 years	Midshipman R.N.	H.M.S 'Prince of Wales'	Enemy Action	English
May 24. 1941	Fairbairn	Male	—	Ord. Sea R.D/F	H.M.S 'Prince of Wales'	Enemy Action	—
May 24. 1941	Barlow	Male	—	Ord. Sea R.D/F	H.M.S 'Prince of Wales'	Enemy Action	—

1325 %c 140°. 1340 %c 180. 1410 %c 200. 1437 %c 190°.

1440 %c 180°. 1445 %c 160°. 1455 %c 170°. 1504 %c 180°.

1518 Sighted 1 Catalina Bearing 210°.

1531 Suffolk bore 255°. 6¾'.

1630. Zig-Zag No. 10.

1715 'Prince of Wales' guides. Co 180°. 24 Knots. Negative zig-zag.

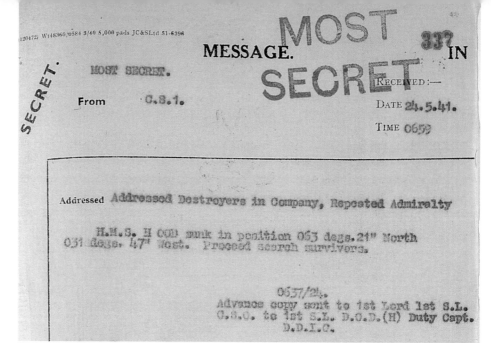

MOST SECRET.

From C.S.1.

RECEIVED :—

DATE 24.5.41.

TIME 0653

Addressed **Addressed Destroyers in Company, Repeated Admiralty**

H.M.S. H OOD sunk in position 063 degs. 21" North 031 degs. 47" West. Proceed search survivors.

0637/24.
Advance copy sent to 1st Lord 1st S.L.
C.S.C. to 1st S.L. D.C.D.(H) Duty Capt.
D.D.I.C.

RIGHT *The second wireless transmission from* Norfolk *(Cruiser Squadron 1) at 06.37 a.m. gave a revised sinking position and the urgent instruction: PROCEED SEARCH SURVIVORS.*

HMS *Norfolk*, the 'County'-class cruiser that shadowed *Bismarck* from the initial sighting to her ultimate demise, conveniently provided the next three sinking positions. From his trailing position 14 nautical miles to the northeast of *Hood*, Rear-Admiral Wake-Walker, who was commanding the First Cruiser Squadron from *Norfolk*, saw *Hood* explode and sink. As *Norfolk* was steaming towards the remains of *Hood*, Wake-Walker apparently instructed the squadron's navigating officer to plot a sinking position for immediate transmission to the Admiralty and destroyers in company. At 6.15 a.m., the first wireless transmission was made: 'HMS *Hood* has blown up in position 63°20′N, 31°50′W.' *Norfolk* continued to close on the spot where *Hood* once was. *Hood*'s remains – some balsa rafts, charred wood and hammocks bobbing about in a spreading pool of oil – would be visible from *Norfolk*'s bridge as she steamed past twenty minutes later in her continued pursuit of the enemy.

At 6.37 a.m., a second transmission was made from *Norfolk*: 'HMS *Hood* sunk in position 63°21′N, 31°47′W. Proceed search survivors.' This second position was clearly a revision of the first, and there is no doubt about Wake-Walker's intention. He was instructing the destroyers HMS *Icarus* and HMS *Achates*, and all other ships in the vicinity, to steam at once to the reported position to rescue any survivors. *Norfolk* could not afford to stop to search for survivors. She, along with *Prince of Wales* and *Suffolk*, gave the Admiralty its only chance of catching the fleeing *Bismarck*. This responsibility was made absolutely clear some hours later in an urgent message from the Admiralty to 'continue shadowing *Bismarck*, even if you run out of fuel'. The search for survivors would be left for the smaller destroyers, but by reporting a second, more accurate sinking position, Wake-Walker ensured that any men left in the sea would have a chance of survival. In the period of almost half an hour that he had before coming upon the wreckage, *Norfolk*'s navigation officer had plenty of time to take a precise bearing from the bridge and plot a position as accurately as he could. He may not have known it, but the lives of three men – Bill Dundas, Bob Tilburn and Ted Briggs – ultimately depended on his skill as a navigator. Sixty years later, I would also depend on it, for I judged his second sinking position to be the most probable of them all.

The third sinking position from *Norfolk* was found tucked away in a folder at the back of the Second Board of Inquiry Report kept at the Public Records Office. The document was a secret tracing from *Norfolk*'s actual plot covering a time period from 5.30 a.m. to 7.06 a.m. on 24 May 1941. The tracing must have been ordered in a gathering of evidence for the inquiry, because it was dated 12 August 1941, which was shortly after the second board began its hearings. When I found this facsimile plot late in my researches, my pulse began to quicken. It was the closest thing I had found to an 'X-marks-the-spot' type of clue to where *Hood* actually sank. It was one of those rare moments in the quiet and scholarly atmosphere of the Public Records Office when you have to resist the urge to shout out with glee and shatter the aura of quiet concentration in the reading room. I decided that, rather than upset my fellow researchers, I would quietly bear the long queue in the copy centre in order to get a reproduction of this prized document that I could take back to my office for careful study.

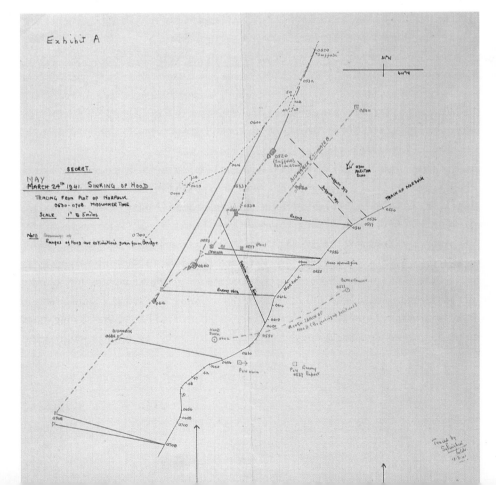

LEFT *This plot of* Norfolk's *D. R. track matched the reconstructed navigation plot I had made, thereby confirming the information I was using was consistent and accurate.*

The value of this plot was more than just the small circle marking the position, which its creator had annotated with the words 'Hood sunk 0602'. Although this position was important because it represented another sinking position for Hood (the fourth), it was the nature of the entire plot that really excited me. This was clearly the actual dead-reckoning plot that was being kept on the bridge by Norfolk's navigating officer. Curiously, the sinking position for Hood on this plot is 4 nautical miles different from the one sent out by Wake-Walker in the second wireless transmission at 6.37 a.m. (63° 21'N, 31° 47'W). The protocol in the 'County'-class cruisers at the time was that the ship's navigating officer would become the squadron navigating officer when a rear-admiral came on board to set-up his flag command (Wake-Walker would not have brought his own navigating officer on board with him). Therefore, all three sinking positions from Norfolk most certainly originated from the same navigating officer. In this case, how is it possible to explain the 4-nautical-mile difference in positions if the same person worked them out? The most sensible explanation is that the sinking position in the second wireless transmission was an estimated position corrected from the dead-reckoning position for errors due to currents and leeway. If this explanation were valid, it would reinforce my feeling that the sinking position given by Norfolk at 6.37 a.m. was the most probable.

Significantly, Norfolk's dead-reckoning plot represents a continuous overview, from a single navigator's perspective, of all the ship's movements for the most crucial hour and a half, centred on the battle. All the vital pieces of information were here on a single plot: Norfolk's precise track; Bismarck's estimated track; Prince of Wales' enemy report; and Hood's sinking position. I had already created the exact same type of plot from numerous separate pieces of information, but it lacked continuity and certain gaps in time had to be filled by assumptions. However, I was greatly relieved to see that my partial plot agreed in every aspect with the actual dead-reckoning plot. This meant that there was a high degree of corroboration between the different sources. The re-navigation was beginning to come together.

The first ships to respond to Wake-Walker's 6.37-a.m. instruction to 'proceed search survivors' were the destroyers HMS Electra and HMS Echo. At 7 a.m. the two ships were some 30 nautical miles to the northeast of the sinking position, but were steaming flat out at a bone-jarring 32 knots towards the scene of the explosion. Forty-five minutes later, the destroyers sighted an oil patch and wreckage right ahead of them and reduced speed to start their search for survivors. To their utter dismay, the rescue operation did not take long – only three men were found clinging to tiny rafts in the freezing water. The three survivors were taken on board Electra and the depressing search continued. By 9 a.m., the search party had been joined by the other destroyers Icarus, Achates, Antelope and Anthony. Hood had by now already hit the seabed 2,800 metres below with a crunching impact. The futility of the destroyers' search amidst the spreading patch of oil still rising from *Hood* was apparent to all and it was abandoned. With *Electra* leading, the ships made for Hvalfjord to deliver their valuable cargo.

There was never a chance for me to get the actual position where *Electra* and *Echo* fished the three survivors out of the sea, for, as is the custom with minor ships such as destroyers, their logs had been destroyed many years ago by the archives. This would have been another crucial position to have, as many shipwrecks have been found on the basis of information from rescue ships, which generally have sufficient time to record their positions accurately. The best I could do without their logs was to create a dead-reckoning track for *Electra* and *Echo* on the information I had and assumptions I made about how they would approach the oil patch and survivors. The result was a position that was in reasonable agreement with the now emerging cluster of four sinking positions.

It would have been tempting to stop the research at this point, as I had accumulated four primary sinking positions which, in addition to being supported by a secondary position (*Electra*'s), were formed in a tight cluster the longest distance of which was about 4 nautical miles. Fortunately, I resisted any temptation to stop.

Throughout this long trail of research I was desperately trying to generate a sinking position from the navigation of *Hood* herself. There were obviously no logs to refer to, as they were lost with the ship. In their jointly authored book *Flagship Hood*, Alan Coles and Ted Briggs wrote of a seemingly accurate position for *Hood* when it made its enemy report upon sighting *Bismarck*. I searched everywhere for the actual wireless transmission matching the details given in the book without ever finding one. I finally concluded that the message had been put together by Alan to make this part of *Flagship Hood* read better (Ted was later to confirm this). I did find a copy of *Hood*'s last wireless message, which had been intercepted by a Royal Canadian Navy 'sparker' (radio man) and ultimately found its way onto the internet when his widow donated his papers to a SPARC Radio Museum when he died in 1999. It was a legitimate message, but the position reference was coded in a way I couldn't understand (013GFVA21D00). I sensed that a final position for *Hood* existed, but I needed to find a way to decipher the code.

The breakthrough I was looking for came as I started work on the Hudson and Sunderland aircraft reports. I could see that they too reported coded positions that were partially similar to *Hood*'s last position. They used an alphanumeric code in two parts, such as 'GFVA 4206'. When I found the coded positions transcribed in several different documents, I knew all I had to do was to compare all the coded and transcribed positions I could find to work out how the alphanumeric code operated.

Once I had five pairs of positions to compare, I was able to make a template that let me work out the rest of the coded aircraft positions. This code operated like the German grid system, but it was much simpler. The alpha component of the code stood for 1°-squares of longitude or latitude, so in the case of GFVA, GF stood for 63°N while VA stood for 32°W. The four digits at the end were not coded. They were simply the minutes portion of the position. Therefore, GFVA 4206 was the code for 63°42′N, 32°6′W.

Having cracked this code, I was sure the GFVA in *Hood*'s last position stood for 63° N and 32°W, but I was struggling to work out the complete position. I then noticed in a list of signals made by *Suffolk* that a few of her positions were reported in a similar manner. For example, a wireless transmission from *Suffolk* at 7.56 a.m. stated: 'Emergency. Repeat back. One battleship and one cruiser bear 182°, 18 miles; approx.

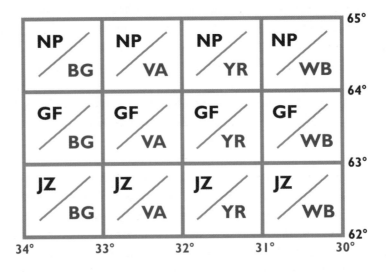

RIGHT *A template I developed to transcribe coded British positions. Once I understood how the code worked I was able to derive a sinking position based upon* Hood's *own navigation.*

true course 200°. My position 048 GFBG 15 x 11.' One minute later, *Suffolk* sent another message reporting, 'Enemy battleship has reduced speed and appears damaged and on fire. My position 63°10′N; 32°34′W x 11.' This time *Suffolk* gave her full geographic position and the mystery was as good as solved. In the minute between the two messages, *Suffolk* could not have travelled far, and so the position given at 7.57 a.m. must be almost identical to the coded position given at 7.56 a.m. After a few moments at the plotting table I had the answer. The coded position 048 GFBG 15 is a range and bearing from a fixed position, as in a range of 15 nautical miles at a bearing of 48° from the position 63°N and 33°W, or when plotted not far from 63°10′N; 32°34′W. The 'x

11′ indicates that the position was based upon a reference position established at 11 a.m. the previous day.

Hood's last reported position, given at 5.43 a.m. when she made her first and only enemy report, could be deciphered as a range and bearing of 13 nautical miles at 21° from the position 63° N and 32° W. I plotted this position and then began to work out Hood's dead-reckoning track up until she was hit and exploded seventeen minutes later, just as I had done for the Prince of Wales. Hood's sinking position, the fifth and final one I would derive, was roughly 8 nautical miles to the west of the cluster of the four other positions.

While it was satisfying to have finally derived a position based on Hood's navigation, I was concerned that it was considerably outside the main cluster of positions. The search box I had in mind would have to expand greatly to incorporate Hood's outlying position. This would add days to my estimate to cover the entire search box. There were no obvious reasons for Hood's position to be so different, especially as she was in company with the Prince of Wales right alongside her. I could only wonder why the squadron navigating officer – Commander Warrand, the man who, in stepping aside to let Ted Briggs off the compass platform first, probably sacrificed his life to save Ted's – had such a different position from the others. I also wondered whether he was right.

There was one last navigation clue to be considered before I finalized my search plans for Hood. The clue came from another destroyer, HMS Malcolm, which had been waiting for an opportunity to join the action against Bismarck when she too received Wake-Walker's order of 6.37 a.m. to 'proceed search survivors'. At 3.06 p.m., Malcolm reached the reported position and found nothing. Malcolm's commander, C. D. Howard-Johnston, then proceeded to another position reported by Vaughan's Sunderland flying boat. Here again nothing was found. So Malcolm began to sweep out an area within 10 miles of the position to pass within 2 miles of any rafts and floats within the area. At 9.45 p.m., the smell of oil fuel was noticed, and the ship immediately altered course upwind. Two hours later, having made 24 miles to windward, they found 'a large patch of oil, 1 mile in diameter, covered with small bits of wreckage and with patches of brown scum. The position was 63° 14′N, 32° 22′W.' Malcolm, who was joined by Antelope in her second stint looking for survivors, searched the area through the night but sadly found no survivors. All the two ships were able to pick up were scattered pieces of wreckage, which they recovered and landed at Reykjavik. But in her scouring of the seas, Malcolm had in fact delivered to me another vital clue.

By the time the destroyer came upon the floating oil patch and wreckage at 9.45 p.m., nearly sixteen hours had passed since Hood sank. During this time, the wreckage would have drifted away from the sinking position, carried and pushed by a combination of current and wind. My hope was to try to confirm where *Hood* went down by backtracking from *Malcolm*'s position based upon an estimation of the total drift. Any position determined this way would be no better than a secondary position, possibly even less useful than *Electra*'s, given the longer period of uncertainty. Nevertheless, the observations made in *Malcolm*'s report were very precise and they had the feel of being accurate. I was hoping the result would at least shed some light on the discrepancy between *Hood*'s position and the cluster of four further east. I started the analysis by compiling all the information I was able to collect on winds and current.

The current that runs over *Hood*'s sinking position is called the Irminger current and it flows west to southwest at an average speed of 0.2–0.6 knots in the month of May. Based on this average speed, I calculated that, in the fifteen hours during which the wreckage had been floating on the water before being spotted by *Malcolm*, it would have drifted downcurrent anywhere from 3.15–9.45 nautical miles. In addition to the current, the wreckage would also have been 'pushed' through the water by the strong winds blowing on the day adding to the total distance the wreckage had drifted. I was able to calculate this component of the total drift, called leeway, using mathematical formulas developed by modern Search and Rescue (SAR) researchers to help them predict how far survivors may have drifted following a vessel sinking. Using the winds logged by four of the British ships on the scene, including *Malcolm*, a leeway drift of 7–9 nautical miles to the south was predicted.

When I plotted both the current and leeway components of drift relative to the position at which *Malcolm* first sighted wreckage I didn't expect the result to be so clear-cut and surprising. The resultant plot transcribed an area within which it was reasonable to expect *Hood* to have sunk. The surprise was that the sinking position from *Hood*'s dead-reckoning track (the one based upon the squadron navigating officer's 5.43-a.m. position) was sitting nearly dead in the centre of this area. The correlation between the two independent loss clues could hardly be better. On the other hand, the other four sinking positions were far to the east, well outside the boundaries predicted by the wreckage drift. Commander Warrand's position was no longer an unexplainable out-lier. It was strongly supported by a credible independent clue and would factor significantly in my search plans for *Hood*.

BISMARCK'S SINKING POSITION

Of all the many British ships and aircraft that took part in the pursuit and sinking of *Bismarck*, relatively few were actually on hand to witness her final moments before she slowly sank at 10.40 a.m. on 27 May 1941. The cruiser HMS *Dorsetshire* was the nearest, as she had been given the responsibility of delivering the *coup de grâce* in the form of three Mark VII torpedoes – two into *Bismarck*'s starboard side at 10.25 a.m. and a final one into her port side at 10.36 a.m. In his report of the action, *Dorsetshire*'s captain, B. C. S. Martin, described *Bismarck*'s last minutes: 'Shortly after this torpedo struck she heeled over quickly to port and commenced to sink by the stern. She then heeled completely over keel up and down by the stern, and then disappeared beneath the waves at 10.40 a.m.'

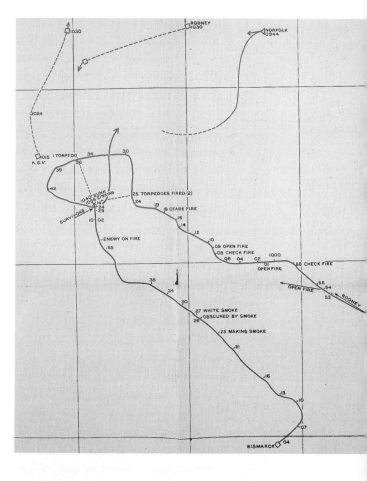

ABOVE *Dorsetshire's track plot as she closed in on* Bismarck *and torpedoed her twice.* Norfolk, Rodney *and* King George V *had already departed.*

Dorsetshire's and *Bismarck*'s minute-by-minute movements in the final action are dramatically captured in a track chart made at sea by a Lieutenant R. D. East on board the British cruiser. The chart has the feel of a proper dead-reckoning plot, but it appears to have been made after the fact (it is dated the following day), probably to accompany the captain's official report which had been requested by the Admiralty as a matter of urgency. The plot shows that *Bismarck* was effectively dead in the water by 10.14 a.m. and sank in the same position before *Dorsetshire* circled to port to return and pick up survivors. The position marked on the chart – 48° 12'N, 16° 4.5'W – was not printed on any of the documents I found in the archives. It is one of only three independent sinking positions reported for the loss of *Bismarck*, all made by the British.

The second sinking position was given in an official wireless transmission made at 11.01 a.m. on 27 May 1941 from the commander-in-chief of the Home Fleet, Admiral Tovey, to the Admiralty. Tovey, commanding from the Home Fleet flagship HMS *King George V*, relayed the news everyone had been anxiously waiting to hear: '*Bismarck* sunk in 48° 9'N. 16° 7'W.' The late reporting of *Bismarck*'s demise (twenty-one minutes after the fact) was the second minor embarrassment Tovey had had to endure that morning. Earlier, he had signalled the flag officer commanding Force 'H'

(Vice-Admiral Sir James Somerville on HMS *Renown*) that he could not sink *Bismarck* with gunfire. Because the fuel situation on board *King George V* and HMS *Rodney* was becoming acute, Tovey decided to break off the action at 10.22 a.m. and steam away to the northeast, leaving *Bismarck* to her certain fate. At 10.38 a.m., Tovey ordered *Dorsetshire* to finish the job using her torpedoes, completely unaware that Captain Martin had anticipated the order and already done the deed. *Bismarck* was seen to have sunk from the after director control tower in the *King George V*, but for some reason this fact did not reach Tovey until 11 a.m.

The third and final sinking position was reported by W. K. Patterson, captain of *King George V*, in his narrative of the action dated 17 June. In his final statement Patterson gives the sinking position as: 'Latitude 48° 10′N, longitude 16° 12′W. Depth 2,500 fathoms.' Patterson's sinking position was the second to be reported from *King George V*, and would have been given to him by the ship's regular navigating officer. Admiral Tovey, who had his full flag staff on board *King George V*, would have relied upon his own squadron navigating officer for the position he reported in his 11.01-a.m. wireless transmission. This explains the unusual situation of two independent sinking positions originating from the same ship. In the official Admiralty version of the complete battle, published years later under the title 'Battle Summary No. 5: The chase and sinking of the *Bismarck*', Patterson's position was adopted as the official sinking position.

The battleship *Rodney* recorded a potential fourth sinking position, but I doubted its value to my search plan. *Rodney*, in company with the *King George V*, did much of the serious damage to *Bismarck* in the final action, clinically pounding her with 16-inch and 6-inch shellfire. In the closing moments of the action, *Rodney*'s range to target was down to 3,800 yards and she was firing full broadsides, achieving up to as many as five or six hits. *Rodney* was certainly close enough to record *Bismarck*'s final position, and she appeared to have done so, as shown by an entry in the 'Remarks' column of her log: '1039 *Bismarck* sunk in pos. 4809N 1607W.' I was immediately suspicious of this position, however, because, along with other notes, it was clearly written between the lines of the main remarks using a different pen. I was pretty sure the position was written in the log at a later time in an effort by someone to get the key events on record. My suspicions were confirmed when I saw that the position was identical to the sinking position given by Tovey in his wireless transmission at 11.01 a.m. What was the chance that two ships navigating independently would record the exact same position down to the nearest second? Not very likely I thought. Never before had I seen a case of one-hundred-per-cent corroboration in Second World War navigation. Certain that the position was copied into *Rodney*'s log only after it was received by radio as part of Tovey's wireless signal, I decided to ignore it.

opens fire. Cos & speeds as requisite for

1026 Cease fire - Co.sp. A.R. rejoin King George V.

engagement. 1039 Bismarck sunk in pos. 4809N 1607W.

1107, - 19 Knts. 1115 A/C 025° In stn. 4ca astern of King George V

1240 A/C 150°. 1130. Hauled down Battle ensign.

H.M.S. "ROONEY", Tuesday 27th day of MAY, 1941.

From CLYDE, To HALIFAX or At SEA: BISMARCK OPERAT.

LEAVE GRANTED TO SHIP'S COMPANY — NIL

Time	Log (Stating type)	Distance Run through the Water Miles	Tenths	True Course	Mean Revolutions per minute	Wind Direction (true)	Force (0-12)	Weather and Visibility	Sea and Swell	Corrected Barometric Pressure in Millibars	Dry Bulb	Wet Bulb	Sea	REMARKS	Initials of the Officer of the Watch
		9	5	030										0000. A/c 088°. 0010 Co B30, 16.2 revs	
0100	17049	2	2	030	140									0022 14 revs. 0025 147 revs. 0030 12 kts. 0031 A/c 022	
		5	7	250										0083 A/c 030°. 0034. 127 revs. 0107 A/c 230. 0125 A/c 270	
		11	1	270											
0200	1717.5	7	0	270	132.8									0228 A/c 220°	
		12	0	220											
0300	1730.2	19	0	220	134.6										
														042 A/c 180°.	
0400	1759.0	3	8	220	134.6	NWbyW	6	c²	34	1007.3	51	48	56		
		15	2	180										0500 A/c 260°	
0500	1777.6	19	0	260	134										
0600	1726.4	19	0	260	134										
0700	1813.7	6	3	260	1183									0720 A/c 180°. 0721 A/c 150°. 0728 A/c together to 125°. 0734 A/c together 050°. 0750 A/c Together 140°.	
		12	7	Vars										0800. A/c together 105°. 0806 A/c together 085°. 0807 H.A.S	
0800	1832.5	20	0	Vars	133.5	NW	6	c²	54	1006.8	52	47		54 Norfolk brg. 022, 12 miles. 0827 A/c 175°	
														0833 A/c Together 110°. 0841. Enemy brg.122.	
0900	1850.0	19	0	Vars	1234									German BS Bismarck 0847. Rooney	
1000	1868.2	20	0	Vars	134.8									opens fire. Cos & speeds as requisite for	
														1026 Cease fire - Co.sp. A.R. rejoin King George V.	
1100	1882.5	19	0	030	1196									engagement. 1039 Bismarck sunk in pos. 4809N 1607W.	
1200	1901.3	12	7	025	123	NW	6	bo²	44	1000.9	51	50	55	1107, - 19 Knts. 1115 A/C 025° In stn. 4ca astern of King George V. 1240 A/c 150°. 1130. Hauled down Battle ensign.	

Distance run through the Water	Position	Latitude	Longitude	Depending on	Currents experienced	ANCHOR BEARINGS			
479.7	0800	48 15N	16 45W	D.R					
Zone Time kept at noon −2	1200	48 55N	15 42W	D.R.					
	2000	50 44	1321W	Obs.	Number on Sick List	5			

Time	Log	Miles	Tenths	True Course	Mean Rev	Wind Dir	Force	Weather	Sea	Pressure	Dry	Wet	Sea	REMARKS	Init
		6	3	150										1300 A/c 020. 1305. DR sighted on Horizon to SE.	
1300	1920.7	12	8	020	123.5									1326 15 speed 17 knots.	
1400	1938.3	4	4	020	125									1415 A/c 037°. 1420 - 18 kts.	
1500	1955.1	12	2	037											
		19	0	037	123										
1600	1973.8	19	0	037	133	NW	7	c²	54	1001.2	52	50	57		
1700	1991.7	19	0	037	133									1705. H.M.S. Jupiter joined screen.	
1800	2007.8	19	3	037	133.6	NW	6	c²	44	1001.5	58	51	54	1820. 12.4 revs.	
1900	2028.3	19	5	037	133.4										
2000	2047.3	19	7	037	134	NW	7	c³	54	998.2	51	50	55	2025 A/c 040°. 2029 A/c 042°. 2032 A/c 023. 2035. N.A℄ by 040° - 1st Degree of H.A.	
2100	2065.1	19	4	037	132									2104 N.A℄ by 070°. 2110 - 133 revs.	
2200	2083.4	19	3	037	133.6									2201. 2210. 2226. N.A℄ by 220°. 2232 131 revs.	

LEFT Rodney's log for 27 May 1941. The entries in the margin using a different pen are a sure sign that the position was copied later from Tovey's 1101 W. T.

When I plotted the three independent sinking positions, they formed a neat triangle with the longest leg representing the 5.4-nautical-mile distance between *Dorsetshire*'s position to the northeast and Captain Patterson's position to the west. Admiral Tovey's position was located to the south of both the others by approximately the same distance (3 ½ nautical miles). Considering the poor weather on the day of the action (winds ranging from Force 6 to 8; *Dorsetshire* recorded 50 knots) there was relatively good agreement between the three positions.

When I began to compare my research with what Ballard had written in his book I was still confident that *Bismarck* could be re-located quite easily, although there were a couple of discrepancies I would need to work out. Ballard's 1989 expedition had discovered *Bismarck* lying on the southern flank of an extinct underwater volcano at a depth of 4,790 metres. The extremely rough terrain of the volcano had plagued Ballard's team throughout their two expeditions and nearly jeopardized their chance of finding the wreck. When I superimposed my plot of the three sinking positions on top of a recent bathymetric chart of the area, I could see Ballard's problem: the volcano's southern flank rose steeply some 800 metres at an average slope of 7 degrees. Ballard's instrument sled, a combination of side-scan sonar and *Argo* cameras had to be towed anywhere from 10 to 25 metres off the seabed to be effective, so it was just barely skimming over the rugged terrain at very slow speed. In contrast, our side-scan sonar tow-fish would be flown at the relatively safe altitude of 350 metres and we could take advantage of the flatter lower slope of the volcano for a safe tow route. Our sonar could search more seabed in one day than *Argo* could in ten, but I was still looking for every advantage I could find to minimize the time we would have to spend re-locating *Bismarck*.

The final and most valuable clues came from Ballard himself. In his book, *The Discovery of the* Bismarck, he writes of the wreck: 'She is less than 2 miles from the sinking position recorded by the navigator of the *King George V*, but I plan to keep the precise coordinates a secret.' From a diagram on the following page, it is clear that the position Ballard is referring to is Tovey's 11.01 a.m. wireless-transmission position – the most southerly position of the three. The diagram also shows *Bismarck* is located to the southeast of *King George V*'s position. Using the 3.2-kilometre range and approximate southeast bearing, I plotted a new position where I reckoned Ballard had found the wreck. Although my bathymetric chart indicated a depth of only 4,500 metres for this position – almost 300 metres shallower than Ballard reported – I knew that our sonar would be able to cover the entire area of discrepancy in a single pass. I had expected to make as many as four sonar passes to re-locate *Bismarck*, each taking fourteen hours to complete, but now I began to revise my thinking. Could we possibly find *Bismarck* on the first pass?

THE SEARCH FOR BISMARCK BEGINS

Despite the last-minute problems with the 60-Hertz generator, the *Northern Horizon* got underway from Cobh in good shape and we had only lost a day on our schedule. I knew there would be many opportunities to recover the lost time, so I could look forward to the transit without concern. There was an exceptional mood of anticipation and purpose on board. Jim Mercer summarized it best when he said to me, 'Everyone here really wants to be here, they are all keen to make a contribution.' There is definitely something about working on shipwrecks that excites people, and we were about to try and find two of the most famous wrecks in the world.

It would be at least a day and a half before we reached the search area, which gave all our people plenty of time to get settled in. On the first day at sea all I really wanted to accomplish was to brief the search team on the *Bismarck* sinking positions and search plan, and to conduct an operational test of the side-scan sonar. Although the sonar tested OK in port, the only sure way to be happy with its tuning was to take it

ABOVE Northern Horizon *'s bow pounds through the sea on our way to the Bismarck search area.*

for a test drive over actual seabed. We launched the 2,700-pound, 4-metre long sonar tow-fish in ideal weather conditions and monitored its descent down to 1,500 metres. I was comforted when the familiar Ocean Explorer imagery began to scroll down our screens and the image quality looked as good as ever. There was a slight hitch when one of our image-processing computers would not read the sonar data correctly because of a software incompatibility. It was the type of problem you could not find at the dock, so I was grateful we had exposed it on the test dive, which left enough time before we arrived on site for a software patch to be created and sent out to us by email. Not many years ago, we would have had to turn back to port to wait for the repair software to be delivered by courier.

As the ship ploughed ahead into the Atlantic Ocean my only serious worry was the prospect of rough weather meeting us when we reached the site. Winds were forecast to veer northwesterly and increase to Force 6, perhaps Force 7, as a frontal system moved east past the search area. Those high winds should only last a day, but in that time the seas would increase to 4 metres, making undersea searching impossible. Any hopes I had of the forecast being wrong were dashed as I watched the ship's barometer fall steadily through the night.

By 8 a.m. the following morning the front was upon us and the wind was steady at 34 knots. It was no longer a question of would there be weather down time, but rather how much? I had budgeted for seven days of down time during the entire expedition, a factor of twenty per cent. What I didn't want, however, was to lose a couple of days before we even got started. Even though the seven days was a contingency, to be used only if necessary, I fully expected to need it, and thus considered it a precious commodity not to be wasted. Problems have a way of compounding themselves when working offshore in deepwater and a perfectly planned schedule can be made impossible by a couple of unlucky breaks or by bad weather at the wrong time. My worst fear was that we would start the expedition on a back foot like this, but there was nothing to do except wait and see how bad the blow would be.

We arrived on site at 7.30 p.m. Our progress had been slowed by the increasing seas and wind – now 38 knots – on the starboard bow. Joe, the chief officer, put the *Northern Horizon* head to wind and swell and the wait began. By midnight the wind was blowing steady at 45–50 knots and the sea was getting angrier and angrier. Our forecasted strong breeze was now a full-blown storm (Force 10).

Conditions moderated slightly the next morning, but the wind continued to blow at 40 knots and greater. In spite of the 6-metre swells, the *Northern Horizon* was only pitching moderately and she was proving her reputation as a good sea-boat. When they were not running to the rails to be seasick, the rough weather gave the filmmakers an opportunity to shoot conditions similar to those that had prevailed on the mornings of 24 and 27 May 1941. Otherwise, not much work could be done and the interminable WOW (waiting on weather) continued.

The wind stayed above 30 knots for the remainder of the day and through to the next morning before it finally started to abate around noon. By 4 p.m., conditions had improved markedly and we began steaming back to the start of our first search line. The winds were dipping below 20 knots for the first time in sixty-three hours. We set up the ship to run a practice search line to see how she would handle on our preferred line heading. Everything was looking good for a launch. Andy Sherrel had his team ready on deck for the real thing and the green light was given. At 6.42 p.m. the Ocean Explorer sonar plunged into the calming sea. A second green light was given to begin her descent. Troy Launay, controlling the winch from his position on the crane, pushed his handle forward to send the first of many thousands of metres of steel tow-cable streaming down towards the seabed. The sonar was on her way. With her went the hopes and expectations of everyone on board that she would soon be sending us back images to show us our quarry had been found.

BELOW *At last, the Ocean Explorer side-scan sonar is launched to start the search for* Bismarck.

Breakout to
Apocalypse

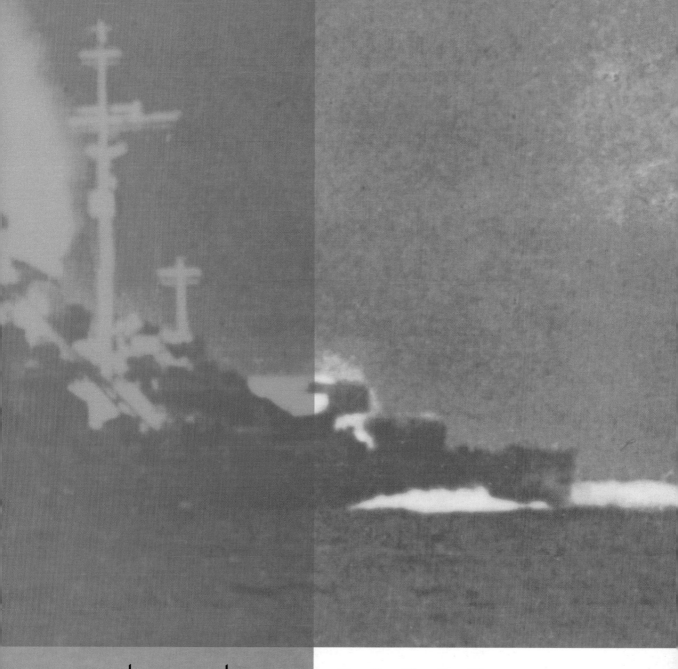

chapter **seven**

JUTLAND UNAVENGED

As Ted Briggs and his two fellow survivors, Midshipman Bill Dundas and Able Seaman Bob Tilburn, began their struggle to survive the unforgiving seas of the Denmark Strait, something resembling an argument seems to have been briefly under way between the two senior officers in *Bismarck*. Watching the wounded *Prince of Wales* turn away, Captain Ernst Lindemann's blood was up. He wanted to go after her. What a victory for the *Kriegsmarine* that might deliver! The overweening reputation of the Royal Navy's dominance over the German navy, unresolved at Jutland, might at last be set down for good. But Lütjens would have none of it. Raeder's last words on 'Rheinübung' echoed in his mind – 'Deliberate, careful operations … a mistake to risk a heavy engagement for limited and perhaps uncertain results … ' Lütjens turned down his captain's request. The master plan must somehow be wrenched back on course. As Dr Eric Grove comments: 'Avoiding unnecessary action was at the core of the German Naval High Command's doctrine and every instinct in Lütjens was calling him to his primary objective – the convoys.'

However, it would not be easy to return to the master plan. *Bismarck*, for all her crushing defeat of the British (one famous battlecruiser destroyed, one brand-new modern battleship put to flight) was hardly unscathed. The worst and most significant part of the damage to her was near the bow. A heavy shell had ripped right through the ship's three compartments back from her graceful 'Atlantic bow', flooding it with almost 2,000 tons of seawater. The shell had also isolated 1,000 tons of fuel, now inaccessible to the ship's engineers. Moreover, oil was actually leaking out at the site of another heavy hit on a compartment directly below the armoured forward conning tower. This leak was leaving a broad, oily band on the sea's surface – a perfect track for shadowers aiming to maintain contact with the injured ship to follow. A third British hit had done relatively little damage, passing across the upper deck without exploding.

It was the first hole that was the worst. It would prove impossible to repair at sea. The hole hit directly at the battleship's performance, putting her 3 degrees down by the head, and giving her a 9-degree list to port. Attempts to plug the hole so as to pump out the seawater had only helped a little. The British had not landed a knockout punch on *Bismarck*, but she was cut and bleeding. And, in effect, *hors de combat*.

'Rheinübung' was dead in the water. How could she fulfil her key role of holding off other capital ships in this state, while *Eugen* ravaged the soft-skinned, defenceless merchantmen in the convoys? And what about *Bismarck*'s fuel state now? Prolonged operations would be extremely uncertain, even with refuelling at sea, which itself would be subject to the usual hazards of war. No, the analytical, methodical Lütjens must have calculated. We will live to fight another day. In the meantime, let us see what our unscathed companion can do, acting independently. So, at 8.01 a.m. on 24 May, just two hours after sinking *Hood*, this signal from *Bismarck* crackled through the airwaves: 'Intention: to proceed to St Nazaire. *Prinz Eugen* cruiser warfare.'

The *Kriegsmarine*'s latest attempt at a deepwater operation was effectively at an end. HMS *Hood* had not died in vain.

SALVATION

Far to the north, almost despairing now of any of their former friends and shipmates, Ted Briggs, Bob Tilburn and Bill Dundas struggled to stay awake and out of the clutches of fatal hypothermia on their three tiny rafts, swaying and dipping on the breaking waves of the Denmark Strait. They could not, of course, know that the action they had fought had achieved its main objective: to stop *Bismarck* getting in among the British convoys like a tiger in bloodlust. Nor could they know that their fight had marked *Bismarck* down to die – an end that would not be long coming. All they knew was the fear of death and of not being rescued from the empty, wide-open seas that stretched as far as their tired eyes could see.

Hours passed. Dundas kept their spirits up and – all-important – their eyes open. He warded off the sleep of death by repeating choruses of 'Roll out the Barrel'. They talked too. All agreed that, mystifyingly, they had heard no sound of the kind of explosion that could have caused such a cataclysm, of the kind that had been heard as *Hood*'s three battlecruiser forebears blew up at Jutland.

Tiredness and cold crept steadily up on the three men in the water. Their rafts began to drift apart, Dundas still indomitably 'rolling out the barrel'. Then, at last, came rescue. Their saving angel was the destroyer *Electra*, part of the force that had accompanied *Hood* and *Prince of Wales* out from Scapa what seemed like an aeon ago. In the punishing weather at the start of the sortie these ships had been left behind because their frail hulls could not keep speed with the capital ships. The three survivors yelled and screamed, waving their arms frantically. Their ordeal was about to end. *Electra* cut her engines and drifted down on them. Despite the cold clenching his hands and fingers, Ted somehow managed to cling onto a line thrown to him. 'Don't you let go of that!' one of their rescuers called. 'You bet your bloody life I won't!' Ted replied. Slowly, in an agony of weariness, the three men began to try to climb the nets slung over the destroyer's side. But Ted, too weak now from cold, exhaustion, from the foul oil he had swallowed and the hours in the water, could not do it. So seamen from *Electra* dropped into the water beside him and pushed and pulled him up the net until he made the deck.

RIGHT *Down by the head: Bismarck shows the effects of the Battle of the Denmark Strait.*

Safely on board, the three survivors collapsed into sleep. Meanwhile, the nightmare continued for the Royal Navy. The destroyers that had roared to the rescue, pushing their speed to the limit to make the wreck scene had prepared hot food, bandages and salving rum for the hundreds of survivors they expected and hoped for. But Briggs, Tilburn and Dundas were the only survivors they ever found. Just three men were saved out of more than 1,400 – men of many ages, nationalities and ranks, from midshipman to admiral, from long-serving rate to newly arrived ordinary seaman.

'With favourable winds', may they all rest in peace.

HUE AND CRY

It fell again to the shadowing cruisers *Suffolk* and *Norfolk* to maintain contact with their enemy. And now a score had to be settled. But which way would *Bismarck* turn? The new senior officer in the task force was now Admiral Frederick Wake-Walker in *Norfolk*, with the badly mauled *Prince of Wales* also under his command. Not called to intervene against *Prinz Eugen* in the disastrous battle of the Denmark Strait, Wake-Walker now had an even more important role. He was to keep the German raiders firmly in his radar plot – through *Suffolk*, with her more modern set – while a shocked Royal Navy collected the resources needed to avenge *Hood*. The additional task of keeping the Germans out of the Atlantic, where they could vanish in the ocean's wide spaces, was more pressing than ever. With every passing hour *Bismarck* and her consort would be getting closer to where they seemed to want to be.

The call went out to gather the clans of the Royal Navy – to bring such a force into battle with *Bismarck* that she and the German navy would bitterly rue the day she set out to challenge her rival's high-seas imperium.

The aim was to amass that 'concentration of force' of which every naval commander dreams. Creating such a force is the high point of strategy – collecting together all the assets you can for a specific and valuable objective. The Home Fleet's commander-in-chief, Admiral Tovey, was already close to *Bismarck* and her consort. His powerful force comprised the battleship *King George V*, the battlecruiser *Repulse*, the aircraft carrier *Victorious* and five cruisers. Two hours after *Hood*'s sinking they were 300 miles to the east of the *'Rheinübung'* force.

Tovey still had a puzzle to resolve: what would his opposite number, Lütjens, do now? Turn back for Norway either through the Denmark Strait or south of Iceland? Head to France for repairs? Or, with the same intent, to a friendly Spanish Atlantic port – or perhaps an Italian or Vichy French harbour in the Mediterranean? He might even continue on into the Atlantic to refuel and resume *'Rheinübung'*. In the absence of certainty and of any knowledge about *Bismarck*'s real condition after her battle in the Denmark Strait every option had to be covered. So Tovey held back, waiting to see which way the cat might jump.

As he did so, capital ship reinforcements were on their way. The battleship *Rodney*, rolling towards the United States for an overdue refit in Boston, was told to turn back and chase *Bismarck*. The old-stager *Ramillies*, escorting eastbound Atlantic convoy HX127, was told to leave her charges and head back a thousand miles. Another veteran, *Revenge*, at ease in Halifax, Canada, was instructed to get up steam as quickly as she could and get to sea. The cruiser *London*, just off Spain, was also instructed to take up the chase, as was her sister *Edinburgh*. And finally, *Hood*'s old Mediterranean friends, Force H, were put on alert to catch the raiders too. It was an impressive cast list. But it had a lot of sea to cover.

Meanwhile, Wake-Walker's cruisers, in company with *Prince of Wales*, were still doggedly pursuing *Bismarck*. Visibility was poor – the weather was still the raiders' friend. Wake-Walker had to rely on *Suffolk* to keep in contact, as the radar in his flagship *Norfolk* was of little use, being unable to sweep from side to side like her sister's. Aside from some heart-stopping moments when *Suffolk* lost contact, this seemed to be working. But Wake-Walker's shadowing approach, waiting for Tovey's force to be in a position to come up and engage *Bismarck*, was making the high command of the navy stir uneasily at their desks back in Whitehall. Eventually, the desire to meddle with the man on the spot got the better of them. One sentence stuck out like a sore thumb from one of their signals: 'Request your intentions as regards the *Prince of Wales* re-engaging?' It may sound innocent enough, but to any career naval officer with a sense of history it spoke volumes, however unreliable and inadequate as a match for *Bismarck Prince of Wales* might presently be. Wake-Walker could not have helped wondering – was he being accused of lacking the fighting spirit – of forgetting Nelson's deceptively understated dictum that 'No captain can do very wrong if he places his ship alongside that of an enemy'? So, under this looming pressure from the 'Whitehall warriors', Wake-Walker devised a plan to draw *Bismarck* away toward his commander-in-chief. And almost lost his major asset, *Suffolk*, and her invaluable radar in the process.

The idea was that *Prince of Wales* would go into the lead and slowly come up behind *Bismarck*, accompanied by the cruisers. On sighting *Bismarck* emerging from the haze, *Prince of Wales* would open fire and then sail off to the east, leading *Bismarck* straight onto the guns and torpedo-bombers of the Home Fleet. Whether this part of the plan worked or not, all would have been well if *Bismarck* had held her course. She did not.

Aboard *Bismarck*, Lütjens had devised a plan to enable *Prinz Eugen* to get away and start work on his fallback plan for her: she was to engage in independent-cruiser warfare in the Atlantic. The idea was that the cruiser would continue on her present southwest course until a rain squall made visibility even worse – at which point *Bismarck* would peel off to the west, drawing away the gnat-like cruisers still buzzing about her ears. The cue to carry this out would be the code-word '*Hood*'.

The moment came. At 6.14 p.m. on the evening of the day that had seen the death of the great British battlecruiser, her name was in the airwaves once again. Round swung *Bismarck*; away went *Eugen*. And *Suffolk*'s radar operator suddenly found himself staring at a plot that showed *Bismarck* dead ahead at only 10 miles. His own frail ship was well within range of the enemy's 15-inch (38-cm) guns – a shell from one of them could finish *Suffolk* in seconds. As *Bismarck* emerged from the rain squall, several of those shells were not long coming. *Suffolk* retreated, rolling violently from side to side, pouring out rolling masses of oily, black smoke to cover her withdrawal. *Prince of Wales* returned fire on *Bismarck* in support, but two of the British ship's guns endorsed Wake-Walker's judgement of her current fighting capacity by jamming once again.

The chase was resumed. The line of light on the darkened radar plot in *Suffolk* now showed just one target: battleship *Bismarck*. Aboard *Prinz Eugen*, Second Gunnery Officer Paul Schmalenbach watched the capital ship go with foreboding:

'Watching our "big brother" disappear gives us a melancholy feeling. Then we saw him again for a few minutes, as the flashes of his guns suddenly painted the sea, clouds and rain squalls dark red … In the fire of his after turrets we saw clearly again the outline of the mighty ship, the long hull, the tower mast and stack, which now looked like one solid, sturdy building … Then the curtain of rain squalls closed for the last time. The "big brother" disappeared from the sight of the many eyes following him…'

STRINGBAG SORTIE

Tovey, waiting for his reinforcements to converge on him and anxiously assessing his enemy's progress, knew he needed to do something to slow *Bismarck* down. But all he had at his disposal were the untested flight crews of the Swordfish torpedo bombers aboard the aircraft carrier *Victorious*. It was a risk, but one worth taking. Tovey ordered *Victorious*, in company with four cruisers, to get to within 100 miles of *Bismarck* and launch an attack.

The exercise looked like a contest between unequals – the antiquated taking on the brand new, a hopeless contest. The Swordfish torpedo bomber – the 'Stringbag' – was a clumsy biplane, with its big engine nacelle (outer casing) up front. The plane's pilots and observers, in leather helmets and goggles, were out in the open air. It was a scene straight from the Western Front. However, appearances can be deceptive – the Swordfish had already proved its worth with deadly effect at the battle of Taranto,

BELOW Stringbag sortie: Swordfish torpedo bombers of R.N.A.S., Yeovilton.

devastating the Italian fleet at its moorings in a night attack. As Dr Eric Grove says:

'The Swordfish was not an old aircraft, it just looked it. It was actually designed at about the same time as the Spitfire. Its role was to take on a range of missions at sea for which speed was not considered vital – reconnaissance and gunnery spotting as much as torpedo dropping. It was in many ways the naval helicopter of its day. Its enormous merit was that it could operate in virtually all weather conditions. In fact it was so well designed aerodynamically that the problem was keeping it down on the flight deck in strong winds, so that it didn't involuntarily take off on its own! Its speed did not compromise it too much against AA fire, especially as the Germans had difficulty in tuning their fire-control systems down to the Swordfish's slow speed of approach – in any case, *Bismarck* did not have very effective rapid-firing AA guns. And if a Swordfish was hit, its great strength helped it to survive. No Swordfish was shot down by *Bismarck*. It did the job.'

Former Swordfish pilot John Moffat also remembers the 'Stringbag' and its extraordinary flying qualities with great affection. 'It really was quite an amazing aircraft. It started the war, and it finished the war, in frontline … When you'd got searchlights on you, you couldn't dive out of them, you couldn't accelerate out of them, but you did the opposite, you closed the throttle. But they couldn't believe you could go that slow. They always went ahead of you, and of course when they went ahead of you, you got the hell out of it!'

Moffat also has good cause to be thankful for the incredible toughness of the Swordfish's stretched-fabric biplane wings and airframe: 'You can come back with fabric absolutely flapping. In fact, I came back on board once, and I had no fabric in my bottom mainplanes at all. They were bare!'

Yet, however strong and effective their 'Stringbags', the inexperienced pilots of 825 Squadron had taken on quite a job. Led though they were by Lieutenant Commander Eugene Esmonde (whose name still resounds in naval aviation), they were facing atrocious weather conditions and a 100-mile flight to find their target. When they got there they would find a welcoming party offering a variety of anti-aircraft dishes for their delectation – heavy, medium and light flak from no less than fifty-two separate gun barrels. Having launched their torpedoes – if they survived – they then had to find their way back through the night and land back on *Victorious*' slippery, heaving deck. They had literally no room at all for error.

The Swordfish pilots began to feel their way over the angry, darkening sea. They were followed later by Fulmar fighters of 800Z Squadron. Homing in with onboard radar, Esmonde led the attack, only to find his squadron overflying a distinctly alarmed US Coastguard cutter, the *Modoc*, on a search for survivors from U-boat attacks on convoy HX126. *Bismarck* lay beyond, and opened up a torrent of fire towards 825 Squadron as Esmonde led them round under cloud cover. With the element of surprise gone, the Swordfish dived in one by one towards *Bismarck*'s port side in the face of a maelstrom of gunfire roaring up. Captain Lindemann and his quartermaster Hans Hansen twisted and turned the huge German ship to avoid the torpedoes. Von Mullenheim-Rechberg watched the resolute attack with reluctant admiration:

'Our anti-aircraft batteries fired anything that would fit into their barrels. Now and again one of our 15-inch (38-cm) turrets, and frequently our 6-inch (15-cm) turrets, fired into the water ahead of the aircraft, raising massive waterspouts. To fly into one of those spouts would mean the end. And the aircraft: they were moving so slowly they seemed to be standing still in the air, and they looked so antiquated. Incredible how the pilots pressed home their attack with suicidal courage, as if they did not expect ever again to see a carrier … Some of the planes were only 6 ½ feet above the water and did not release their torpedoes until they had closed to 360 or 460 yards. It looked to me as though many of them intended to fly on over us after making their attack. The height of impudence, I thought.'

But Hansen and Lindemann's manoeuvres worked – until the last Swordfish made its attack run from the starboard side, unnoticed by *Bismarck*'s gunners until it was too late. A white column of water shot into the air amidships on the battleship, followed by a great cloud of black and white smoke.

However, despite all their efforts, when the Swordfish (and all but two of the Fulmars) made it back to *Victorious*, it was clear that their bold and courageous attack had failed in its objective of slowing the German battleship down. The single torpedo hit had spent its force slightly displacing part of *Bismarck*'s massive, thick armour belt, hardly marking her. The hit had caused one casualty – it had knocked down Warrant Officer Kurt Kirchberg with such force that he had been killed instantly. Apart from that loss and some minor internal damage, *Bismarck* was in no worse shape than before the attack. She continued her relentless progress towards the coast of northern France and safety.

OUT OF THE NET - AND INTO THE TWILIGHT OF THE GODS

Worse was to come for *Bismarck*'s pursuers. The faithful *Suffolk* was still tracking the raider, roughly parallel to her out of gun range, but on a zigzag course designed to throw off U-boat attacks. *Suffolk*'s crew had kept contact with *Bismarck* for more than thirty hours by the early morning of 25 May. Although the German ship had occasionally disappeared, *Suffolk* had always got her back. The British crew had come to expect that their target would disappear from their screens when *Suffolk* was on the 'zig' away from *Bismarck*, only to reappear again when the cruiser was on the 'zag' back towards the German battleship's normal course.

Lütjens decided it was time to get rid of this nagging presence that threatened the very life of his ship. He ordered *Bismarck* to turn in a huge loop back behind *Suffolk*, and then set a new course to the southeast, closer still to safety. The cruiser noticed nothing amiss at first. But when *Bismarck* failed to reappear in her expected position after first twenty minutes, then nearly an hour, and then longer, it was clear to *Suffolk*'s Captain Robert Ellis that his quarry had slipped the noose he had held around her for so long. By 5.15 a.m. on Sunday, 25 May 1941, the British knew the worst for sure – *Bismarck* had escaped.

But only for Lütjens to put her back in the trap in one of the most extraordinary twists of fate in the whole pursuit.

Believing himself still firmly in the spider's web of *Suffolk*'s radar, Lütjens took a fateful decision. If his shadowers still had a clear fix on him, nothing could be lost by making a signal to his operational overseers, Group West in Paris. Even if the British picked it up and used it to locate him, it would not add to the information they already had about his position, and it would enable him to make a full report to Group West. He may have come to this inaccurate 'appreciation of the situation' because *Bismarck*'s electronic equipment was still detecting radar pulses coming towards her from the British. But to be useful, a radar pulse has to get back to its sender. By now, *Suffolk* was getting nothing back, and the various scattered units attempting to converge on *Bismarck* were beginning to conduct a diverse set of searches to locate her again.

But why did Lütjens send a signal? Why take the risk? Why do anything that might help your pursuers, if only fractionally? After all, your radar detectors – and radar was a technology still in its infancy – might just be wrong. Ironically, Lütjens' own *B-Dienst* (radio-intelligence staff) – who had previously supplied him with a good deal of inadequate or faulty intelligence – had assessed the situation correctly, realizing that the British had completely lost *Bismarck* for the first time.

So what motivated Lütjens' actions? Here we must speculate. But it seems likely that a combination of bureaucracy and fatalism acted together.

History shows that the Nazi regime had a deep love of reports and paper work, even sometimes incriminating itself in its own crimes against humanity by methodically listing details of its extermination campaigns against European Jews and others. '*Alles in Ordnung*' – 'Everything in good order' – was truly their mantra. Forms had to be made out; the great god of bumf had to be worshipped. And the navy of the Third Reich, with its highly centralized bureaucracy based on orders, reports and radio messages, was no exception to this rule. The opportunity this gave to British intelligence was already contributing to the neutralization of the U-boats, and would be a vital factor in their final defeat. Now it would also betray *Bismarck*.

At 7.27 a.m. on 25 May Lütjens sent a short signal reporting the wrong information – that a battleship and two heavy cruisers were still in contact. He then settled down to write a much longer signal, sent in four bursts between 9.12 a.m. and 9.48 a.m. The message contained a detailed account of his action against *Hood* and much more besides, including his own present position. It was a gift to his enemies.

That message was also evidence of Lütjens' fatalism – the British had never lost contact yet, so why should they have done so now? Here, once again, the admiral's methodical and analytical mindset seems to have overwhelmed any confidence he might have had about bringing his great ship safely to port. Even before he set out on '*Rheinübung*', he had confided to a friend:

'I realize that in this unequal struggle between the British Navy and ourselves I shall sooner or later have to lose my life. But I have settled my private affairs, and I shall do my best to carry my orders out with honour.'

This '*Götterdämmerung*' spirit seems to have infected Lütjens' attitude towards his crew too. It so happened that 25 May was his birthday. Following congratulations on the tannoy from the ship's company, Lütjens responded with the following message about the present state of affairs for *Bismarck*:

'Seamen of the battleship *Bismarck*! You have covered yourselves with glory! The sinking of the *Hood* has not only military, but also psychological value, for she was the pride of England. Henceforth, the enemy will try to concentrate his forces and bring them into action against us. I therefore released *Prinz Eugen* at noon yesterday so that she could conduct commerce warfare on her own. She has managed to evade the enemy. We, on the other hand, because of the hits we have received, have been ordered to proceed to a French port. On our way there, the enemy will gather and give us battle. The German people are with you, and we will fight until our gun barrels glow red-hot and the last shell has left the barrels. For us seamen, it is now a matter of victory or death!'

As a morale booster, that speech (a reconstruction from the debriefings of *Bismarck* survivors) is roughly on a par with the black humour of 'Floggings will continue until morale improves!' Its effect on the *Bismarck*'s young and optimistic crew can readily be imagined, and it is a course of conduct bafflingly alien to anyone who knows a little of the qualities of leadership expected in the British armed forces. Lütjens' address could hardly have been better calculated to depress the morale – and so, possibly, the fighting spirit – of *Bismarck*'s crew. But, as Dr Eric Grove explains, such an attitude had deep roots:

'German culture, especially naval culture, differs from British culture in many ways. The British expect to win; there is a reason for optimism even in adversity. The Germans expect to lose, after exacting the maximum price. Lütjens' coldly analytical mind, which had marked him out for this difficult mission, now prevented him making an up-beat exhortation to his flagship's crew. All he could do was communicate his own depression and anxiety. The game was up, and now everyone on *Bismarck* knew it.'

The deepest of ironies in all this is that Lütjens had far better cause for a more optimistic view than he knew. For the British were busy wasting the gift he had given them with his long radio messages.

When the Radio Direction Finding (DF) teams in Britain picked up Lütjens' long report to Group West, they knew he had delivered himself back up to them after the long, anxious hours in which *Bismarck* seemed to have vanished in the wide Atlantic spaces. The teams quickly computed *Bismarck*'s position – which showed clearly that she was heading for France – and the data was flashed back to Tovey in *King George V*. However, as agreed in procedure, the raw figures were sent, not the fix worked out from them. At this point, the Admiralty still thought that Tovey had specialist help, in the form of two DF destroyers, to assist him in working out an accurate position. But one of these specialist ships had been forced back to port early in the operation, and the other one had been fitted with a u/s DF kit. Next, the figures were plotted wrongly on board *King George V*. Finally, just to finish off this comedy of errors, the Admiralty refused to advise Tovey that he might have got his figures wrong, despite the urgings of their own specialists that the fleet was burning up precious fuel and time on a wild-goose chase. This refusal seems to have arisen partly out of a sense that the man 'on the ground' was the best one to decide what to do next.

Such finer feeling, of course, had not stayed Whitehall's hand in nudging Wake-Walker to bring *Prince of Wales* into action against *Bismarck* earlier. Now, just when a little intervention might have been helpful, Whitehall held back.

The consequence was that Tovey signalled his entire task force to search in exactly the wrong direction – back towards the north – in the mistaken belief that *Bismarck* was trying to return to Germany the way she had come, through the Denmark Strait.

So now Lütjens – although he did not know it – had been given another chance to escape. For five hours, *King George V*, *Prince of Wales*, *Victorious*, *Suffolk* and four other cruisers steamed northeast, towards waters empty of their quarry.

BACK IN THE NET

To be fair to the 'Whitehall warriors', their unease mounted as new data came in through the morning and early afternoon of 25 May. They even began to include in their signals estimates of what the DF fixes meant for *Bismarck*'s course – to the south, to France and safety. But as so often in great affairs, it seems to have been a small human touch that clinched the matter and convinced Tovey and the Admiralty that southeast was the course to take.

Far away in occupied Athens, a senior *Luftwaffe* officer made a family enquiry – about his son, a midshipman 'somewhere at sea'. The officer wanted to know where his boy's ship was heading. That ship was the *Bismarck*, and the answer to his enquiry came back encrypted in the *Luftwaffe*'s version of the Enigma code, which had been unravelled by the Ultra codebreakers at Bletchley Park near London. The reply was straightforward, and it fell into the hands of the Royal Navy almost as soon as it was sent. *Bismarck* was making for the west coast of France. So – another grim irony – this officer had helped to reset the jaws of the British trap around his own son.

For the British, valuable time – and fuel – had been lost. When Tovey turned back

BELOW *'Sighting the* Bismarck *– the beginning of the End, North Atlantic 1030 hours, 26 May 1941': Robert Taylor catches the moment when the RAF Coastal Command Catalina found* Bismarck *again. (Reproduced courtesy of the Military Gallery, Bath, UK.)*

from his pursuit of northbound phantoms, his reckoning was that he had handed the enemy a 100-mile lead. But knowing where *Bismarck* was heading was one thing. Knowing where she actually was, quite another. The task of solving that puzzle fell to RAF Coastal Command.

TARGET ACQUIRED

The Catalina, later to win fame as the workhorse flying boat of the Second World War, was at this time not so familiar a sight in British skies. It was an American import – a state-of-the-art machine from the nation that led the world in aviation manufacturing.

So it was that although the US was not yet at war against Germany, an American officer played a key role in the destruction of the *Bismarck*. For the aircrew of Catalina Z of 209 Squadron, based at Lough Erne in the northwest of Iceland, included Ensign Leonard Smith of the United States Navy. Smith was there to help his future allies familiarize themselves with their new aircraft. It was as though Grand-Admiral Raeder's forebodings about the prospects for the *Kriegsmarine* once the Americans entered the war were already being played out in miniature.

At about 10.15 a.m. on 26 May, after a six-hour flight to the search area, Catalina Z was flying at 500 feet above the wind-tossed waters of the North Atlantic. Visibility was poor. But gradually, to the aircrew's astonishment, a low, menacing shape began to emerge from the murk a few miles ahead. Ensign Smith banked the Catalina away up into the cloud, planning on coming in astern of the target to identify her. But as he emerged again from the cloud, he realized to his consternation that he was right alongside the ship, and just 500 yards away. It was *Bismarck* all right. She greeted this new spy in the sky with a roar of anti-aircraft rage. Fire rippled along her bulwarks and burst all around the seaplane, rattling along the aircraft's hull with its message of death. Banking sharply away, the Catalina radioed in the momentous news as fast as she could: *Bismarck* had been found again.

The German raider was back in the net. And just as the trap around her was set from the air, so it would be closed by aircraft too. Powerful, modern, apparently invincible as she was, *Bismarck* would no more escape the frequent fate of the battleship in the Second World War than so many of her contemporaries.

SWORDFISH ATTACK

On board *Bismarck*, the depression induced by Lütjens' apparent consignment of his ship to Valhalla had been marked. A further address by Captain Lindemann gave the crew some cheer, but morale, which had been high until then, had nevertheless taken a knock. A passing distraction was provided by the construction of a dummy funnel, designed to fool the enemy into thinking *Bismarck* was another ship, but the decoy was never to be erected. And then came the Catalina.

As *Bismarck*'s anti-aircraft armament erupted in a bid to shoot down the Catalina, Lindemann and his staff considered sending up an Arado floatplane to destroy the shadower or chase it off. The plan was soon abandoned; one look at the sea state convinced everyone that recovering the aircraft would be too risky. Now, as Mullenheim-Rechberg remembers, the fake funnel was truly redundant:

'The dummy stack still lay where it was built on the flight deck. It had not been rigged … If it was to serve its purpose, we would have had to set it up when we were out of sight of the enemy, so that the next time they saw us they would immediately think they were seeing a two-stack ship. Instead of playing our trick, we confirmed our identity by firing at the enemy aircraft … we even spared him the trouble of making completely sure who we were!'

But still *Bismarck* had a chance. If she kept up her speed, by midday on 26 May she would make it under the cover of U-boats and aircraft on the approaches to the French port of St Nazaire, where the British would not dare to follow her. As it was, she could not go all out – her fuel situation was too delicate for that, with the precious store of 1,000 tons tantalizingly shut off from her in the damaged fore part of the ship.

And then, as the day turned to dusk, everything changed at the hands of a squadron of old-fashioned-looking Swordfish.

For the British now, the key issue was whether or not they could slow *Bismarck* down enough to allow the big ships to catch up with her and destroy her before she got under the cover of her own forces. The omens were hardly good. Fuel was running low in many of the ships that had been chasing *Bismarck* for hours. The only option left was another attack by Swordfish torpedo bombers, aiming to cripple the battleship sufficiently to bring her to action with the avenging British capital ships closing in on her.

With sad justice, it was aircraft from *Hood*'s old partners in Force H that were to avenge her now. On Admiralty orders, and with Vice-Admiral Sir James Somerville in command, Force H had been steaming away from its stomping ground in the Mediterranean and towards *Bismarck* since the previous day. Progress had been hampered by a wind that had forced the ships to reduce speed.

These were terrible flying conditions. The great, flat top of the force carrier, *Ark Royal*, rose and fell to the long Atlantic swell. She was sometimes engulfed by green seas, even though she stood more than 60 feet out of the water. She was torn at by a wind speed over her flight deck of 50 miles an hour. Nonetheless, a reconnaissance sortie to find *Bismarck* had to be flown. The biplanes trundled slowly down the flight

deck, seeming to drop like stones as they left it. Sometimes the planes actually touched the wave tops as they fought to gain enough height to fly. In fact the mission was all in vain, as Ensign Smith's sighting of *Bismarck* came through loud and clear before the Swordfish could get a fix on her too. But they counted them all out, and they counted them all back, although one crew only just made it, their aircraft crashing and smashing onto the flight deck when the *Ark*'s huge stern jerked suddenly upwards as they were landing. The crew were unhurt; the fragments of their aircraft were pushed into the sea and the rest of the landings were completed safely.

As if one flight like that in a day were not enough, the Swordfish crews now had to prepare for a torpedo attack on *Bismarck*. Pre-flight briefings were held and the aircraft were fuelled and armed with torpedoes with magnetic detonators, set to explode beneath the vulnerable underbelly of their quarry. Just before 2 p.m. on 26 May, fifteen 'Stringbags' once again lumbered slowly into the air to begin a last-ditch attempt to stop *Bismarck*.

As it was, the Swordfish almost stopped the cruiser *Sheffield* instead. Unalerted to her presence in their attack area, and seeing what they thought must be *Bismarck* on their on-board radars, the Swordfish dived on one of their own with deadly intent. Some nine torpedoes were launched in all. *Sheffield*'s Captain Charles Larcom threw his ship from side to side to 'comb the tracks' of the torpedoes. Skill won the day and not a single one hit. Realizing their mistake, the Swordfish pilots turned back crestfallen to the *Ark* – one signalled apologetically to *Sheffield*: 'Sorry for the kipper!' However, this near-disaster was, in fact, vitally useful. Five of the torpedoes launched at *Sheffield* had exploded on hitting the water, clearly revealing that the magnetic pistols, whatever their advantages against a heavily armoured ship, could not be relied on. Back on board *Ark Royal*, the Swordfish armourers loaded their aircraft with torpedoes fitted with the more straightforward contact detonators. Next time there would be no mistakes – it would be hit or miss.

At 7.10 p.m. on Monday, 26 May 1941, the Swordfish took to the air once again. This time they used *Sheffield* as a datum point to begin the final approach towards their real target, 12 miles dead ahead of the cruiser. And then suddenly there was *Bismarck*, her great, black bulk shouldering the high seas aside as she headed onward towards France. Safety was so close.

The alarms on board the battleship shrilled again as the Swordfish curved down to begin their final attack.

SWORDFISH TRIUMPHANT

This really was the 'last-chance saloon' for the Royal Navy. Unless they stopped or slowed *Bismarck* now, the great battleship would make it back to St Nazaire and safety. Everything was running out for the British: time, opportunity, fuel and tactics. Soon their quarry would find herself protected by the prowling menace of the U-boats and the ferocious power of the *Luftwaffe*. Both were forward positioned in occupied France, just itching to acquire the kind of juicy targets that the Royal Navy was offering them in their desperate gathering to destroy the *Bismarck*. And the outcome of all of this hung on fifteen aircraft seemingly straight out of a bygone era.

Led by Lieutenant-Commander Tim Coode, the Swordfish lined up on their target. They dropped out of the cloud on *Bismarck*'s port side to be greeted by another inferno of anti-aircraft fire. The tracer bullets reached out yearningly towards the flimsy planes, every one intent on tearing the Swordfish out of the sky. As that cacophony burst all around them, the pilots and their observers not only had to keep flying as directly on target as possible, but they also had to make sure that every torpedo (each Swordfish carried just one) dropped into the trough between one wave and the next. It was crucial not to drop the torpedo onto the wave itself or the weapon would skew crazily into the air or down into the depths, and fail to settle on the run that would lead to its target. As pilot John Moffat remembers all too clearly, this vital attack saw some unorthodox actions definitely not found in the Fleet Air Arm's training manuals:

'I heard this voice in my ear … this was my observer, my navigator … and he was

saying, "I'll tell you, I'll tell you! … I'll tell you when to let it go!" … Next thing, I'd just looked out the side of the aircraft, and there he was just hanging over the side. I'm not kidding, I mean hanging over the side! There he was leaning right out, and his head down, and he kept saying "Not yet! Not yet!" – and then I realized what he was on. The idea is you see, the sea was so bad … that if you didn't set that torpedo into the trough properly, if you hit the top of the wave and it porpoised, it wouldn't run. You had to get it so it went straight in, and he held me there far too long. It was a few seconds, but it felt like years!' Meanwhile, the attack, far from taking the orderly and co-ordinated approach planned aboard *Ark Royal*, had become something of a scrum, as heavy cloud cover confused and disorientated the 'follow-my-leader' plan of attack. The result was a maul, with aircraft approaching from all angles, making their run-ins and torpedo launches as best they could. And some torpedoes at least were striking home – Mullenheim-Rechberg clearly recalls two hits forward of his position in the gunnery director above the two after 15-inch (38-cm) turrets 'Caesar' and 'Dora'. But just there *Bismarck*'s underwater protection had been designed to take that kind of damage.

Then came the hit that would make history. Mullenheim-Rechberg remembers:

'The attack must have been almost over when it came, an explosion aft. My heart sank. I glanced at the rudder indicator. It showed "left 12 degrees". Did that just happen to be the correct reading at that moment? No. It did not change. It stayed at "left 12 degrees" … we were in a continuous turn.'

Mullenheim-Rechberg's despondency was matched in the British fleet, as the

Swordfish strike leader radioed in: 'Estimate no hits.' That was it then. The game was up. It was now nearly half-past nine in the evening. Night was approaching and the dawn would see *Bismarck* under the air cover of the *Luftwaffe*. And fuel was running lower and lower. Already the cruiser *Edinburgh* had felt compelled to break away.

But then, at the darkest hour, the last of the spotter Swordfish that had been clinging onto *Bismarck*'s coat tails ever since the attack lurched to a halt as its hook caught the arrester wire on *Ark Royal*'s still heaving flight deck. It was now just before midnight and the Swordfish crew had a strange story to tell. They reported that after one torpedo was seen to hit home, the German battleship had turned through two huge circles on the ocean and then dropped her speed. This report – added to an earlier one from the shadowing cruiser *Sheffield*, greeted with disbelief, that *Bismarck* had turned almost due north at the end of the attack – suddenly lifted the gloom among her British pursuers. *Sheffield*, after absorbing a straddle from *Bismarck* that had raked her upperworks injuring twelve men (three of whom later died), had made a most puzzling report: the battleship was steering just west of north, a complete change of course from the one she had held for so long. *Bismarck* was, in effect, now going in exactly the wrong direction and she was holding that course when last sighted by the cruiser. So could the Swordfish attack really have pulled off the miracle that the British had all been longing for, and damaged the raider so badly that she could not be controlled?

That this was indeed what had happened was in no doubt on board *Bismarck*. The Swordfish torpedo had smashed into the starboard quarter of the ship, jamming the steering permanently over to that fateful 'left 12 degrees'. The same hit had torn a huge hole in the ship and flooded the compartment so completely that all the steering rooms had had to be abandoned to the inrushing sea. Attempts to pump the compartments out failed because the pumps had also been disabled. When repair teams opened a hatch into the steering compartments, they looked down to see the terrifying sight of the Atlantic rising and falling within their ship, shooting up through the hatch as her stern dug into the swell, disappearing completely as it rose again, and flooding out through the torpedo hole that was letting it in. Although volunteers had come forward to take on the task, it was all too clear that any attempts to get into this compartment to free the steering gear from its drive motor – and so regain some control – would fail. All sorts of ideas were thought through, only to be abandoned: even a virtual suicide plan involving divers going over the stern of the ship to cut or blow the rudders off was rejected, because its chances of success were so low. Bill Jurens comments:

'Ships use their rudders – and the key is moving rudders – to maintain directional control. So once *Bismarck*'s rudders were jammed, they ceased to work as true rudders at all. Ships lacking rudder control but still under power tend to swing into the oncoming wind, which is exactly what *Bismarck* seems to have done. In some ships with damaged or missing rudders steering can be somewhat regained by varying power between the engines so that the propeller(s) on one side turn faster than those on the other, and so take the ship in the direction of the side with the faster-turning propeller, but this did not seem to work on *Bismarck* at all. Even if it had worked, she would probably still have been caught, as the consequent reduction in speed is usually substantial.'

As Lindemann made attempt after attempt to steer his ships with engines alone, and failed, the situation facing the crew of *Bismarck* became clear in all its horror. Not only was their ship now uncontrollable – all thanks to one tinpot little torpedo that their main armour would simply have shrugged off – but its general direction was taking it back from where it had come.

And that meant the accursed rudder was driving them straight into the maw of the Royal Navy.

COUNTDOWN TO THE RECKONING

Revenge would not be long in coming now for the British. As they tracked the crazy course *Bismarck* was pursuing, each twist and turn seeming to end up pushing the ship back towards them, they realized that their luck had finally and conclusively turned. At last, they would be able to bring their enemy to battle and finish off the work the Swordfish attacks had begun.

As a preliminary strike, the Royal Navy had a weapon to hand – one of the most ruthless and energetic destroyer commanders of the Second World War. Captain Philip Vian was leading the Fourth Destroyer Division: four modern 'Tribal'-class destroyers, and the Polish *Piorun*. Detached earlier from Atlantic-convoy duty, the division's task would be to maintain contact with *Bismarck* until first light – no chances would be taken that might allow her to slip away again. Then the heavy ships that had so long been converging on *Bismarck* would come in like matadors to finish the great wounded beast off. To attempt such an attack during the night hours, Tovey reasoned, would be far too risky. The writer and broadcaster Ludovic Kennedy, who was on the scene himself as a junior officer in the destroyer *Tartar*, commends what must have been a hard decision to make:

'Tovey did a very brave thing – he told his rather horrified staff that there were so many ships now around the *Bismarck*, destroyers going in to make torpedo attacks and that kind of thing, that he wasn't going to risk being unable to distinguish friend from foe, and therefore would lay off until the morning. He was pretty certain that if

Bismarck was unable to repair the damage, he would be able to catch her up … but it was a very brave decision, and it was the right decision, but it required a lot of guts to do it.'

For Vian and his destroyers, it was now a clear case of 'engage the enemy more closely'. The 'Tribals' continued to smash their way forward through the brutal Atlantic weather, green water streaming off their foc'sles as the lithe destroyers rose and fell in the waves. By 11.30 p.m., the five destroyers were in position and the attacks began. They were to go on for more than seven hours as the ships of the division charged in under intense enemy gunfire to deliver their attacks as closely as they could. But as the weather worsened, co-ordination became harder and harder, and Vian ordered each ship to take her chances when she could. So one by one, in they went, taking death by the horns, and launched their torpedoes; and one by one every one of them missed, despite early claims that there had been hits. In the face of 50-foot high waves, the black darkness and the longer range of launch forced on them by the fire pouring out of *Bismarck*, there was no surprise in that, but they had certainly kept the German battleship under pressure, and ended the night still in contact.

On board *Bismarck*, all attempts to repair the jammed rudder had come to an end. As the alarms shrilled once again, it must have been a welcome distraction for many to work the ship and her guns to fend off the buzzing attacks of the destroyers that persisted through the night. But for those not directly engaged, their own thoughts crowded in on them as they felt their own ship drag them slowly towards death and destruction at the hands of their enemies.

'That was the worst part of the whole operation,' recalls Mullenheim-Rechberg, 'the certainty that we were powerless to escape our fate. We were wishing that day had broken and that the battle had begun. Anything but this waiting around, being powerless to do anything but wait … It was a real voyage to Golgotha.'

In that twilight world of fear and dread, strange scenes were to be witnessed. The crew were given permission to help themselves to anything they wanted from the stores. Officers sat in silence in the wardroom, occasionally exchanging a few words. Then one spoke suddenly, expressing the thoughts that were preoccupying all on board: 'Today my wife will become a widow, but she doesn't know it yet …'

When Mullenheim-Rechberg went up to the bridge, at first it seemed almost deserted. Then his eyes picked out men here and there, stretched out in corners. Lindemann – already wearing a life jacket – looked back at Mullenheim-Rechberg without even returning his salute; no words for a man who had once been the captain's personal adjutant. Later still in the night, when asked by men in the engine room what revolutions to put on *Bismarck*'s stopped engines in order to keep the overheated turbines in running order, Lindemann simply replied, 'Ach, do as you like.'

In the charthouse, a single lamp lit the position marked on the chart showing *Bismarck*'s crazy, swerving course – the scene gave an agonizingly clear picture of what the jammed rudder had done to the great ship. No one was on duty; on the deck in a corner, two men lay asleep.

On his way back to his action station Mullenheim-Rechberg passed the fleet commander, a man he had served under as long ago as 1934. Accompanied by one of his staff officers, the commander was probably heading for the admirals' bridge. This time the salute was returned, but again in silence. Lütjens went on his way. Mullenheim-Rechberg was never to see him again.

But one part of the ship was certainly active – the radio room. Through the night, messages passed back and forth between the ship, Group West in Paris and Berlin. Early on (well before all attempts to free the jammed rudder had been exhausted) Lütjens had sent the terse message: 'Ship unable to manoeuvre. We will fight to the last round. Long live the Führer.' One more salutation to Adolf Hitler was to follow. Messages of support came by return, and even news of the award of a Knight's Cross to Chief Gunnery Officer Adalbert Schneider for the sinking of *Hood*. Finally, Lütjens even radioed for a U-boat to be sent to take off his War Diary. (An earlier attempt to fly it off in the Arado seaplane, along with other papers and film of the battle of the Denmark Strait, had been foiled by a fractured compressed-air pipe on the aircraft's launch catapult.)

So now, as the dawn slowly broke over their crippled ship, all the crew of *Bismarck* could do was watch and wait as their fate bore down on them across the cold, grey sea.

THE RECKONING

The same frightful destruction that *Bismarck* had visited upon *Hood* was now to be visited on her – but *Hood*'s agony had, at least, been over in minutes. *Bismarck*'s would last for almost two hours.

From all points of the compass the Royal Navy now closed in for the kill. From the northwest came the Home Fleet flagship, *King George V*, accompanied by the low hull of the battleship *Rodney*, unmistakable with her long foc'sle bearing three triple 16-inch (40-cm) gun turrets and her superstructure piled up towards her stern. From the north came the cruiser *Norfolk*, anxious to see an end to this battle-chase, for she had been in on its beginning. Out of the west came the cruiser *Dorsetshire*, leaving the convoy she was escorting behind. From the south, *Bismarck*'s nemesis, Force H with its aircraft carrier *Ark Royal*, was steaming hard to reach the scene.

At a quarter to nine on the morning of Sunday, 27 May 1941, the largest guns spoke first in this battle – *Rodney* fired from her A and B turrets. Bearing straight at her enemy in a line abreast with *King George V* – 'as imperturbable as though they were on their way to an execution', says Mullenheim-Rechberg – the two battleships held their fire until the range had closed to under 12 miles. All this time *Bismarck*, still not under full control, was approaching her attackers head on too. Her opening salvo reconfirmed the high opinion the Royal Navy already had of German gunnery. By the third salvo she had straddled *Rodney* – the naval gunner's prelude to a direct hit.

But within minutes, as the two British ships brought all their guns to bear, the weight of metal and the unequal nature of the fight began to tell on *Bismarck*. Just after 9 a.m., a 16-inch shell hit the German battleship fair and square on her forward section. That was the end of turrets 'Anton' and 'Bruno' – half *Bismarck*'s big-gun power was gone at a stroke. Torpedoes from *Norfolk* were also on their way. Now *Bismarck* could only trade blow for blow with her after turrets, 'Caesar' and 'Dora', under the command of Burkard von Mullenheim-Rechberg in the heavily armoured after director. And he would have to run the big-gun battle from there: the main fire-control station had fallen silent as the British shells continued to wreak havoc on the forward part of the German battleship. Mullenheim-Rechberg's target was in plain sight: Tovey's *King George V* was sailing less than 7 miles away and visibility was excellent. Now would *Bismarck* get her own back?

'"Passing fight to port, target is the battleship at 250 degrees," I told the after computer room,' recalls Mullenheim-Rechberg, 'and, upon receiving the "ready" report from below, "One salvo." Boom!'

Once again, by Mullenheim-Rechberg's reckoning, *Bismarck* was getting close to her target, straddling *King George V* – one salvo short, three over. Then, suddenly, he was operationally blinded.

'The director gave a violent shudder and my two petty officers and I had our heads bounced hard against the eyepieces. What did that? When I tried to get my target in view again, it wasn't there; all I could see was blue. I was looking at something one didn't normally see, the "blue layer" baked on the surface of the lenses and mirrors to

BELOW Rodney *and* King George *shower* Bismarck *with shells in the final moments.*

make the picture clearer. Damn! I had just found the range of my target and now I was out of the battle. Though no one in the station was hurt, our instruments were ruined. Obviously, a heavy shell had passed low over our station and carried away anything that protruded ... Two metres lower and it would have been the end of us. The armour of our station would not have been enough protection against a direct hit at that range.'

But now, as Mullenheim-Rechberg struggled in vain to get some information about what was happening to *Bismarck* outside his action station, evidence of the carnage being wrought on his ship was coming into the very director itself. Men were climbing up an internal companion ladder into the director, wounded and desperate to find shelter from the shell-storm engulfing their ship. That one shell that had carried away the range-finding equipment over Mullenheim-Rechberg's head was, by chance, the only major hit on his director, but in the rest of the ship it was a devastatingly different story.

Refusing to let the men who had taken shelter with him leave the director, even when he judged that the order to abandon ship might well have been given, Mullenheim-Rechberg held them there until all the firing had ceased. He had decided that to leave would have been 'nothing less than suicide'. It was only later that he was able to piece together just how right he had been.

Because *Bismarck*, modern and so strongly built, was refusing to sink and – following to the last her navy's traditions – would not strike her colours, the Royal Navy saw it as their only option to continue pouring shell fire into her until she went under. But the German battleship had been built precisely for the kind of close-range gunfight in which she now found herself. It was a long time before she slowly began to sink. Attempts by *Norfolk* and *Rodney* to torpedo *Bismarck* seem to have been largely unsuccessful due to her erratic course. Nevertheless, as the toll of damage relentlessly mounted and shell splashes from near misses deluged her with water, the list to port with which she had started the action grew worse. She continued to settle further into the water. *Bismarck* was clearly sinking – but still she would not surrender.

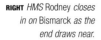

RIGHT *HMS* Rodney *closes in on* Bismarck *as the end draws near.*

Bill Jurens comments: 'It would have been more "efficient" – a cleaner kill – to have had the British battleships pull off to long range once *Bismarck* was helpless and sink her with plunging fire that would have cleanly penetrated her decks with the aim of exploding her magazines. It would have been less brutal to try to dispatch her with torpedoes from cruisers and aircraft, which were available in abundance. But Tovey chose, for reasons which remain controversial even to this day, to close in and inflict what amounted to the "death of a thousand cuts" on his enemy.'

For Ted Palfrey aboard *Norfolk*, the sight of his cornered enemy being beaten to pieces in this way was a grim one:

'I thought at the time how very sad it was that this beautiful ship should be pounded as she was being pounded. But later, of course, I realized it was necessary. It would never have done for the Germans to have been able to have towed the *Bismarck* back to France, even if she was finished. That would have been a great victory for them.'

What denying that victory meant for the officers and men of *Bismarck* beggars belief. As those whose action stations kept them below decks and in relative safety heard the order to abandon ship, they climbed out into the open air. The few who survived described the scenes from hell that met their eyes:

A crowded compartment just below the upper deck and the open air – 300 men are struggling towards the ladders to the upper deck, desperate to escape. There is a direct hit. At least a hundred die, many are frightfully injured, disembowelled, mutilated, torn by the thousands of razor-sharp splinters released when a shell explodes against the steel of a warship.

An engineer petty officer escapes to the upper deck, after flooding a blazing 4-inch (10.5-cm) magazine, to find his hands running with blood as he emerges into the open air. Bodies are piled three or four deep all around him. He dashes for shelter to the aircraft hangar, but shrinks back: it too is filled with the dead bodies of those who had sought shelter there before him.

A shell tears down below the aircraft catapult into the ammunition storage area below, killing anti-aircraft gun crews sheltering there from the inferno above them.

There are screams and yells from inside one of the 6-inch (15-cm) twin turrets. The men are trapped. The door is jammed shut and will not open. The ship will sink with them still inside their turret.

The radio room, the heart of the ship's communications system, resembles a slaughterhouse – every man in it dead.

Luftwaffe men, in despair, shoot themselves as the carnage rages on all around them. Two men running aft through the smoke fail to see a great hole in the deck – they plunge straight down into the fires roaring below.

A direct hit on one dressing station kills all the medical staff and most of the wounded there. Still the other medical teams continue to work without thought for their own safety. There is little they can now do except administer morphine, but they stay with their charges to the end. None of the orderlies or doctors will survive the sinking.

A man about to abandon ship by the starboard rail is, for some reason, struggling to remove his trousers – perhaps so he can swim better. A shell explodes. When the smoke clears, the lower half of his body has vanished; his head and torso tumble into the sea.

And for every one of these terrible moments, how many more occurred in the heart of the ship as buckled hatches and destroyed ladders, collapsing bulkheads and exploding ammunition, fires and fumes and flooding water trapped *Bismarck*'s people so they had no chance at all? Only the cold Atlantic knows.

May they, too, rest in peace.

END OF A GIANT

When the British guns fell silent, the sea was covering much of *Bismarck*'s upper deck as she rolled in the steep Atlantic waves. Deep in the ship's engine room, staff led by Engineer Officer Gerhard Junack (who was to survive) set explosive charges to complete the process of sinking their ship. The charges were attached to cooling water intakes on a nine-minute fuse. After a last check around the turbine room, Junack climbed up through the decks to the open air, on the way calming a crowd of men who were convinced they could not get out. The problem was an armoured hatch that was jammed half open. Organized by Junack, the group made it out by taking off their life jackets and squeezing through.

For the crew of *Bismarck* it was now a struggle between every man and the implacable ocean. But even getting off the ship into the sea presented perils, despite the closeness of the water as the ship slowly capsized, her decks awash, the dead and wounded sliding off her into the water as she rolled wearily from side to side. Still defiant, Junack gathered a group of men around him and tried to cheer them: 'Don't worry comrades. I'll be taking a Hamburg girl in my arms again, and we'll all meet once more on the Reeperbahn.' However, as they abandoned ship, some made the fatal error of going down the port side nearest to the water; the rolling of the sea threw them back against the side of the ship, knocking them out as they were smashed against the steel.

As Mullenheim-Rechberg prepared the party with him to abandon ship, he too rallied his survivors. 'A salute to our fallen comrades!' he cried. They saluted with him – and then, with one look at their ensign, still flapping in the breeze over their stricken ship, into the water they went.

The survivors swam away from the ship as fast as they could in their waterlogged clothes and their clumsy life jackets. Hundreds of heads now dotted the heaving waves of the North Atlantic. Far away stood *Dorsetshire*, who had fired her last three torpedoes some time before, aimed at sinking her stubborn enemy. Soon the cruiser would be the saviour of at least some of *Bismarck*'s crew.

As the survivors, crowded together now in the water, turned for one last look at their ship, they witnessed an extraordinary sight.

' … they saw Lindemann standing on the forecastle in front of turret "Anton". His messenger, a seaman, was with him. Soon, both men went forward and began climbing a steadily increasing slope. Lindemann's gestures showed that he was urging his companion to go overboard and save himself. The man refused and stayed with his commanding officer until they reached the jackstaff. Then Lindemann walked out on the starboard side of the stem [at the bow of the ship] which, although rising ever higher, was becoming more level as the ship lay over. There he stopped and raised his hand to his white cap.

'The *Bismarck* now lay completely on her side. Then, slowly, slowly, she and the saluting Lindemann went down. Later a machinist wrote, "I always thought such things only happened in books, but I saw it with my own eyes."'

It was 10.40 a.m. on Tuesday, 27 May 1941. *Bismarck*'s first and only voyage had lasted just over eight days.

Flying his Swordfish torpedo bomber from *Ark Royal* on his way to a final attack to finish off *Bismarck*, John Moffat witnessed the death throes of the battleship from the air:

' … when we got about 1,000 yards from the ship, it suddenly turned on its side, just like that! It was as quick as that. And I flew over it … maybe 50 feet off its deck, and all those poor people in the water, hundreds of them. Terrible. In those terrible waves … '

The *Bismarck* survivors, their ship gone, were left floating in their hundreds in the oil-covered sea, fighting the cold. The waves constantly swept Mullenheim-Rechberg from one group to another. There was no sign of any rescue ship. Then, at last, after an hour in the water, the crest of a wave lifted him up and he saw the familiar three-funnel profile of a 'County'-class cruiser. These cruisers had been the *Bismarck*'s nemesis from the first, with the pursuit by *Suffolk* and *Norfolk* all the way from the Denmark Strait. Now another of the class, *Dorsetshire*, was standing by to rescue him and his shipmates.

Slowly the *Dorsetshire* steered for the largest group of survivors, and then stopped engines. Her great, grey sides formed a steel wall rising up and down above the exhausted survivors. Lines snaked down from the upper deck and crewmen stood by to help their vanquished enemies climb on board. There was no scrambling net, but a wooden raft was lowered into the sea for the *Bismarck* crewmen to hold onto before their final effort. Then, just like Ted Briggs, Bob Tilburn and Bill Dundas only three days before, the German survivors struggled up the sides of the ship to safety. Despite their desperate will to live, this was far from easy: the lines were slippery; the ship rolled away, snatching the ropes out of their grasp; frozen hands could barely close on their last chance of rescue. But some of the lines had a bowline, a loop in the lower end to put your foot in, so your whole weight did not hang on your exhausted arms. Mullenheim-Rechberg tried to get the nearest survivors to him, many of them technical people inexperienced in seafaring skills, to use these. Then he swam for one such line himself, but when he was hauled up, just as he reached out for safety, his grip on the rope failed and he fell back into the water. But fortune was shining on him that day, for he found the same line again with the same two British seamen hauling on it. This time there was no mistake, and he made it to safety on the deck of HMS *Dorsetshire*.

However, by a dreadful twist of fate, Mullenheim-Rechberg was destined to be one of a select few saved from the sinking of the *Bismarck*.

While the German surface raiders had had only mixed success in their attacks on the British, their U-boat colleagues had wrought havoc in the Atlantic almost since the start of the war. The U-boats, which had adopted 'unrestricted' warfare, were not to be trifled with. *Dorsetshire* was all too aware that U-boats would have been ordered to close on *Bismarck* in her last hours and to help her if they could. A fat, heavy cruiser, stopped in the water; now that would present a juicy target for a U-boat which would have little chance of observing, at periscope depth, that survivors were being rescued, would not know for sure in any case that they were from *Bismarck*, and might not stay its hand even if it suspected the truth. The U-boat war was a war to the knife.

So when a watchkeeping officer in *Dorsetshire* reported a smoke discharge on the water, suggesting the presence of a submarine close by, there was no alternative for the cruiser's captain, Benjamin Martin. His first and last responsibility, as always, was to his men and to his ship. With terrible irony, the known tactics of the U-boat colleagues of the men in the water gave him no choice. He must leave the scene, and as quickly as possible. He had done what he could for *Bismarck*'s survivors. Now he must clear away and leave them to take their chances in the wastes of the North Atlantic. He rang down for revolutions; in the destroyer *Maori*, nearby, her commander did the same. The hundreds of *Bismarck* survivors awaiting rescue must have known that their last chance had gone as the water foamed under the cruiser's stern and she gathered speed to get to safety, away from the threat that could destroy her in an instant. In minutes they were alone again – and now no one would come for them in time: none of their own ships nearby; too far out for aircraft to spot them; too far out for the Spanish rescue ships, already despatched, to win the race against the hypothermia that would claim them; beyond rescue, beyond redemption from the unforgiving sea.

Between them, *Dorsetshire* and *Maori* picked up 110 *Bismarck* survivors. U-74 found three more; the weather ship *Sachsenwald* another two. That was all. They were indeed the lucky ones, for well over 2,000 of their shipmates died, in their ship and in the water – joining their former adversaries of HMS *Hood* in that most unmarked of graves: the wide, wide ocean, stretching out like the eternity that had claimed them.

LEFT *Piteously few survivors of* Bismarck *are rescued by* HMS Dorsetshire.

Relocating
Bismarck

chapter **eight**

FIND IT FAST

As the *Northern Horizon* moved steadily towards the start of our first search line, pulling the Ocean Explorer sonar along at the bitter end of 7,800 metres of cable, I could finally assess the impact of all the delays to our schedule. It was day ten of the estimated thirty-five-day expedition and we were already four days behind schedule. I had raised expectations that we could find *Bismarck* fast, almost promising to locate her on the first line, but now the pressure was on to do just that so we could claw back some of the time that had been lost. Seven hours after it was launched the sonar had reached the start of line number one, and in as little as two hours' time it would be passing the position where I had predicted *Bismarck* would be found.

Luckily, one last clue came to me in the strangest way. It turned out that another expedition using the Russian *MIR* submersibles and support ship *Akademik Keldysh* had been to the wreck of *Bismarck* less than a month before us, which had led to some television news coverage in Germany and America. One of our film-makers had been in Germany at the time so he had taped the programme and brought it to sea with him. We watched this together. Part of the story revealed how it had taken the *MIR* pilots a long time to find the wreck because the position they had been given was incorrect by about 1,500 metres. I couldn't be sure how they had acquired this piece of information, but it was obvious that the other expedition was using Ballard's positions – the *Akademik Keldysh* had no side-scan search capability like we did. Whatever the case, the news report showed charts that confirmed the error. I wasn't about to ignore this gift from heaven.

We were using the Ocean Explorer's low-frequency sonar set to search a total swathe of 4,800 metres, or 2,400 metres to either side of the sonar's central track. I was expecting to see *Bismarck* on the starboard channel of the sonar display but I was also mindful of the 'blind spot' directly beneath the sonar towfish which makes it possible to pass directly over the top of a wreck the size of *Bismarck* and miss it completely. We were trying a new technique (using high-frequency sonars pointing forward to fill the gap) to minimize the blind-spot problem, but we weren't sure how well it would work with the towfish flying 350 metres above the seabed.

Quite unexpectedly, we had a very good sonar target on the port channel just thirty-seven minutes after the start of the first line of our search. To a trained eye like Richard Dailey's, the big, gregarious Texan who had spotted it first, the small, bright sonar target was clearly a shipwreck. But just as clearly it was not *Bismarck*. The wreck was no more than 100 metres long and there was no debris field around it. What disaster had befallen this unknown ship of an unknown age was not a question for us to answer. I was grateful the wreck was there to prove that everyone was sharp and

LEFT *This graphic illustrates the very wide coverage of the Ocean Explorer side-scan sonar, but also the problematic 'blind-spot' which can mean that large objects are missed.*

focused, but other than that I disregarded it immediately. Still, I copied its position down in my log by force of habit.

The sonar slowly advanced on my predicted position, now highlighted as a small, red circle on the navigation screen everyone was watching. Each of its 'ping' noises, timed at four seconds apart, would build up the sonar image line by line. If the sonar was positioned parallel to the wreck, as I hoped it was, it would take about four minutes to image the entire hull yielding a multicoloured shape some sixty 'ping' noises long. To keen sonar operators like myself, every next 'ping' held promise of great excitement but to everyone else it was like watching paint dry. We were now in the area of the red circle where the wreck, or more likely, debris, would start showing up. We passed the red circle but the seabed was barren. Five minutes, ten minutes, fifteen minutes passed and the same barren seabed continued to scroll down our screens. Had I made a mistake or been too presumptuous about the clues I was taking for granted?

Then, as if on cue to relieve the tension that was building up in the room, the first sign of a definite hard target started to light up the screen. More bright yellow rectangular shapes followed. Was this the debris field or signs of the hull itself? Or was it just a rocky outcrop in the wrong place at the wrong time? It was impossible to tell because the targets were too close to the sonar's centre track and were being distorted by the same phenomenon that causes the blind spot. But then a curved dark pattern began to appear. It wasn't hard, but it was long and linear and I optimistically identified it as a possible slide scar, where the hull had slid down a slope. The head of the 'scar' widened and darkened and bits of yellow targets appeared around its edges, just as you would expect had this been the impact crater left from *Bismarck*'s first powerful contact with the seabed. Further down the track was another hard, square target that was a dead ringer for wreckage – possibly one of the missing turrets.

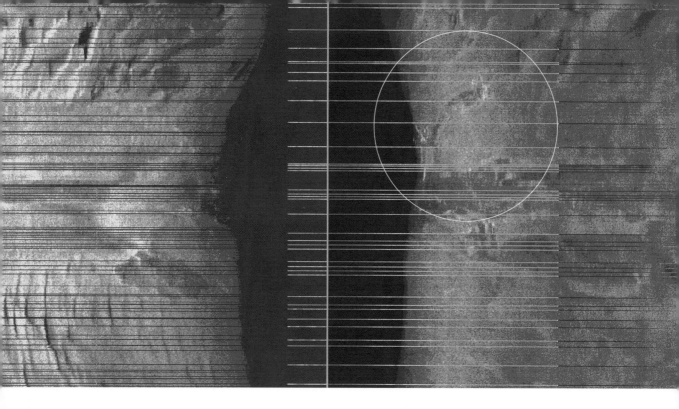

I was very sure the targets we found were the remains of *Bismarck* but a higher resolution sonar pass would be necessary to be one hundred per cent positive. Once I had determined the path for the next line, positioned to show up the full extent of the debris field in the highest possible resolution, I decided to abort the current line early so we could start the long turn for a reciprocal course as soon as possible. The questioning voices I heard in reply suggested that not everyone shared my confidence in the targets but I saw no sense in wasting time. Eleven hours later the sonar was at the start of the high-resolution pass, which was based on a swathe width of 2,400 metres so we could try and get the entire debris field covered by one 1,200-metre-sonar channel. When the towfish is 3.5 nautical miles behind the ship you cannot be certain whether it is towing directly behind or off to one side. For this next line to be a success our tolerance for off-track error was about 200 metres. When the sonar targets began appearing on the screen I thought the sonar had hit the line as well as we could have hoped.

This time the targets were shown on screen in yellow with green and blue centres, indicating that they had echoed back nearly one hundred per cent of the pressure wave transmitted by the sonar. There were also more of them. At least fifteen major targets were resolved with plenty of smaller 'hits' surrounding them. The slide scar showed far more detail and once again it appeared to take a curved path down the slope leading straight to the largest target of them all. Rectangular, with very straight sides and, most importantly, a shadow caused by its structure blocking the pressure wave, this target had all the earmarks of the hull itself. Moreover, it was pointing in the same direction Ballard had found the hull and it measured precisely the length of the hull minus the stern, which had broken away. There was a good-sized target at the extreme edge of the sonar's range that was only partially imaged but I had to be satisfied with this result. I felt that up to ninety per cent of the debris field had been mapped, with the hull located at the terminus of the slide scar, and not much more could be gained by another sonar pass. It was time to get Magellan in the water to confirm our findings.

Even though our fast location of *Bismarck* had shaved thirty-two hours off the schedules, the pressure to make efficient progress had not lifted. We were still in catch-up mode and the morning's weather forecast indicated we had a window of two and a half days of good conditions before another gale would hit and shut down our operations. As the Oceaneering team reconfigured the back deck of *Northern Horizon* from sonar to ROV work, Bill Jurens and Eric Grove waited anxiously and prepared for their first glimpse of *Bismarck*. They had been together solidly for a week now, and had been engaged for most of it in detailed and animated dialogue about their thoughts and theories, which they would soon learn were correct or not. They continued to wait as the deck reconfiguration took longer than usual and a problem with the fibre optic cabling delayed launch of the ROV until the evening. I counted the lost hours as the already narrow weather window narrowed even further.

Anticipating that our planned ROV dive time would be curtailed, I had the memorial plaque prepared to be taken down to the wreck on the first dive. I had been going to leave this until the second dive after the initial reconnaissance work had been completed but my hand was being forced by the unsettled weather and I was keen to get on with this important task. The plaque's additional 40 kilograms of weight would not help the ROV's manoeuvrability, but I counted on being able to find the hull quickly and lay the plaque somewhere on the bow to free the ROV of its precious payload. With the plaque firmly secured in its port manipulator arm, Magellan dived into the darkness on her way to visit yet another illustrious shipwreck.

The first image to appear on our screens when Magellan reached the seabed four hours later was a pair of leather boots. A chilling and poignant reminder that we were working around a mass grave for 2,131 men, the boots were also the first thing reportedly sighted by the previous two expeditions to *Bismarck*.

ABOVE *A close-up view of the slide scar and debris field. The 1.5 kilometre-long slide scar appears to lead directly to a group of large sonar targets.*

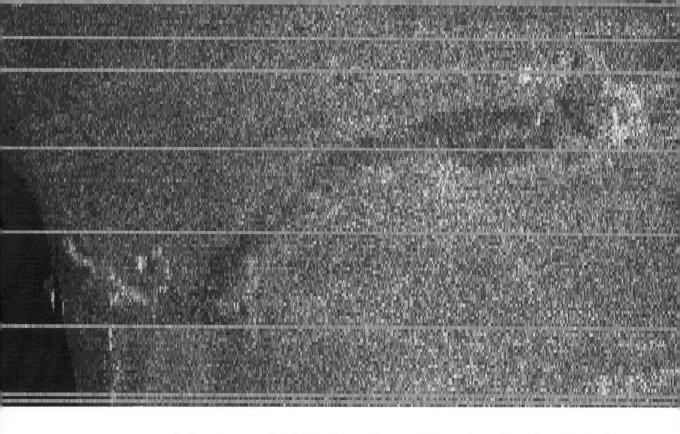

As Troy Launay piloted Magellan north towards the estimated position of the hull, Richard Dailey worked the scanning sonar looking for targets beyond the vision of our cameras. We had purposely landed down the slope from the wreckage which meant we were coming across very light debris, such as floats and small pieces of structure. Our progress up the slope was extremely slow, exacerbated by the long time it took to move both the ship and the ROV in coordinated jumps. Several hours passed before we found the first piece of heavy structure – a curved piece of armour plate estimated to be 7 inches thick, using the albino crab which was perched on one corner for scale. Somehow we had missed the large sonar target, so we decided to head for the densest part of the debris field to find our bearings.

Any doubts that the debris we were filming belonged to *Bismarck* were firmly laid to rest when we came across the next two pieces of wreckage. The first was part of *Bismarck*'s mast, snapped in two and folded upon itself, but clearly identifiable by the distinctive crosstree support and crow's nest; the second was one of *Bismarck*'s fearsome 15-inch gun turrets. Like the turret found by Ballard in 1989, this one was inverted and lodged deep into the muddy seabed – a sure indication of the turret's extreme top-heaviness. The sides of the gun house showed the first evidence of shelling. Her grey paint, surprisingly fresh after sixty years of submergence, was marred by streaks of rust radiating out from a shell hit.

We were now in the thick of the debris field and the sonar screen lit up with hard targets showing as bright red shapes against the blue-green background. As Troy flew Magellan towards a large target, the seabed we passed was littered with small, mostly

unidentifiable debris. Every so often something recognizable would stand out – a section of deck railing and chain, grating, a ladder. But then we found something completely out of place with the setting of a Second-World-War naval battle – a modern underwater telecommunications cable running over a piece of wreckage and directly through the debris field. We found this rather amusing, as usually wrecks are purposefully avoided by cable companies, but we weren't about to complain, as the cable would later prove to be a great help to us in navigating around the debris field.

The ROV continued to close in on this very large sonar contact that was standing so high off the seabed it left a shadow behind it. As our powerful HMI lights punched through the darkness, the tall object came into view. It was *Bismarck*'s superstructure! Upside down and impaled into the seabed, the superstructure appeared to be torn off at main deck level like it had been wrenched from the ship when she had turned over and sunk. The Admiral's Bridge, where Fleet Commander Lütjens had been heading when last seen, was cocked at an angle and covered by a forest of rusticles, each several feet long and still growing like undersea stalactites. There was so much to take in and the rust obscured much of the surface, but it was possible to spot some smaller shell holes in several locations. The great height of the superstructure made it a perfect reference point for navigating to other pieces of wreckage, as it was possible to identify it in the high-resolution sonar image because of its long sonar shadow.

Confident that we could find the large sonar target representing the hull by following a range and bearing from the superstructure, we moved the ship 320 metres into the shallow valley just east of the debris field. Our search for the hull was

ABOVE *In this higher resolution image the two debris fields are more apparent. The largest sonar target with the acoustic shadow behind appears to lie at the end of the slide scar.*

painstaking but ultimately fruitless. We spent seven hours crossing and re-crossing the valley but had very little to show for our efforts. I was barely keeping my frustration in check when Magellan suddenly dropped into the seabed, kicking up a huge cloud of sediment. Mixed within the cloud I could see small, red globules floating slowly upwards – a sure sign that the vehicle had just suffered a serious hydraulic leak and would need to surface for repairs. While the break to repair Magellan would be a welcome relief after our poor performance searching for the hull, we could scarcely afford any more down time during this critical phase of the expedition. Still, we had found one of the missing turrets as well as the superstructure, so dive number one had had some measure of success.

FRUSTRATION

When Magellan reached the surface later that evening the cause of the hydraulic failure was readily apparent. One of the steel pipes feeding hydraulic fluid to a main thruster had pulled out of its fitting, draining the reserve oil volume in seconds. Hydraulic failure can be time-consuming to repair and this case was no different. By the time Magellan was repaired and back down on the seabed searching for the missing hull, twenty hours had passed. Our objective was the same as the previous dive: to find the hull as quickly as possible, lay the memorial plaque on the bow, and begin the detailed filming of the hull.

This time I had a new plan. Rather than search the barren valley for the hull using the scanning sonar we would find the slide scar and follow it directly to the hull. We had spotted the slide scar during the previous dive and were able to relocate it within five minutes of being on the bottom in dive number two. The scar looked like a huge, shallow trench in the seabed where the sediment had been smoothed by the force of the hull sliding down the slope. Mike Schick was now piloting Magellan and he had to fly the vehicle down the slope keeping a close eye on one edge of the trench as a guide. Every so often the ROV would leave the trench to investigate large sonar targets but it would always return to pick up the slide scar. The ship and ROV were moved towards one another in 75-metre increments, but any forward progress we were making was at a snail's pace. Each time a move was made 100 metres of cable had to be recovered and the ROV lost contact with the seabed. The pilots were concerned about letting out too much cable for fear it would get tangled, or even worse, severed by the sharp wreckage strewn everywhere. This cautious approach was making our search for the hull impossible. After two hours had passed, we had covered just 350 metres, most of the time spent with the ROV high up in the water column or straining at its short tether. The other problems were that we were heading

RIGHT *Richard Dailey helps me rig a lifting loop to the* Bismarck *plaque.*

away from the large sonar target I believed to be the hull and we had lost the trail of the slide scar. Something was amiss with the direction in which we were heading, so I decided we should regroup back where we had started the dive.

It was becoming increasingly apparent that we would never find the hull at the rate we were going. The ROV pilot was being severely constrained by the short tether, which was having a knock-on effect on the sonar operator's ability to effectively scan the seabed for targets. At one point the ROV was actually pulled backwards 50 metres, losing all the ground it had just struggled to cover. I wondered how easy this would all be if I was inside one of the *MIR* submersibles and could fly straight down the slide scar unencumbered by an annoying leash to the surface. The team was growing frustrated and tired and I could see their morale flagging. A radical change was needed in order to reverse our situation from one of futility to one of productivity.

As much as I loathed the idea, the only way to improve the ROV's manoeuvrability was to rid it of the 40-kilogram memorial plaque, by laying it earlier than planned. The ROV pilots felt hamstrung by this additional weight and there was little doubt they could move much faster without it. It was an important decision and one only I could make. I had met the *Bismarck* survivors personally, and had promised them that a memorial plaque would be laid on the wreck. Like Ted Briggs with *Hood*, they had felt the bow to be the most appropriate location for the plaque. So to have to leave it anywhere else was a deeply disappointing decision, but one I was forced to make in view of our other objectives.

There was really only one other appropriate place to lay the plaque – *Bismarck*'s superstructure. The superstructure was a major recognizable part of the ship, that housed many of *Bismarck*'s crew so there would be a direct connection with the men the plaque was meant to honour. Knowing that his understanding of the ship and naval tradition in general would be a good guide to follow, I turned to Eric Grove for his opinion about this choice. Eric's reply was immediate. He felt the superstructure was symbolic of the people who had served on *Bismarck* and an entirely appropriate place for the plaque. In particular he thought the bridge, from which the respected Captain, Ernst Lindemann, had led his crew from in their final battle, would be the perfect spot.

Fortunately, we had found the superstructure and knew how to relocate its position quickly in the debris field. After making one more unsuccessful attempt to find the hull in the valley, based upon a newly calculated position about 100 metres further east than where we first believed it to be, we returned to the superstructure and selected a precise landing spot for the plaque. Ron Schmidt took control of the manipulator arm and got ready to hit the switch which would open its jaws at the exact moment Mike had positioned Magellan over the spot. In the final moments Magellan lurched spasmodically, a sure sign that Mike was struggling to keep the 4,500-lb vehicle from touching any of the nearby structure. Finally, Mike had Magellan on target and I asked Ron to drop the plaque. Liberated of its payload, Magellan drifted upwards as the gold Roll of Honour blazed brightly through the almost impenetrable darkness. I too felt a weight lift off my shoulders. My promise had been fulfilled and we could now search for the hull unhindered.

LEFT *The bronze memorial plaque that incorporates the name of every person lost on* Bismarck *now rests on the underside of the Admiral's bridge.*

Whether it was the weight released from Magellan or the midnight change in shifts that brought a fresh ROV team, I wasn't completely sure, but we began to make real progress again. First we found one of *Bismarck*'s stereoscopic range finders, probably from the foretop gun director. Two large shells had hit it from opposite directions and most of its roof had been blown away. In an impressive display of its destructive power, one shell, possibly one of HMS *Rodney*'s 16-inch salvoes, had passed clean through the gun director from one side to the other. It is inconceivable how anyone inside or nearby could have survived such a heavy blow.

We began to find a number of significant pieces of wreckage close to where we were without having to reposition the ship and ROV – another 15-inch gun turret lying upside down; the starboard side crane with its upper half sheared clean off by an apparent shell hit; the topmost section of the main mast. We were making great progress and everyone's morale had quickly picked up. Chris Jones, our navigator, was dutifully plotting each piece of identifiable wreckage which was found on a map which would help our next attempt to find the hull at the bottom of the slide scar. I expected it to be a long and sleepless but exciting evening, when suddenly without warning the video monitors went blank. I jumped from my chair and rushed out to the ROV control van to find the Oceaneering team sitting in darkness. There had been a major power failure and although the lights immediately flashed back on, the status of the ROV was still unknown. Several attempts to restart the ROV's 25-horsepower motor failed. The exact cause of the failure was still being debated but one thing was certain – the ROV was on its way back to the surface. Once again our momentum had been blunted by an equipment failure.

By the time Magellan reached the surface the wind was blowing 35 knots and 3- to 4-metre swells were running. The conditions were not ideal for a 'dead vehicle recovery', but Ron Schmidt and Andy Sherrel had the whole team on hand to ensure a calm and safe recovery. Through the thick acrylic cover of the electrical junction box in Magellan's depressor, the extent of the failure was clearly visible: an angry black patch on the inside of the cover marked where there had been a serious short in the wiring carrying 2,600 volts of power. The fierce arcing that had resulted had damaged everything in its path. Deeper inside the junction box, the main transformer was found to have shorted as well, and would have to be replaced. A lot of work was required to Magellan up and running again.

After a largely frustrating dive the only consolation I could find was that the equipment failure had hit at the same time as the bad weather, so either way our work would have been halted. Ron and his team had quickly diagnosed all the electrical problems and I knew I could count on them to put Magellan right. My faith in the co-operation of the weather was considerably less. I retreated into my office to see how far behind schedule we had fallen. It was day fourteen of the expedition and today we were meant to have finished with *Bismarck* and be on our way to *Hood.* The fact that we still hadn't found *Bismarck*'s hull was difficult to accept, but I couldn't afford to dwell on it. I was positive we could find the hull if we just got back to the slide scar and followed it doggedly to the end

FOLLOW THAT TRAIL

By the time Magellan was ready for action again, the weather, to my great relief, was also improving. In the early morning of 11 July, everything was set for launching Magellan for her third and, hopefully, final dive. As the depressor was about to be lifted by the crane Richard Dailey noticed that one of the two pins connecting the cable termination to the depressor had been sheared off; by doing so, he averted a definite disaster. With one pin gone, as soon as the depressor was pulled upwards by the heaving motion of the ship, the second pin would have surely followed. With its mechanical termination destroyed the depressor would have fallen to the seabed, taking with it the Magellan ROV and any hopes we had of finding *Bismarck* and *Hood*. Although we had a spare ROV on standby in America, losing both the depressor and the Magellan ROV was a disaster scenario from which we would have had no realistic chance of recovering. Because of Richard's alertness, we had dodged a fatal bullet.

A replacement pin was quickly fitted to the depressor termination and Magellan was ready for take two on the third dive. As before, the plan was to find the slide scar and follow it directly to the hull. The easiest way to find the slide scar was to locate the underwater telecommunications cable and follow it to the point where it crossed the slide scar at a 90° angle. This time I was intent on keeping the pilots in visual contact with the slide scar at all times. There would be no chasing of sonar targets or any other distractions that would pull us away from the trail.

As Magellan reached the bottom and the seabed came into view, I was amazed to see that we had landed right on top of the underwater cable at the point where it crossed the slide scar. Was this a sign that our luck was about to change? This was an important reference point on the seabed to which I wanted to be able to return in case we lost our way, so we spent some time double-checking its position. First we moved west following the cable to a piece of wreckage we had seen on dive one. This allowed us to take a sonar range and bearing to the superstructure, our other key reference point. We then flew back eastwards along the cable to the slide scar. I wanted to be absolutely sure this was the slide scar and not some freak geological feature, so I asked Troy to follow the scar up the slope to the north. Troy and Andy also agreed to keep the ROV in visual contact with the slide scar whenever we had to move the ship. This important change in method eliminated the leapfrogging of the ROV that made us lose visual contact with the seabed and thus our bearings. By following the slide scar, we were able to get our first true feel for how its appearance could suddenly change. One moment the edge of the trench was steep, well defined and easy to follow, and the next moment it would flatten out and change colour with no discernible continuation.

Once I was one hundred per cent positive we were in the main slide scar where *Bismarck* had slid to her final resting place, I asked Troy to turn Magellan south and follow the trail. Andy's shift – which consisted of Troy flying Magellan, Richard on sonar, and Neil Corliss on the winch – were especially keen to find the hull on their watch so they could claim bragging rights as the first ROV pilots to have flown over *Bismarck*. I encouraged their motivation by naming them the 'bloodhounds'. Whenever they became unsure about the trail or picked up a large sonar target off to the side, I would keep them focused on the slide scar by saying: 'Follow that trail like a bloodhound!'

At first the slide scar was easy to follow. We decided to follow the eastern edge of the trench, which was several metres high in places and visually distinct. The sediment cover was quite deep, so it was easy to imagine the 35,000-ton *Bismarck* ploughing her way down the volcano's slope, pushing aside great volumes of sediment. Unperturbed by current, bioturbation (surface sediments disturbed by biological organisms – in extreme cases, completely altering the appearance of the seabed's surface), or falling sediment, all of which are generally negligible in the deep ocean, the trench left by *Bismarck* was remarkably fresh despite being sixty years old. We once flew over to the other side of the trench to see the western edge and there was a clear symmetry to the grooving of the sediment. Although we had no means of measuring the width of the trench, it did appear to match the breadth of *Bismarck*'s hull. All the signs encouraged us into thinking we were on the right trail.

We made the first 100 metres down the slide scar moving at 150°. This put us on course to intercept the very large sonar target that I had originally believed was the hull, so I had no reason to worry about our progress. The next 100 metres started to trail off to the south, however, and move away from the sonar target, which was now far to the east. I was faced with exactly the same problem we'd had the first time we had attempted this at the start of dive two. It was a very difficult moment because I was still truly undecided about the two options which were staring me in the face: I had every reason to believe that the large sonar target was the hull, but how could I ignore the absolute physical certainty that the hull would be at the end of the slide scar, even if the scar pointed in a different direction. Each time we ventured off into the valley looking for the large target using Magellan's sonar we came back empty-handed. I had little confidence in the result differing if we tried this again.

The bloodhounds continued their way down the slide scar, hugging the trench edge. Magellan's compass now read 200°. We had been on the seabed for four hours working at an extremely high level of concentration. Our navigation was based on a combination of DGPS (Differential Global Positioning System) positions for the ship on the surface, dead reckoning of the ROV on the seabed, sonar navigation of targets on the seabed, and pure guesswork – an exhausting combination. In my mind I had decided to stay committed to the decision of following the trail no matter what. To do that I had to completely disregard my original beliefs about the large sonar target. As long as the trail didn't go cold I was sure we would find the hull.

Deeper and deeper Magellan pushed down the slope. After each forward movement of the *Northern Horizon*, Magellan would have to pull all of her cable with her to make any forward progress of her own. It was an agonisingly slow process that increased the already thick tension inside the survey lab. Suddenly, we came to a section where the trench edge flattened and there was nothing in our screen to indicate which way we should go. The trail had gone cold. Various suggestions were being made to turn left or to turn right towards a different coloured patch of sediment. I listened to the suggestions but decided we should stay committed and maintain the course in which we were heading. I was sure the slide scar would soon re-emerge. When it did about 40 metres ahead, I once again urged Troy to: 'Follow that trail like a bloodhound!' My anxiety was beginning to turn to excitement as I could sense the trail was coming to an end.

In the last 100 metres, the more I wanted Magellan to pick up speed, but the slower she seemed to go. I couldn't understand why we hadn't already picked up the hull on Magellan's scanning sonar. The trench edge was now steep and well-defined again, so there was no worry about losing our way, but I desperately wanted to find the hull before the tide of fortune changed again. We came across a section of ladder-way lying across the trench edge, which provided a brief distraction from our search for the hull. It was obvious the ladder had fallen to this spot after *Bismarck* had slid past, as it was undamaged and had not been pushed into the sediment, as it would have been had *Bismarck* slid over it. The ladder, its full length spanning the trench edge, was also useful in illustrating the depth of the trench.

Up until this point every repositioning of the ship had been made in 100-metre increments. I called up to the bridge for the next 100-metre move, but Troy cut in to say that they only wanted 50 metres this time. I was baffled as to why, but for some reason did not question him. I continued to stare at the screen, looking for any clue that we were nearing the end of our search. Will Handley was sitting to my left and I

BISMARCK DEBRIS FIELD

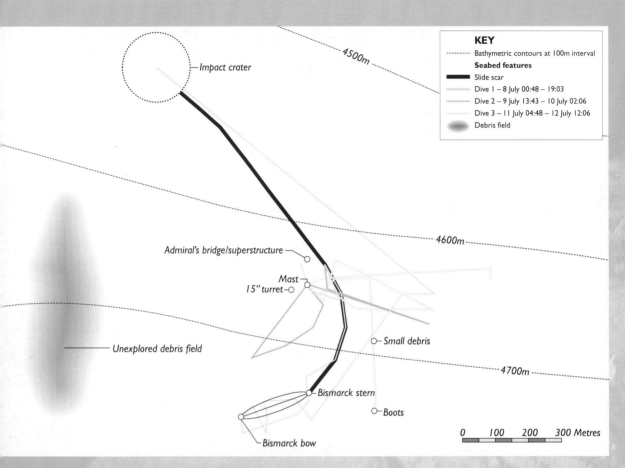

Impact crater

4500m

4600m

Admiral's bridge/superstructure

Mast

15" turret

Unexplored debris field

Small debris

4700m

Bismarck stern

Boots

Bismarck bow

0 100 200 300 Metres

ABOVE *The deep crater where Bismarck first hit the seabed is located nearly 1,500 metres further upslope.*

ABOVE *Two shells hit this stereoscopic range-finder from opposite directions. The exit hole from one is just above the impact mark of a second shell that didn't penetrate.*

LEFT *The mainmast is broken just above this platform.*

BELOW LEFT *Leather boots and jacket.*

BELOW RIGHT *From the upturned superstructure hangs a forest of rusticles, which made it difficult to spot shell damage.*

ABOVE *One of two 15-inch gunhouses we found upsidedown on their roofs. The second was heavily damaged.*

ABOVE *A steel cabinet.*

pointed out to him a change in the background picture. We were approaching something very big, but why hadn't it been picked up on the sonar? I called over to Richard on the sonar and asked: 'What is that?' and he answered: 'It's the *Bismarck!*' The lab erupted in a cheer and just then the fractured stern of the hull crept slowly into view. The ROV team had found the hull on sonar minutes earlier (thus explaining the shorter, 50-metre move) but they had kept it quiet to give us a surprise. It was a cheeky trick to play at such an important moment but when it was all over I couldn't be upset with them: we had found *Bismarck*'s hull and I was delighted.

PROUD AND DEFIANT

They may have thought of her as 'The Invincible *Bismarck*', but the events of 27 May 1941 proved that *Bismarck* was no more invincible than *Titanic* was unsinkable. However men have tried, they have not been able to build ships that are truly unsinkable or invincible. *Bismarck* was a strong and well-built ship, and that strength is still apparent in the wreck that lies at the bottom of the ocean. Although stripped of her main 15-inch gun turrets and much of her topside structure, *Bismarck* is still remarkably beautiful. Her lines are as graceful as ever. But look closely, as we have been able to do, and the extraordinary pounding she absorbed at the hands of the British fleet is also plain to see.

In the final action against *Bismarck*, starting at 08.47 a.m. with *Rodney* firing the first of her 113 16-inch, multi-gun salvoes and ending at 10.21 a.m. with *King George V*'s order to cease fire, the British fleet fired a total of 2,876 shells at *Bismarck*. How many hit and how many were telling in their impact was anyone's guess. British estimates ranged from 300 to 400 hits. *Bismarck* was also struck by as many as nine torpedoes in her last three days – witnesses on both sides observed at least six definite strikes. Was the cumulative effect of this concentrated British onslaught sufficient to sink *Bismarck* or was it the scuttling action taken by the German crew in her final moments that finally brought this great ship down? This deeply rooted historical controversy has never been fully resolved.

With the Magellan ROV being able to fly freely around the entire wreck and film all its surfaces, both horizontal and vertical, we were in a position to shed the first real light on this question. Our plan was to conduct a systematic visual census of all the shell hits and torpedo strikes to the hull and wreckage, and compare this census to the historical record of the action as reported by the eyewitnesses. This complete counting and mapping of the shell hits will hopefully be an ongoing project, to be taken up by experts such as Bill Jurens in the months and years following our expedition. My preliminary findings, however, strongly suggest that *Bismarck* was more vulnerable than was originally believed.

It must be stressed from the outset that our objective technical study of the damage suffered by *Bismarck* is not a comment on her ability as a fighting unit, which had been amply proven in her first engagement at sea. On the morning of 27 May *Bismarck* was crippled as a warship and the fighting spirit of her officers and crew was sapped. She was no longer the same fighting unit that sank *Hood* so convincingly and made *Prince of Wales* turn away to lick her wounds. Despite outmanoeuvring the British throughout the North Atlantic, *Bismarck*, with her rudders jammed to port and her speed severely reduced, was effectively cornered and unable to defend herself. The punishment delivered upon her by the British, without the fear of *Bismarck*'s usual counterpunch, throws into sharp relief how well *Bismarck* had been designed to withstand attack.

From the concentration of shell hits we have been able to document, it is clear that the British guns were aiming at *Bismarck*'s armament and gun directors, and that they were quite accurate in their fire. The first telling blow was struck by *Rodney* at 09.02 a.m., firing straight ahead and landing a 16-inch shell on *Bismarck*'s upper deck, putting the two forward turrets 'Anton' and 'Bruno' out of action. That shell must certainly have been the one we found to have hit the conning tower square in the middle of its forward-looking face. Although the shell didn't fully penetrate, it put a hole in the 1.4-inch (350-mm) armour belt, surely killing or disabling everyone inside, and destroying the communications link with the forward turrets. Around the conning

RIGHT *Evidence of a 16-inch shell hit from* Rodney *that knocked out turrets 'Anton' and 'Bruno' fifteen minutes after the action started.*

tower and turret, 'Bruno', we found at least six other heavy shell hits that had followed the first, but the fatal damage had already been done.

About the same time, an 8-inch shell from *Norfolk*, which had been firing from a position north of *Bismarck*, destroyed the foretop gun director. The stereoscopic range finder for this director was probably the one we found in the debris field that had been struck by two shells coming from opposite directions, as it was located very close to the upturned superstructure. The smaller of the two shells, which had hit with deadly force but had not penetrated, could have been in this salvo from *Norfolk*. With the forward turrets and the foretop gun director negated, one half of *Bismarck*'s main firepower had been rendered useless in the first fifteen minutes of the battle.

As *Bismarck* limped on her meandering course into the teeth of the firefight, *Rodney* and *King George V* continued to pile shells into her port side. This is where the British gunnery got the measure of *Bismarck* and hit her with devastating effect. Each of *Bismarck*'s three 5.9-inch, secondary gun turrets on the port side were hit by single, well-placed shells which penetrated the turret and exited the other side. The forward turret appears to have been hit by a large-calibre shell with the added effect of its entire back end being blown away. The centre of the ship, adjacent to the port catapult, was also hit very badly. There is not the huge shell hole described by Ballard, which he put down to a magazine explosion, but rather the penetration of the deck by a number of shells on both sides of the catapult. The damage is heavy.

By 09.15 a.m. the aft gun director under Mullenheim-Rechberg's command had been knocked out by a heavy shell hitting the telescopic range finder overhead. We weren't able to find that range finder or evidence of any other hits to the top of the gun director. There was a single shell penetration at the base of the director but this surely was not the hit Mullenheim-Rechberg was referring to. Of his very detailed account, the only thing we could document was his path of escape, along with the other men who sought the refuge of the armoured director, through the forward hatch marked 'U145'. Today, it remains eerily ajar.

Captain Dalrymple-Hamilton of *Rodney* reported that by 09.19 a.m., only turret 'Caesar' of *Bismarck*'s main armament was still firing, and only very intermittently. Perhaps by then the sternmost turret 'Dora' had already been eliminated by the heavy shell that had hit the barbette on the port side, leaving an impressive hole in its rim and a gaping hole in the main deck. A smaller hit on the other side of 'Dora''s barbette must have come from *Dorsetshire* which was trailing *Bismarck* from the southeast. Admiral Tovey's view from *King George V* was that: 'After half an hour of action the *Bismarck* was on fire in several places and virtually out of control. Only one of her turrets remained in action and the fire of this and of her secondary armament was wild and erratic. But she was still steaming.' It would be another hour and twenty minutes before *Bismarck* was sunk. Her colours were still flying – proud and defiant – but as a warship she was finished.

From then on, the action carried out by the British fleet to sink *Bismarck* was like a form of target practice. In discharging their duty to sink *Bismarck* as rapidly as possible the British officers did not find the task pleasant. Dalrymple-Hamilton observed that: 'Broadsides fired at close range, although spectacular, failed to produce any disruptive effect, neither did the fires raging all over the ship cause a major explosion. The ammunition expended in this effort therefore seems to have been largely wasted...' While the broadsides of armour-piercing (AP) shells did not lead to a cataclysmic explosion or rapid sinking of *Bismarck*, our investigation of her sides and armour belt clearly shows *Bismarck* was heavily damaged by this close-range shelling. Of the dozens of hits we saw there were quite a few outright penetrations in the armour belt on both the starboard and port sides. The neat holes left by the AP shells gives the false impression that damage to the ship was superficial. Of course, what we couldn't see was the damage incurred behind the armour plating as the shell burst, sending red-hot fragments scattering throughout the ship, killing everyone in its path and starting internal fires. While these shells apparently didn't reach *Bismarck*'s vitals – her magazines and engine rooms – they were causing serious damage and some flooding that ultimately contributed to *Bismarck*'s slow death. Perhaps in a normal encounter where *Bismarck* was able defend herself, the enemy would not have been able to deliver so many serious blows – without taking an equal or greater measure in return – and her armour would have kept the ship alive in a fight to the finish. Sadly for her, this encounter was anything but normal.

With her guns silenced, the most serious damage to *Bismarck* was yet to come. At approximately 09.40 a.m., *Rodney*, who had crossed *Bismarck*'s bow to the northeast, fired a spread of four torpedoes at a range of 4,000 metres from her port tube. One torpedo was observed to hit amidships. At 10.10 a.m., *Norfolk* fired four torpedoes, also at *Bismarck*'s starboard side, from a range of 4,000 yards. Two possible hits were observed, one abreast the mainmast and one abaft turret 'Dora'. By 10.15 a.m., *Bismarck*, which had entered the action with a 3–5° list to port, was very low in the water and men were seen to be jumping in the sea. The order to set off the scuttling charges in the engine room was given at about this time, but it was complicated by the fact that the port side of the ship was already heavily flooded. At 10.20 a.m., *Dorsetshire*, which had caught up with the immobile *Bismarck*, fired two Mark VII torpedoes into her starboard side from a range of 3,600 yards. One torpedo was seen to explode under her forebridge; the other is thought to have struck further aft. At 10.36 a.m., *Dorsetshire* circled *Bismarck*, which was now wallowing beam-on to the sea, and from the north sent a final Mark VII torpedo slamming into her port side from a range of 2,600 yards.

Never before had anyone been able to say precisely how effective these torpedo strikes had been in damaging *Bismarck* below her armour belt. Because she had avoided so many of the earlier torpedo attacks and had seemingly shrugged off all those that did reach her hull, with the sole exception of the fateful strike on her rudders, perhaps people were led to believe that *Bismarck* was immune to torpedoes. We can reveal for the first time that she was not. Our investigation along both her starboard and port sides shows most definitely that *Bismarck* was mortally wounded by the British torpedoes. In total we found four gaping torpedo holes – two on the starboard side and two on the port side – that were clearly sufficient to sink *Bismarck*, without the aid of additional water ingress due to the scuttling charges. The locations of the torpedo holes – firstly, abreast the conning tower, starboard side, secondly, abreast the rear AA gun director, starboard side, thirdly, abreast the bridge port side and fourthly, slightly abaft the turret 'Caesar' – match well with the eyewitness testimonies. The second and third torpedo holes were probably enlarged in the course of *Bismarck*'s slide down the volcano slope, but there is a distinct possibility that the second hole was formed by two strikes from *Norfolk* and *Dorsetshire*. The first hole was probably from a *Dorsetshire* strike that exploded against the hull and distorted the armour plates immediately above. The position of the fourth hole suggests that it was from the *Ark Royal* Swordfish on 26 May, causing far more damage than anyone realized, thus explaining the flooding that caused *Bismarck*'s initial list to port.

Confirmation of the torpedoes' effectiveness against *Bismarck* validates Tovey's decision to cease the gunfire and the senseless slaughter of escaping German sailors.

He correctly instructed: 'Any ships still with torpedoes to use them on *Bismarck*.' While the British guns made *Bismarck* a wreck, it was the torpedoes that sank her. The scuttling action taken by the Germans may have hastened the inevitable, but only by a matter of minutes. However, Tovey's unfortunate radio transmission to Vice-Admiral Somerville on board *Renown*: 'Cannot get her to sink with guns', timed some five minutes after *Bismarck* had already sunk, is what initiated this lingering idea that British guns were not up to the job. The ironic truth is that they were.

Shortly after *Dorsetshire*'s final torpedo struck *Bismarck*, she heeled over to port and started to sink by the stern. She then turned over completely onto her keel and sank by the stern at 10.40 a.m. The very clean fracture of the stern, particularly along the welded seam of the main deck, is a strong indication that the stern did in fact break off at the surface, as Ballard has postulated. Investigating the break around its entire circumference, we found no evidence of impact damage with the seabed, nor did we find any part of the stern in the impact crater. The stern appears to have been welded directly onto the hull without the use of longitudinal strength members, as if it was nothing more than a decorative appendage. The bulkhead forward of the break is perfectly intact (Ballard shows this bulkhead to be missing, but it would have been impossible for his downward-looking camera sled to see it was still there) and the remains of two lower decks are folded over the back end. The force that ripped the stern off at the surface was probably due to the difference in buoyancy between the air-filled stern and the flooded hull.

Bismarck's superstructure was probably wrenched off at the same time, by the same forces that separated the stern at the surface. The deck plates that remain where the superstructure once was are remarkably undamaged. This had led Bill Jurens to question the quality of the welding, which, at the time *Bismarck* was being built, was still in a relatively primitive state of development. As *Bismarck* rolled over her main turrets, which were held in the barbettes by gravity alone, they all fell out of the hull, and, along with large amounts of debris that had accumulated on the decks during the battle, started its long plunge into the abyss. Because she was close to being fully flooded, *Bismarck*'s journey to the seabed would have been quick. Her speed through the water would have rapidly increased until it reached a terminal velocity – something on the order of 20 knots – dictated by the hydrodynamic drag on the hull's shape. Along the way, those same hydrodynamic forces would have exerted themselves and righted the hull again, so that when she hit the seabed some ten minutes later she would have been perfectly upright.

The impact of *Bismarck*'s hull on the seabed would have been colossal. What remains today is a huge impact crater several hundreds of metres long and tens of metres deep – the most impressive I have ever witnessed. After completing our

RIGHT *The hatch in the aft gun director through which Baron von Mullenheim-Rechberg made his escape is still open.*

BELOW *A huge gash in the port-side decking forward of the conning tower.*

BELOW RIGHT *The back roof of this secondary gunhouse was blown off by a heavy shell.*

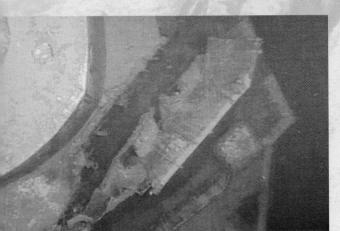

ABOVE *The entry hole of a smaller shell that exited on the other side.*

ABOVE *The final port-side secondary gun to be taken out of action with a shell through its roof.*

survey of the hull we flew Magellan north to try once more to locate the large, mystery sonar target before moving on to investigate the impact crater and the up-slope end of the slide scar. It was our third try with the large sonar target but again the hilly nature of the valley prevented its location. (We later discovered a flaw in our sonar image processing computer which had exaggerated the measured size of the targets, and had fooled me into thinking the target was precisely the correct length of the hull minus the stern. The precise location of the hull was ultimately found to coincide with the blind spot directly beneath the sonar towfish on our first search truckline. Based upon corrected measurements I believe the mystery target is likely to be the missing funnel.) However, there was no missing the impact crater. When *Bismarck* had hit the seabed the force of her hull, now weighing an estimated 35,000 tons, kicked up massive waves of sediment that remain ominously perched on the volcano's slope. There was no landslide that carried *Bismarck*'s hull down the slope. Rather, the hull slid down the slope itself, carrying its own momentum forward from the initial impact. Our proof of this is that the distinctive trench cut through the sediment starts right below the impact crater and extends all the way down to where the hull rests. The tons of sediment that can be seen at the bottom of the open barbette where turret 'Anton' once rested testify to the spectacular ride the hull had had. It must have tobogganed down the slope, ploughing up huge plumes of sediment. By the time the hull came to rest, it had travelled 1,450 metres down the slope and turned southwest, lodging herself into a thick pile of sediment. The hull now lies in 4,700 metres of water with the bow pointing at 290°.

In the evening of our final dive from *Bismarck* we held a simple service in remembrance of the 2,131 men that lost their lives here. Eric Grove read a lesson and a specially written prayer in German, which Rob White repeated in English. It was a beautiful evening. The wind was still and the sea calm; the mood was sombre. I placed a wreath on the waters above where the men lie. The few words I chose to say summed up my feelings as I thought of their sacrifice: 'We came to honour you with respect. May you rest in peace.'

There was much more I would have liked to investigate before leaving the site. Our search of the eastern debris field could have gone on for at least another day, and we hadn't even peeked into the equally large debris field located nearly 1 kilometre to the west. What those investigations could possibly have revealed about *Bismarck*'s final moments would have to be left for another expedition. The same can be said for the large sonar target which we had not found.

Finding the wreck of *Hood* – the part of the expedition we had presumed to be the hardest – was still ahead of us, however. Unlike *Bismarck*, which had been found in a matter of hours, its location would be measured in days or possibly even weeks. My worry shifted back to the weather. We had suffered more weather down time than I had bargained for at the *Bismarck* site, and I was beginning to fear that there was more in store for us when we reached the Denmark Straits. The time had come for us to leave *Bismarck* and steam north to find another famous warship, forever linked to *Bismarck* in history by the battle they fought sixty years ago. It was time to hunt for the *Hood*.

Two basic mosaics highlight shell damage to Bismarck: *starboard side mid-ships* (above) *and on the bow near the starboard anchor capstan* (right). *The mosaics are created using powerful computer software to piece together many video frames.*

The Hunt
for Hood

chapter **nine**

A TARGET IN THE NIGHT

The circular route from *Bismarck* to *Hood* covers slightly more than 1,100 nautical miles. At an average of only 10 knots (survey vessels are not known for their speed) I was expecting the transit to *Hood* to take us about four and a half days, which would give everyone plenty of time to recover from the sleepless finale of *Bismarck*'s investigation, and then to gear back up for the search for *Hood*. The long-range weather forecast for the *Hood* site looked good but there was an annoying low-pressure system with gale force winds blocking our preferred route. *Northern Horizon*'s captain, Keith Herron, and I were keeping a close watch on this weather system and had agreed upon a Plan B if it began to move in our direction. Meanwhile, the Oceaneering team was busy changing the deck around to prepare for side-scan sonar operations. I had asked Andy Sherrel to reconfigure the Ocean Explorer sonar by moving the 120 kHz transducers back to their normal side-scan location. For the *Bismarck* search they had been situated in the towfish's nose, looking forward to cover the blind spot, but the technique had not been as useful as I had hoped. If we were lucky enough to find *Hood*, I wanted to be able to get some high-resolution images of the wreck, so the transducers would be of more value looking sideways than looking forwards. I had no other option but to accept the risk that we could miss *Hood* in the blind spot at the front, in the same way as we had initially missed the hull of *Bismarck*.

The following day the annoying low-pressure system had become a real problem. It had deepened and its southerly gales would have hit the *Northern Horizon* square on the nose, had we continued our course. I was considering changing course and heading towards Reykjavik, Iceland, because we had an urgent crew transfer to make and film needed to be sent to London as soon as possible for editing. I had lined up a transfer boat to meet us at the *Hood* site but if the seas were rough the transfer would not be possible and we would have to call into Reykjavik anyhow. Because we had fallen behind schedule, the crew transfer was becoming our main priority. Keith thought we could skirt around the low-pressure system by staying just east of the worst winds but still make decent progress to the north. The course change he suggested was a compromise that allowed us the flexibility to choose one direction or the other when the situation was reviewed in twenty-four hours. Four hours after Keith had altered course 11° to the north, the wind had freshened to 35 knots against us, causing our speed to drop below 8 knots.

The poor weather continued into the next day and I was beginning to contemplate the impact of another period of weather down time, when just after noon the wind began to ease. It dropped further throughout the day, and by the following morning it was down to 5 knots. This latest threat of bad weather disappeared as quickly as it had materialized. The *Northern Horizon* was practically sprinting northwards at well over 11 knots and the weather forecast for our arrival on site was good. The transfer boat rendezvous was back on and the port call in Reykjavik, to the dismay of many on board wishing to have a drink in hand and a firm ground underfoot, was off. It was time to finalize my search plan for *Hood*.

After the many months of research and navigational analysis that had preceded it, the final formulation of my search plan took about an hour. I had three main decisions to make: firstly, the size of the search box, secondly, the orientation of both the search box and the tracklines, and thirdly, the sequence in which we would follow the tracklines in order to find *Hood* as quickly as possible. The first two decisions were dictated by the simple application of the navigational errors we had found to exist in the reported sinking positions during the First and Second World Wars. The errors that I chose to apply in this case were divided into two different categories: the worst

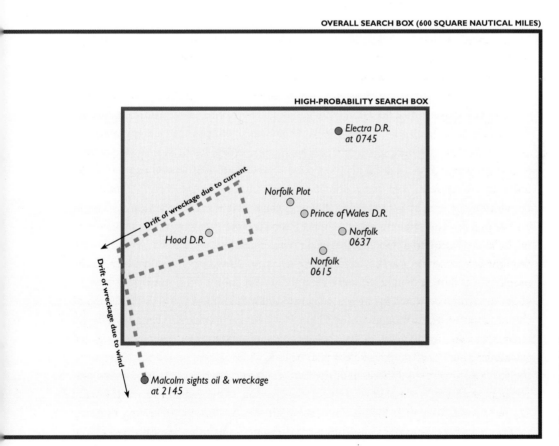

LEFT *All the primary sinking positions and secondary clues are plotted in this diagram. The overall search box of 600 square nautical miles is four times larger than the area searched to find* Titanic, *but we can cover it five times faster.*

error reported by a surface ship and the average error reported by a number of surface ships. These circles of error were drawn around each of the five most likely sites for *Hood* to have sunk. After this had been done, two rectangular boxes could be plotted: the overall search box and the high-probability box. Because these error values are company secrets of Bluewater Recoveries I can only reveal that the size of the overall search box was less than 600 square nautical miles and the high-probability box was significantly smaller.

The third decision – which tracklines to search first – can generally be made either on the strictly statistical basis of choosing the sequence of lines which would cover the largest amount of high-probability area in the shortest time, or on the basis of having a hunch where the wreck actually lies. Despite the enormous effort that goes into the quantitative formulation of a search plan, I've always believed that it is important to look beyond the numbers, develop a gut feel for the wreck's location and factor that into your plans. There are plenty of stories of fortunate shipwreck-searchers who relied on a hunch to lead them straight to their quarry. In selecting my trackline sequence I decided to go with Ted Briggs' hunch that the squadron navigator on board *Hood*, Commander Warrand, would have been the most accurate navigator on the day. Although Ted's hunch was based on a personal bias – it was Warrand whom Ted credits with saving his life – there was also a sound reason for it. Warrand was the squadron navigating officer reporting directly to Admiral Holland during the pursuit of *Bismarck*, which meant that he was the most senior British navigator in the fleet, and presumably the best. Warrand also had the advantage of navigating from the largest, most stable ship, which would have helped make his sextant readings and D.R. track calculations more accurate. You only had to look as far as our search for *Bismarck* to see that this theory had some validity. Of the three British reports for the sinking position of *Bismarck*, the closest to the actual location of the wreck was made by the squadron navigating officer reporting directly to Admiral Tovey.

Dawn was breaking on the morning of day twenty-one of the expedition when the

Northern Horizon arrived at the *Hood* search site. I came up to the bridge to look on the radar for the Icelandic transfer boat that was supposed to meet us before the search began. It was another fine and clear day – absolutely perfect for a ship-to-ship transfer at sea. Instead of a single transfer boat steaming towards our location, however, the radar screen was unexpectedly awash with bright yellow dots moving slowly along the eastern edge of our search box. It was a fleet of fishing boats, a dozen in all, that were trawling with mid-water nets. Generally, you look forward to seeing other ships far out at sea, as it is the only thing to connect you to the outside world. But these boats, with their large nets and heavy rigging, were far too close for my liking. Keith and his mates would need to keep a very close watch on their movement in order to avoid a potentially dangerous situation, as we would be competing for the same space with our respective tows in the water, which would restrict each ship's manoeuvrability.

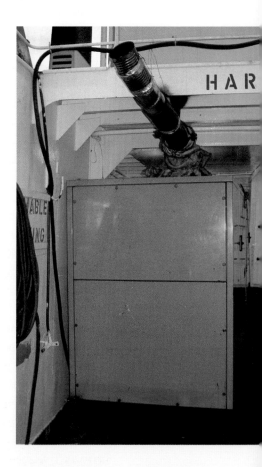

Once the transfer boat had made it to our location, she tied up alongside the *Northern Horizon*. In a matter of thirty minutes the transfer was complete – one film-maker and boxes of *Bismarck* videotape off, and a two-person *Channel 4 News* team and some spare parts on. The response to the underwater footage of *Bismarck* – the first high-quality colour film of the wreck to be broadcast in the UK – had been so positive that *Channel 4 News* decided to send a team out to do live coverage of our hunt for *Hood*. The appreciation of our initial success, which the reporter, Lindsay Taylor, was able to relay was nice, but I was more interested to hear how he had fared on the eighteen-hour journey from Reykjavik on a 23-metre transfer boat. In one sense this transfer was a dry run for the journey we were all hoping Ted Briggs would be able to make, if and when we found his former ship. Having met Lindsay during the mobilization in Cobh, I knew him to be a keen boater, and so I valued his opinion. He reported that the trip had been very good, but as the sea conditions were near-perfect it wasn't necessarily a good indicator of how easy Ted's transfer would be.

ABOVE *This generator took up our last remaining deck space, but in the end it saved the expedition from costly downtime.*

During the transfer the fishing fleet had moved south, away from the search box, leaving us an unobstructed path to start our first trackline. However, just as *Northern Horizon* got into position to launch Ocean Explorer, the Chief Engineer, Krzyzstof, came to me with a harried look on his face, and said that there was another problem with the 60-Hz generator. The generator had been the cause of our earlier electrical failures and Krzyzstof had already rebuilt it once on the job, but I could see in his eyes that he had lost confidence in its reliability. Fortunately, we were able to fall back on the spare deck generator that Steve Spivey had been so determined to get on board during the mobilization. It had sat silent since we left Cobh, taking up our one precious patch of free deck space. But due to Steve's good judgement, it would now save us from a potentially schedule-killing trip to Reykjavik for repairs.

By noon, with all the niggling problems behind us, the Ocean Explorer sonar was launched into the cold waters of the Denmark Strait and was heading down to the unexplored depths of the Irminger Basin. Three hours later I was getting the first glimpse of the type of seabed we would have to contend with while trying to pick out possible sonar targets. While the seabed was as flat as I expected, the surface geology was far more active than I had hoped. There were large patches of rocky outcrops scattered about, as well as some indications that actively mobile sand-waves were travelling across the seabed in response to a bottom current. We had started the search from the eastern side of the search box, which coincided with the lower slope of the Reykjanes Ridge. The geology we were seeing was not out of the ordinary there, but it was still potentially troublesome if *Hood* had happened to sink on this side of the box.

As we moved west into the slightly deeper waters of the basin, the rugged geology disappeared and the seabed turned into a carpet of soft, sandy sediment. The resulting sonar images had the ideal background that wreck-hunters like me pray for – a uniform tableau of burgundy, providing a stark contrast with the bright yellow, green and blue shapes that depict a shipwreck. We were searching on the line closest to the *Hood*'s supposed sinking position, hoping that Ted Briggs's hunch would hold true. The sonar moved past the high-probability circle of the sinking position, which had been derived from Commander Warrand's calculations, but no shapes appeared. The end of the line was not yet in sight but I was already thinking about my next series of moves. I had decided to turn south to run one search line before moving back north for the next nearest line to the *Hood*'s supposed sinking position. In addition to covering the highest probability zone first, the pattern I had devised was designed to minimize the amount of time spent in making each turn.

The next trackline, on a reciprocal course of the first, began with equal promise of finding *Hood*. Because the wind on the morning of the battle sixty years ago had been blowing from the north, the leeway drift of the ships would be to the south. I had no way of knowing for sure whether the respective navigators had corrected their positions for leeway. If they had not, it was possible that *Hood* was actually south of the positions they had reported. On the other hand, the leeway of heavy, deep draft ships like *Hood* would be very small – possibly even nil. After all, they didn't call *Hood* the biggest submarine in the British Navy for no good reason. As the seabed was

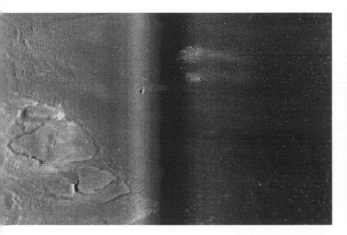

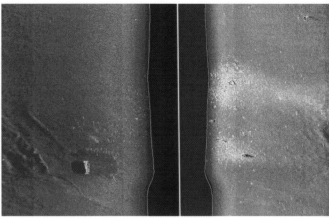

scanned on this southern trackline, I wondered whether leeway would be a factor in our location of *Hood*. I got my answer when the line was finished nine hours later and our list of sonar targets was essentially blank.

We were back on the eastern side of the search box ready to start the next turn when Keith spotted a problem with a few of the fishing boats that had moved north back into our area. We had over 6,300 metres of towcable streaming behind us and needed to turn to port to head up to the next line. Unfortunately, one particular trawler was moving in the same direction and looked set to cross directly in front of our intended course. His nets were out and he had just as much right to continue his course as *Northern Horizon* did. If he kept his northern course we would have to either turn to starboard or recover the towfish as fast as possible in order to slow down and let him pass ahead. It was a tricky situation which could have ended up in a large loss of time for our search, or worse. Keith raised the opposing captain on the radio and informed him of our situation, and, to our great relief, the trawler decided to bear off to the south, thereby clearing our path to the north and the next trackline.

Other than this anxious moment with the fishing boat, the search for *Hood* was proceeding well and was taking on a predictable rhythm, which I was prepared to follow all week if necessary. It was taking ten hours per trackline, during which I'd be glued to the sonar display. This was punctuated by five hours per turn, which was all the time I had to catch up on sleep and any other business. The next trackline, our third, would also pass close to the *Hood*'s supposed sinking position, and would also pass the cluster of four suggested sinking positions on the eastern side of the box. The patterns of geology on the seabed were now becoming familiar to us, to the point where it became possible to say which part of the search box the sonar was in, on the basis of a quick look at my computer screen. The current ten-hour stretch was taking place from the evening to the early morning, which meant that it was quieter than usual in our control room. I had always preferred working the night shift: there were fewer distractions and it seemed that the best results were always achieved then. We

ABOVE LEFT *The first side-scan sonar image showing a classic debris field, which came up on our screens thirty-nine hours after we started the hunt for* Hood.

ABOVE RIGHT *The width of this second pass was 1,800 metres. At the time I was still hoping the large sonar contact on the left side was* Hood*'s bow.*

were more than halfway through the line and I was alone in front of the sonar display. The sonar had just reached the flat and featureless abyssal area when I turned to see the first few pixels of a yellow and green sonar target emerge from the top of the screen. Another eight seconds passed, producing two more scan lines, and the target was just as strong, with a sharply defined shadow behind it. The next ten minutes of sonar data were to confirm my immediate impression, but I was certain I was looking at the remains of HMS *Hood*.

For the second time running, the sonar trackline had passed directly over the wreckage field. This time we had been left with a beautiful image that was easy to interpret. One large section of hull, possibly the bow, was lying by itself, separated from two, discrete oval debris fields with long tails which winnowed to the north as if a current had scattered the lighter debris in that direction. The debris fields were full of individual hard contacts, including one that had a long angular shadow and all the earmarks of being the broken stern. There was no reason to continue the line any further. This was the *Hood*, and I wanted to have a high-resolution image as soon as possible.

Because we had hit the wreckage field with perfect orientation, I asked Chris Jones to set up a reciprocal line just 50 metres south of the original trackline. I had the sonar's swathe reduced to 1,800 metres to frame the entire debris field. Eight hours later, the first pieces of debris were being picked up by the sonar. This image was every bit as stunning as the first, but far more informative, given that the wreckage was magnified by about three times. The large section of hull had what appeared to be a pointed end, with a high, square shadow behind it, and was framed by a subtle impact crater. Thinking back to Ted's description of how he saw *Hood*'s intact bows sliding back into the water as she sank, I was already calling this target the bow. The two debris fields, separated by at least 250 metres, were extremely dense with wreckage, confirming the extraordinarily violent explosion that *Hood* had suffered. A sonar target with a long angular shadow on the edge of the eastern debris field remained my favourite choice for the stern. Surprisingly, there was one other significant target on this image that was hardly picked up on the first pass. It was an extremely hard, rectangular target that was located by itself approximately 900 metres from the nearest debris field and 2 kilometres away from the large hull section. I was very curious to learn the identity of this piece, to understand how it could have ended up so far away from everything else.

Remembering the agonizingly drawn out search for *Bismarck*'s hull, I wasn't about to take any chances with *Hood*. So I asked Chris to set up one final trackline that would yield the best possible image and seabed position of the large hull section and impact crater. We narrowed the swathe right down to 500 metres and had the Ocean Explorer towing at an altitude of 75 metres in order to try to produce distinctive acoustic shadows, which would allow us to positively confirm the target's identity. *Northern Horizon* ran straight down the trackline but for some reason the towfish was off line by about 75 metres and we only got a partial image of the hull directly beneath the towfish. However, the image of the impact crater was spectacular. For years I had struggled, trying to convey to people the extent of the force with which shipwrecks hit the seabed in deep water. This one picture, which showed in detail the radiating sediment mounds formed by the shock wave from the hull's impact, said it all.

Ron Schmidt's shift recovered the Ocean Explorer for the last time on the expedition and began the changeover to ROV operations. It was day twenty-four of the expedition and our speedy location of *Hood* – thirty-nine hours from the time the sonar was launched – meant that instead of being four days behind schedule we had caught up and were suddenly one day ahead. The best news of all, however, was that Ted Briggs' hunch had been right. On 24 May 1941, Commander Warrand had been by far the most accurate navigator.

BELOW *This high-resolution image shows only a part of the hull (centre), but it perfectly illustrates the tremendous force of the impact on the seabed.*

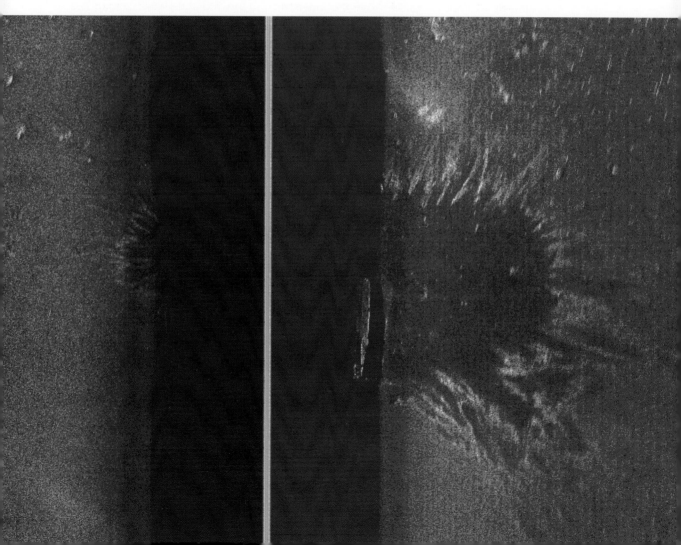

RIGHT *Captain John Leach's drawing of what the explosion on* Hood *looked like to him.*

SHE'S FOUND

As I absorbed the information contained in the beautifully illustrative sonar images we had collected of *Hood*'s wreckage, I began to revise my expectations of the condition in which we would find the wreck once Magellan had reached the seabed. Originally, I'd thought we would find *Hood* to be broken in two, or possibly three pieces, with the bow intact from the superstructure forward and sitting more or less upright on the seabed. I had expected a large part of the stern to be intact and sitting upright, as well. The explosion *Hood* suffered near her mainmast, depicted most vividly in a drawing Captain John Leach had drawn for the second Board of Inquiry, would have caused a lot of destruction in the region of the engine rooms, and would have left a single debris field scattered between the bow and the stern. These expectations were in line with the extensive eyewitness testimonies I had read, as well as my own experience investigating shipwrecks caused by massive explosions. In the light of this fresh information from the high-resolution sonar images, however, I was slowly being forced to the conclusion that the damage suffered by *Hood* was far greater than I had originally imagined.

Three things concerned me. For a start, the size and density of the debris field strongly suggested that a very large percentage of the hull had been ripped apart by the explosion. I had been thinking that as much as a quarter of the hull could have been destroyed to the point of being unrecognizable. But now I was thinking that half of the hull, or even more, could have sustained that much damage. Secondly, the spread of wreckage was more than twice what I had expected. I could understand it being larger because it was likely that what I believed was the bow had planed (descended at an angle) away, scattering debris behind it on its path to the seabed. But I couldn't account for the large sonar target which we had located so far in the opposite direction. What was it, and how had it got there? It didn't seem like the type of structure that was capable of planing away. Finally, and most distressingly, I had to consider the possibility that the bow was not upright, but on its side. The acoustic shadow caused by the sonar target that I believed to be the bow was very straight, indicating that the upper surface was smooth. Even with her turrets removed, as *Bismarck*'s had been, the barbettes on the bow would have created distinctive shadows in the sonar image. But there were none.

Will Handley had spent the previous three days preparing for the ROV investigation by making an identification booklet for *Hood*, based on close-up photographs of our model. The idea had worked a treat with *Bismarck* and the booklet had been referred to constantly whilst filming on the hull. But with Magellan just hours away from her first meeting with *Hood*, I wondered aloud if his efforts were all to be in vain. What if *Hood* was so damaged she was virtually unrecognizable?

When Magellan did reach the seabed, the first pieces of debris we found were easily identified by their sheer ubiquity. They were the long, cylindrical crushing tubes that had been hidden behind *Hood*'s outer bottom plating as a defence against torpedo strikes. They had been meant to absorb a torpedo's impact and thus hopefully prevent the ship from being badly damaged. Someone did a quick calculation based upon a drawing and thought there could have been as many as 12,000 crushing tubes loaded in *Hood*. Magellan had been on the seabed for two hours and we had already found five: there would be many more to follow.

The plan of the dive was simple: to find the large sonar target and identify it. On the way through the debris field we were finding quite large pieces of shell plating and structural frames but it was impossible to say which part of the ship they had come from. Miscellaneous plating and hull structure is very difficult to identify in the best of circumstances, and these pieces were fractured, twisted and heavily corroded. To make matters worse, a thick layer of fluffy sediment covered the wreckage and they were becoming overgrown with anemone-like organisms. The covering of sediment had been caused by a surprisingly strong bottom current. This had stirred up sediment from the seabed and plastered it over the surfaces of the debris, where it had eventually stuck and then gradually built up over the years. For relatively deep water, the visibility was awful. The effect in our video cameras was like that of driving with your headlights on in a heavy snowstorm. I had experienced conditions like these in 280 metres of water but never in 2,800.

By the time we had worked our way over to the large sonar target and begun inspecting its upper surface, the current and visibility had become twice as bad. We had found one fractured end of the wreckage and had known immediately that we were working on a major section of the hull, but we couldn't tell much more than that. The upper surface was completely flat, thereby confirming that the hull wasn't upright, and one entire section of shell plating was missing, exposing the internal structure. Ron Schmidt was struggling to make even the slightest amount of forward progress with Magellan against the current in search of some recognizable feature. Finally, a square vent covered by a heavy grating was found, and then a second, identical vent was found nearby. Vents like these could have been situated either on the side of *Hood*'s hull, or on the bottom. I desperately wanted them to be side vents, which would mean that *Hood*'s deck would still be accessible to us for filming. We repositioned the ship and ROV to look at the other side of the hull, but before we could find anything, Magellan's video screens flickered and then went dark.

BELOW *Ron Schmidt pilots Magellan around another famous shipwreck.*

All of the topside equipment was working fine, so the problem had to be with Magellan. We could have been minutes away from discovering that the hull section we were working on was the bow, but the dive was now over and Magellan was on her way back for repairs. I was frustrated by the day's events, but I had to put this out of my mind because I had an important phone call to make. Just as Ted was seeing us off in Cobh I had told him that he would be the first person I'd call once I was sure we had found the *Hood*. It was Friday night and I knew he would be at home waiting for my call. When I told him that I had just spent the last hour looking at pictures of his ship his reply was short and choked with emotion. He asked where I had found her and was pleased to hear that it was close to Commander Warrand's estimated position. We kept our conversation short because I knew that Ted had his own important phone call to make. He wanted to call Commander Warrand's widow (mother of Joanna Warrand of the Hood Association), who was now living in Australia. Ted had been carrying the memory of Commander Warrand's kind act of self-sacrifice with him all these years and he wanted her to know that her husband's grave had been found.

BELOW *Commander Warrand, the squadron's navigation officer on board* Hood.

By 09.45 a.m. the next day Magellan ROV was repaired and back in the water to start the second dive. We were lucky to still have her with us at all – we'd been within a quarter of an inch of losing her completely, and with her, the expedition itself. When she was recovered in the early hours of the morning we could see just how lucky we'd been. The electrical failure had been caused by Magellan's depressor being rotated again and again by the strong bottom currents, twisting the electrical conductors and optical fibre core until they had both snapped. When the fibres had snapped we had

THE HUNT FOR HOOD

lost the video feed. This had alerted us to the problem just in the nick of time before the depressor and Magellan were lost for good. It turned out that the depressor's mechanical termination, which connected it to the steel umbilical cable, had unscrewed to the point that only three threads had been left holding the two ends fast. Normally all fifteen threads of the termination are screwed lock-tight. With twelve of the threads already unscrewed, the remaining three could have been undone in less than an hour and both the depressor and Magellan would have joined *Hood* on the seabed as wrecks. It was the second time during the expedition we had dodged a fatal bullet.

WHAT SANK HOOD SO FAST?

The sudden loss of *Hood* and her crew of 1,415 men was utterly unimaginable to the Royal Navy and the British people until it actually happened. The mighty *Hood* was the most feared and respected warship afloat. For two decades she had been the world's heavyweight champion and she stormed into battle with *Bismarck* with full confidence that she could more than match her younger challenger. In less than eight minutes her confidence and reputation were proven to have been grossly misplaced. Eight minutes and forty

shells were all that it took to fell the mighty *Hood*. Once hit by *Bismarck*'s fifth salvo, she exploded and sank in two to three minutes. Within approximately ten minutes, *Hood* was transformed from a fiercely proud and determined flagship of the Royal Navy into a burning patch on the water, with just three men out of her 1,418 left struggling for their lives. How was this possible? What caused the mighty *Hood* to sink so fast?

This was the question that drew me to *Hood*'s story in 1995 – a question I hoped we would be able to answer, in spite of the obvious challenges we would face. My main concern was that her destruction would be so complete that identifying the precise trigger for the explosion and the ship's consequent demise would be impossible. In preparation for the investigation I had asked Bill Jurens to list all the possible scenarios that could explain *Hood*'s sudden loss. He developed a comprehensive list with a total of ten different scenarios each with a theory of how we could prove or disprove each one. The scenarios ranged from the most obvious (15-inch shell penetration of magazines with an above-water hit) to the most controversial (poor quality armour or steel), with all kinds of other suggestions between. Still, there was a distinct chance that we could come away from the investigation empty-handed, with nothing learned or gained. The second Board of Inquiry had stated: 'As noted before, much of the evidence is contradictory and inconclusive, and we realize that many points in connection with the loss of the *Hood* can never be proved definitely.' I was reasonably confident that our investigation would provide some of the missing evidence that had left the key question unanswered for sixty years.

After her near loss, Magellan was sent back into the cold, dark waters of the Denmark Strait sporting a newly modified termination (a simple set-screw through its body solved the problem) which would not unscrew in the current. Over the next five days Magellan made three more dives to the wreck and spent a total of sixty-six hours on the seabed filming and investigating *Hood*'s wreckage. There was some more excitement in the form of another electrical cable failure, and a patch of rough weather causing a day of down time, but in general our progress was good and we covered as much of the debris fields as we could have hoped. The strong bottom currents were still a problem but because they were tidally induced (the currents reversed on a routine basis) we had slack periods when the visibility cleared up very well. We took advantage of the slack periods in our filming and set about finding the evidence to explain her loss. *Hood*'s wreckage tells a surprising story – one that I had not expected.

Contrary to accepted British opinion at the time, the first shell that hit *Hood* was an 8-inch round from *Prinz Eugen*, and not one of *Bismarck*'s heavier salvos. The confusion stems from the fact that both German ships had opened the battle by firing on *Hood* alone. However, the reconstructed version of *Bismarck*'s war diary has an entry confirming it to have been *Prinz Eugen* who had first drawn blood at 05.57 a.m.: 'Observing a fast spreading fire on *Hood* in front of the level of the quarter mast. Probably plane hangar or gasoline fire at impact of the second salvo from *Prinz Eugen*.' Although we were unable to find the area of this hit in the wreckage, the witnesses who had testified to the Board of Inquiry had firmly described the resulting fire as being on the port side of the boat deck and abaft the mainmast. The fire burned with a clear flame and spread quickly along the deck before dying down a couple of minutes later. The Inquiry concluded that the fire had been due to some of the 4-inch and Unrotated Projectile ammunition catching fire, but that this fire hadn't caused the explosion. Fundamental to their latter conclusion was factual information that: firstly, the fire had been dying down before the explosion; secondly, the hatches in the train of supply had definitely been closed; and thirdly, *Hood* had been hit by another shell after the fire had started, and almost immediately before the explosion.

Just before 06.00 a.m. Vice-Admiral Holland signalled another turn to port of 20°, in order to bring his after guns to bear on *Bismarck*. Although the flag for this turn had been hoisted and seen by the *Prince of Wales* stationed just 4 cables (741 m) away on the starboard quarter of *Hood*, it was uncertain whether *Hood* actually made the turn because she was immediately hit and mortally wounded by a shell from *Bismarck*. In fact, the second Board of Inquiry concluded that the turn was never executed. Had *Hood* made this turn that had been intended to let her take on *Bismarck* on an equal footing: eight guns versus eight guns?

The second shell that hit *Hood* was not clearly seen, but it apparently hit on the boat deck near the mainmast, close to where the first shell had hit and started the fire. It was a shell from *Bismarck*'s fifth salvo, which was seen to straddle *Hood* with some shells falling short. Captain John Leach, who was on the compass platform of the *Prince of Wales* and looking directly at *Hood* when the explosion occurred, saw a funnel of flame between the after funnel and mainmast shoot up to double the height of the mast (approximately 300 feet, although others claimed it to be double this). He estimated that the base of the explosion had been from 20 to 30 feet. He had seen heavy debris thrown into the air, but had heard very little noise. He described the effect of the conflagration that erupted as 'a vast blow lamp'. Chief Petty Officer French, who had been on the pom-pom platform, had actually seen the boat deck lift and 'X' turret falling over (*Hood*'s forward turrets going from bow to stern were named A, B, X, Y). Others testified to seeing big objects (15–inch turrets and guns) being thrown high up into the air.

When we found the stern of *Hood* we were surprised to see that she was resting on the remains of her keel at an odd angle, which made the point formed by her stern castings jut upwards into the water column. Her fragile-looking ensign staff was untouched and the teak planking was remarkably intact, belying the extraordinary scene of destruction waiting for us at the forward end of the stern. There, where the stern met the seabed at an angle of about 45°, the quarterdeck was fractured straight across, from one side of the ship to the other. This break appears to have happened on impact as the light decking, unsupported by any structure below, cracked under the full weight of the stern as it rammed into the seabed. The other side of the quarterdeck was lying flat on the seabed and the position of its forward break – at the aft end of the opening for turret 'Y' – meant that the length of this entire piece was about 40 metres.

Around the back of the stern on the port side the damage was completely different. This damage was not the result of impact with the seabed. A major piece of the port side plating – at least 15 metres – had peeled backwards and was now lying perpendicular to the stern. Bearing evidence of the great force that ripped it away from the hull, the plating was severely bent and fractured. Our view of the wreckage made it impossible to say whether the damage in this area included the outer bottom plating but I suspect that it did. Here was all the proof that was needed to confirm

HOOD DEBRIS FIELD

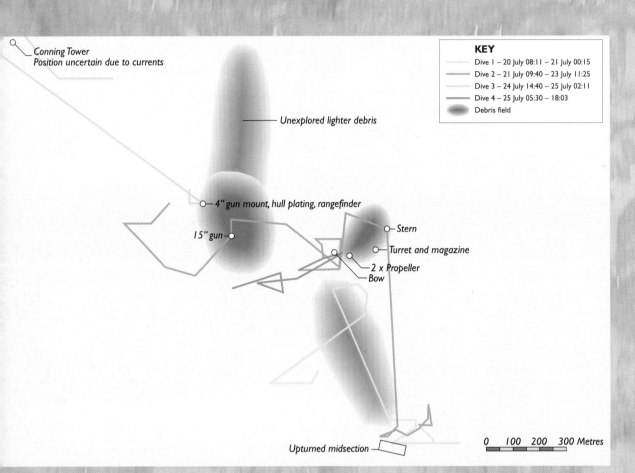

Conning Tower
Position uncertain due to currents

Unexplored lighter debris

4" gun mount, hull plating, rangefinder

15" gun

Stern

Turret and magazine

2 x Propeller
Bow

Upturned midsection

KEY

—— Dive 1 – 20 July 08:11 – 21 July 00:15
—— Dive 2 – 21 July 09:40 – 23 July 11:25
—— Dive 3 – 24 July 14:40 – 25 July 02:11
—— Dive 4 – 25 July 05:30 – 18:03
Debris field

0   100   200   300 Metres

ABOVE *One of two forward propellers lying next to each other.*

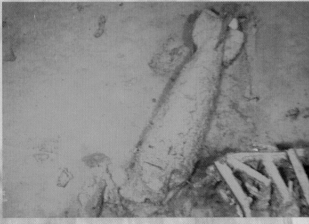

ABOVE *The back end of one of Hood's torpedoes. We could not confirm, one way or the other, whether it exploded in the intense conflagration.*

LEFT *A truly remarkable find: one of* Hood*'s bells lying in a pile of debris.*

BELOW LEFT *A teapot.*

BELOW RIGHT *A pair of boots.*

ABOVE *A 4-inch shell casing sitting upright on the seabed.*

ABOVE *One of* Hood*'s 15-inch gun turrets lying on its side. The base structure on the left appears to have been blown upwards.*

that the 15–inch magazines had exploded as was universally believed. The force of the explosion and the extreme heat generated by the burning cordite had broken *Hood*'s back just below the aft turrets, and had blown back the side shell plating on the port side. Had only the 4-inch magazines exploded, such serious damage to the hull wouldn't have extended this far aft.

Further evidence that both 15-inch and 4-inch aft ammunition magazines had exploded was the apparent obliteration of a 70-metre section of the hull, extending from the aft curvature of 'X' turret forward to the after bulkhead of the forward engine room. The smaller, eastern debris field appears to mark the position of this explosion, as key pieces of wreckage found here can be identified from this part of the ship. The wreckage includes both of *Hood*'s forward propellers lying next to one another with a length of their shafts still attached; two complete stern tubes, broken at or near the shaft couplings on either end; and one of the after turrets lying on its side and missing its gunhouse. Heavy plating at the base of the turret appears to be bent upwards, as would be expected if the explosion had originated from the magazines directly below.

Unfortunately, the precise location of *Bismarck*'s shell penetration will probably never be known. The remains of the 70-metre section where the shell hit is so completely and utterly destroyed that even the task of identifying the wreckage is nearly impossible. (Considering the difficulties of picking out individual items, we were amazed and very fortunate to have found one of *Hood*'s bells hidden deep in a pile of debris.) To make matters worse, any debris lying on the seabed is covered with an unusually thick layer of sediment and rust due to corrosion. The fragmented and contorted appearance of the wreckage found in the eastern debris field is a testament to the violent power of the explosion that broke *Hood* in half. The aft magazines were to have contained a total of 112 tons of cordite and there can be little doubt that they exploded simultaneously after being ignited following the impact of *Bismarck*'s shell.

Every description of the explosion given by eyewitnesses has been surpassed by what we found on the seabed. The entry in *Bismarck*'s war diary reads: '0601'20' Extraordinarily violent detonation on the *Hood*. A high pillar of metal debris is visible. A heavy black cloud of smoke envelops the ship that sinks rapidly by the stern while twisting about 180°.' Lieutenant-Commander A.H. Terry, who had observed the explosion from a position high up on the port side of the ship on board the *Prince of Wales*, was one of the few to see any specific damage to the hull of the battleship before she sank. In his testimony to the Board of Inquiry, he said he thought that the side and bottom of the ship had been blown out, as he observed what he had considered to be the frames of the ship abreast the mainmast as she had keeled over. However, like others, he had heard no great noise. A few talked of a rumbling or muffled sound, but that was all. From more recent experience, I was aware that a ship could be blown up at sea without even those on board hearing a classic explosive 'bang'. In one case, a 15,000 ton cargo ship (MV *Lucona*) was blown up by a time bomb containing 500 kilograms of TNT. But of the six crew that survived, including the Captain, not one had heard an explosive sound, or had even been aware that an explosion had occurred. I suspect that in the seconds that *Hood* was hit and exploded, the eyewitnesses had not – even collectively – been able to take in all the unbelievable and horrifying things they were seeing and hearing.

Given the extent of the damage we had already documented and the disappointment of not being able to say more about the fatal shell hit on *Hood*, we were grateful to be able to answer one important historical question: Had *Hood* executed the last 20° turn to port? As Magellan was manoeuvred along the port side of the stern, where it rested on the seabed, the aft propeller and rudder came clearly into view. The rudder was undamaged and fixed in the exact position Holland had ordered: on a turn of 20° to port. To be precise, it appears that *Hood* had been still in mid-turn when hit. A number of historians, including Dr. Eric Grove, have already commented on the bad luck that had accompanied Holland's choice of tactics. Had this turn been completed just thirty seconds sooner, *Hood* would have moved out of the shot pattern of *Bismarck*'s fifth salvo and probably not been hit.

Upon relocating the major hull section, which we had only begun to film on the aborted first dive, my worst fears were confirmed when we found it to be lying upside down on the seabed. This was a first for me in deepsea shipwreck investigations. I found it quite shocking because in the dozens of deepwater shipwrecks I had found, never before had I found one – or even a section of one – to be completely inverted. This did not bode well for this section: it was a strong indicator that the section had been heavily damaged – and that is exactly what we found. It turned out to be a mid-ship section of hull about a hundred metres long, extended from the after bulkhead of the forward engine room to the forward curvature of 'A' turret. The break at the engine room bulkhead was jagged and very irregular, but the side and bottom plating were not splayed out. Unlike the stern break, it did not appear to be close to the seat of the explosion. The break near 'A' turret, on the other hand, was the worst of them all. Extremely large pieces of plating on the side and bottom were bent outwards, this time on the starboard side. In fact, the entire starboard side shell plating – the full hundred metres – appeared to have been ripped from the hull. On the port side, the top decks adjacent to the two turrets were missing, which enabled us to get close to the barbettes for turrets 'A' and 'B', despite the hull being upside down. Oddly, the rotating structure of 'A' turret had not fallen out of the barbette although the gunhouse had been blown away. 'B' turret could not be located.

RIGHT *The port-side torpedo mantlets – a distinctive feature that proved beyond doubt we had found Hood.*

BELOW LEFT *An example of the limited implosion we saw on the underneath of Hood's mid-section.*

BELOW RIGHT *The shell plating (left) at the forward end of Hood's mid-section appears to have been blown backwards by an explosion in the forward ammunition magazines.*

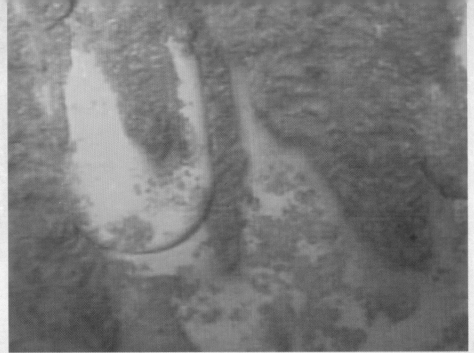

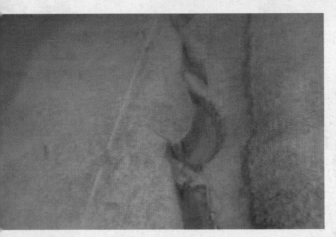

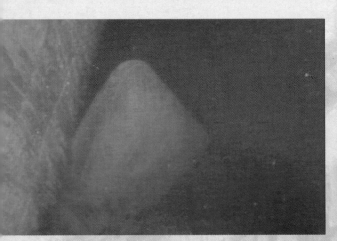

ABOVE *Hood's rudder stuck forever in a 20°-turn to port.*

ABOVE *Port-side shell-plating blown backwards towards the propeller bracket from the aft magazine explosion.*

BELOW Hood's bow lying on its port side.

BELOW The 650-ton conning tower was found over 1,000 metres away from the nearest debris field.

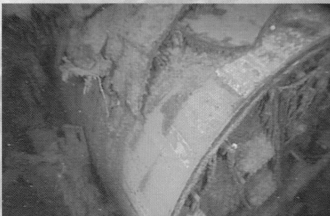

ABOVE LEFT Turret 'A', in its barbette in the upturned mid-section. The gunhouse roof is missing, thereby exposing several hand wheels.

ABOVE The side shell-plating along the entire starboard length of the mid-section was ripped away.

LEFT A curious rat-tail fish investigates the memorial plaque that Ted Briggs has just placed at the foot of Hood's bow.

The bottom plating of the inverted mid-ship section had experienced some implosion damage that Bill Jurens, in particular, found remarkable. He describes it as: 'characterised by long, parallel, longitudinal trench-like depressions in the bottom plating, terminating, apparently, at major transverse bulkheads. The shell plating covering the depressed longitudinal trenches has exhibited remarkable ductility before failure. Some preliminary measurements of the bottom plating suggest that the elongation at failure was probably in the vicinity of 35–40 per cent, indicating that the steel was well into the plastic stage.' This should finally put to rest the controversial speculation that *Hood*'s steel was in some way substandard and prone to brittle failure.

Up to this point we had accounted for roughly 210 metres of *Hood*'s total length of 262 metres, in the two major sections found (stern and mid-ship) and the missing 70 metres, which is actually represented by several large pieces scattered in the debris field. All that was missing was the bow, and, true to form, it was eventually found lying port-side down. Anchor cable was strung out in several different directions, inviting us to follow their links in search of *Hood*'s anchors. Sadly, none were found. The undamaged forward part of the bow evoked *Hood*'s former beauty and power, but the break aft told the true story of her loss. It, too, was badly broken, with the teak deck and internal structure aft of the second hawsepipe cover completely gone. Viewed from one angle, the bow was merely a shell, without any of her massive ground tackle on show to impress. This section of the bow measured approximately 30 metres, meaning that a further 20 metres were missing. Sections of it, including part of the breakwater, were found later in the western debris field.

It has been difficult to reconcile the damage *Hood* suffered forward of the superstructure with the various eyewitness testimonies. Ted, himself, recalls seeing the bow intact and the guns of 'B' turret slumped hard over to port as he swam away to safety. Given that he had escaped from the compass platform on the superstructure without injury, it is understandable that Ted expected the forward half of the ship to be largely intact – so did I. After all, the main explosion was aft near the mainmast. Could there have been a second explosion in the forward magazines that had ripped the bow apart as dramatically as the stern had been? Certainly the breaks near the forward turrets support this. The implosion damage we documented was very limited in scale and could not account for the massive destruction and outward-splaying of shell plating, whereas a second magazine explosion could.

A final piece of wreckage adds fuel to the fire. The conning tower – all 650 tons of it – was found over one kilometre away from the majority of the debris and two kilometres away from the upturned mid-ship section. While it appears that the mid-ship section planed away from the surface position where the ship sank, it is hard to imagine the extremely heavy, cylindrical conning tower going anywhere but straight down to the seabed once it separated from the hull. Could the conning tower have been blown free by an explosion of the forward 4-inch and 15-inch magazines and propelled away from the rest of the ship? Several eyewitnesses had noticed one particularly large piece high in the air. Was this the conning tower, or had the explosion taken place largely underwater?

In the light of what we had found on the seabed, it was necessary to reconsider all the eyewitness testimonies in case certain statements had been overlooked, or initially discounted when compared to the testimony of seemingly more credible witnesses. Two such witnesses on board the *Prince of Wales*, Chief Petty Officer French and Chief Westlake, had testified to seeing the bows broken, in the vicinity of the breakwater and forward of 'A' turret, respectively. French had also seen flames come up from under the water and run along the waterline for the greater part of the ship's length. This later observation was important because there would have had to have been a pathway of fire from the explosion aft to the forward magazines for this theory to have any validity. In describing his escape, Tilburn said a 'flash of flame came between the control tower and 'B' turret above the forecastle deck just as we were going in the water.' Similarly, Ted remembered a 'gigantic sheet of flame around the compass platform.' The origin of this flame could be the same that caused the 'spurt of orange' seen by Mullenheim-Rechberg coming from *Hood*'s forward guns as the bow slid back into the water. Even if the flame outside the ship had not ignited the forward magazines, it does suggest that the tower of fire that had vented upwards near the mainmast had also vented horizontally. This 'vast blowlamp' was being fed by 112 tons of cordite and would have been burning the guts out of *Hood* at the same time as she was being torn apart by the explosive pressures building up inside her. If these flames could vent 300 to 600 feet high could they not also vent 400 feet horizontally to the forward magazines in a ship that was rapidly breaking apart?

Our expedition to investigate HMS *Hood* was meant to answer one question: What caused her to sink so fast? *Hood*'s wreck surprised us in many ways and what we saw has unexpectedly led to other, possibly unanswerable questions. There can be no doubt, however, that *Hood*'s loss was due to a catastrophic explosion of her aft ammunition magazines, which had been ignited following a 15-inch shell hit from *Bismarck*. *Hood*'s back had been broken immediately: the obliteration of a 70-metre section of her hull is a testament to the violence of the original explosion. Precisely where that shell hit and how *Hood*'s armour was penetrated will probably never be known. The massive damage to *Hood*'s forward section points to a similar explosion in her forward magazines, occurring just before the bows slipped beneath the waves. The fact that *Hood* sank in less than three minutes, taking 1,415 brave men with her is no longer a surprise to me. The surprise is that anyone survived at all.

RIGHT *Magellan has a tight grip on the memorial plaque as she descends for the last time on the Hood/Bismarck expedition.*

TED BRIGGS' RETURN TO HOOD

The chance to be over the site of *Hood*'s wreck and to personally say goodbye to all his shipmates was very important to Ted. This was something he had longed to do since we first raised the idea of the expedition six years ago, and he had been deeply disappointed that his temporary ill health had prevented him from making the trip on HDMS *Triton* in 1997. As one of the three lucky ones who had survived, he felt it to be his responsibility to go back and pay tribute to the bravery of his friends and the sacrifice they had made sixty years ago. It was a personal pilgrimage that he would be making, one which we and the HMS *Hood* Association were absolutely determined to help him make.

Although the planning for Ted's return had been going on for months, the question of whether it would actually happen was totally dependent on the weather. We needed calm sea conditions, like those we'd had for the first transfer, but since that day, the seas had been too rough for another safe transfer. On Monday, 23 July it was publicly announced that *Hood* had been found. Ted was interviewed in London by Jon Snow for *Channel 4 News*, after which he caught an evening flight to Reykjavik. The following morning Ted boarded a tugboat I had hired to take him the 250 nautical miles out to where we were diving on the wreck. At the eleventh hour, I'd replaced the first transfer boat with the tugboat because it was bigger and safer, and Ted's safety and comfort was paramount in my planning. The round trip on the tugboat would take nearly two days – the longest time Ted would have been on a ship at sea since he had retired from the Royal Navy in 1973.

It was day twenty-nine (Wednesday, 25 July) of the expedition and because of the gale force winds which had been forecast for the next three days, it was to be the last day of diving on *Hood*. We needed to leave the site that evening to miss the approaching storm and start the long transit back to Cobh for demobilization. But in total contrast to the bad weather which was well on its way towards us, we were blessed with an absolutely perfect day for Ted's visit. It was fine and clear, with 5-knot winds and a low to moderate swell running. The Icelandic tugboat appeared in my binoculars exactly on time, her bow pushing out a wall of water in her haste to join *Northern Horizon* over *Hood*'s position. Ten minutes before she'd appeared, Magellan, with the memorial plaque gripped firmly in her left manipulator, had reached the seabed and was off to locate *Hood*'s bow. We were ready to receive our VIP guest.

I went over to the tugboat in the *Northern Horizon*'s rigid inflatable boat (RIB) and greeted Ted with a bear hug. I was so pleased to see him out there with us and in such

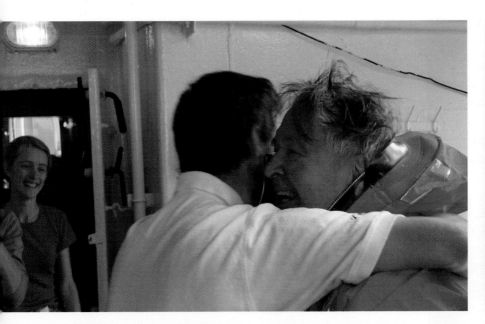

good spirits. In spite of his long and tiring journey, he felt very well and was keen to get aboard the *Northern Horizon*, and so I bundled him into a survival suit and we got into the RIB for the quick transfer. The RIB was winched up to the main deck and Ted was helped on board and into a crowd of people waiting to greet him. He headed straight for Rob White and embraced him. First around the neck, in a mock gesture of 'What have you got me into?', and then warmly around the chest. Ted's sense of humility and his humour – were already on active display. As we struggled to get him out of his clumsy all-over suit, he fixed us with a grin and said: 'I can't recommend the tailor!'

Liberated from his suit, Ted joined me in the lounge for a detailed look at the video we had shot of *Hood*'s wreckage. In the studio with Jon Snow he'd only been able to see snippets of what we'd found, so now he was seeing for the first time the full-scale destruction that had been levied on his former ship. Ted watched the horrifying

ABOVE LEFT *I am so delighted that Ted is safely on board the* Northern Horizon *I give him a second bear hug.*

ABOVE *In the RIB after having just picked up Ted from the Icelandic tugboat.*

pictures quietly, every now and then relating a personal memory about certain areas of the ship he recognized from his service on-board, despite their dramatically altered state. Without prompting, Ted wondered whether the first magazine explosion aft had triggered more explosions in the bow – a conclusion I was beginning to draw myself. It would have been completely understandable for Ted to have been upset by the images of the fractured and mangled wreckage, but more than anything he was greatly relieved: relieved that the death of his shipmates had been so mercifully quick. I told him he was a very lucky man to have survived this, but he made no reply. I think he had come to terms with his luck, but as the lucky one he clearly felt the responsibility to return to his ship and his shipmates for one last salute.

Magellan was hovering at the point of the bow as Ted and I climbed into the ROV control van. Troy Launay eased Magellan towards the anchor cable, which was draped over the bow, and down onto the seabed while Ron Schmidt positioned the left manipulator to lay the plaque in the spot Ted had picked out. For Ted, the bow was the enduring symbol of *Hood*'s beauty in life, and now the entombment of her crew in death. Sixty years after his service on the ship as a boy signalman, Ted's brave return to this place was the fulfilment of a promise he had made to himself and to his shipmates. Once the plaque was resting against the anchor cable Ron gave the manipulator controls to Ted for him to open the jaws and release the plaque. As if he was reaching down to the wreck with his own hands, Ted pressed the switch and let the plaque go: 'Farewell good friends, I have never forgotten you.'

As the clouds of sediment swirling around the plaque settled, Rob White joined Ted and me on the back deck of *Northern Horizon* for the service of remembrance to *Hood*'s crew. Each of us was to read during the short service, after which Ted would place a wreath on the water as I had done for *Bismarck*. We had halted the ROV dive to allow everyone on board to witness the service. The back deck, which was normally devoid of people, was now suddenly crowded. I had chosen to read a sonnet written by Lieutenant Steegman RNVR, (Royal Naval Voluntary Reserves) who had served as an ordinary seaman on *Hood*. He had read the poem over the site whilst on patrol there years later. I thought that it was beautifully poignant and I was grateful to be able to repeat Steegman's tribute to his and Ted's friends.

We pass, alert and cautious, o'er your grave
Now sixty years old. A thousand friends and more
A thousand fathoms deep. I humbly crave
Forgiveness for my tears; my heart is sore.
What blessed hopes would I not now forswear,
Deny my faith, distort the desperate truth,
If, by some miracle, the sounding gear
Could echo up the voices of your youth.
Rage on, ensanguined seas; hurl on your heads
The ancient curse of sailors yet unborn.
Not all the storms in hell can rock the beds
Of *Hood's* great company. No more I'll mourn
For now I know no sailor ever dies.
We pass right on. 'All's well', her echo cries.

Ted closed the service saying the familiar lines that I had heard him read in other services: 'At the going down of the sun, and in the morning, we will remember them.' Invariably, on other days, his voice would falter at the end, but not today. Ted had lived with the sinking of *Hood* as a dreadful memory, but now he was proud that he had returned and made his peace with it. The day was more of a celebration than a mourning, and so, with a broad smile, Ted thanked everyone on board who had worked so hard to make it possible.

I rode with Ted back to the tugboat in which he was to begin his long journey back to England. Rob joined us, and together we said our goodbyes from the tugboat's deck while a school of dolphins swam playfully between the two ships. We too had a long journey, back to Cobh, and there was little time to waste with the storm bearing down on us. This expedition had started as a personal journey for Ted to say a final farewell to his friends. For Rob and I, and for countless others in Britain and Germany who had supported us and joined us in spirit on board the *Northern Horizon*, it had become our journey as well. A journey to respectfully honour two great battleships and the crews that had served on them. Once they had been pitted against each other in war but now they were joined together in our peaceful memory. 'We will remember.'

Basic mosaics of Hood*'s bow (opposite) and stern sections (above). Note the plaque at the foot of* Hood*'s bow for scale.*

chapter ten

Drawing the **Threads Together**

Just as many minds and talents had come together for the expedition to find the wrecks of *Hood* and *Bismarck*, so too had the voyage itself drawn together many ideas about what had happened during those tumultuous days in 1941. Time alone will show the full story of what we found and what these great ships have to tell us, eloquent from their resting places in the depths of the North Atlantic and the Denmark Strait. Already the ideas of our experts, Dr Eric Grove and Bill Jurens are changing and developing as they pursue their studies into what was found and revealed.

For **Dr Grove**, perhaps the most significant lesson from finding the wrecks is an historiographical one. He writes: 'No single form of evidence is enough. What we found on the floor of the Atlantic alters our interpretation of other evidence which might have been dismissed at the time for lack of corroboration. This is true of both *Bismarck* and *Hood*.

'In the case of the wreck of the German battleship, listing to port, her stern sheared off, her shell plating below her armour devastated, one is the more struck by the state she was in even before the final action to destroy her began. The three *Ark Royal* Swordfish torpedo hits (as reported by *Bismarck*'s Fourth Gunnery Officer, Baron Burkard von Mullenheim-Rechberg), even though they were only from relatively light torpedoes, had clearly caused serious flooding as well as the crucial damage to the steering. Moreover, her list got much worse after about forty minutes of bombardment, as the British shells opened up numerous holes through which the masses of water thrown up by numerous near miss shell splashes could pour. The Germans themselves admit that the flooding on the port side was so bad they could not carry out their scuttling work there. So we have a ship in sinking condition, a condition that could not be reversed because of the devastating bombardment, before *both* the scuttling measures and the serious underwater hits by *Dorsetshire*'s 21-inch (53-cm) Mark VII torpedoes – with

warheads that *Bismarck*'s anti-torpedo protection had not been designed to withstand. Both are best described as a joint coup de grâce to a defeated and sinking ship.

'Neither the one nor the other, whatever the claims over the years, sank her alone. Also of significance are the hits that very clearly wrought havoc with her armament and its direction quite early in the action. Those hits so tellingly recorded on *Bismarck*'s forecastle demonstrate truly crippling damage to the forward armament, just as the lighter holes in the foretop tell of equally devastating fire control damage. To sum up, *Bismarck* was not an immobilized giant which committed suicide; she was a thoroughly defeated ship, sunk by the overwhelming power of the side that controlled the surface war in the Atlantic.

'As for *Hood*, I have now abandoned my support for the Director of Naval Construction's (DNC) claim that the torpedoes were the prime cause of the ship's loss. The picture is of an explosion with its origins in the after magazines wreaking havoc with the rest of the ship. The fact this did not happen in the USS *Arizona* at Pearl Harbour provides no firm evidence against it happening in *Hood* – *Arizona* had been heavily reconstructed, with better precautions against the spread of serious fires. I now believe that the 100 tons or so of cordite in *Hood*'s X and Y magazines suffered a massive deflagration that burned its way like a blowlamp through the ship. As it reached the engine room vents it shot upwards into the sky – but much also went forward through the machinery spaces, killing and burning as it went, venting upwards as Ted's "sheet of flame" around the bridge and igniting the forward magazines. Even before the ship sank, according to several witnesses (whose evidence must now be reassessed), flames were seen shooting out of *Hood*'s forward guns. The 100 tons of cordite went on burning as the ship went down, loosening the conning tower and causing the explosion, which we can now guess was what propelled a drowning Ted Briggs back up to the surface.

'But I do still find it most unlikely that all eight inboard torpedo warheads escaped the inferno; some must have exploded, perhaps contributing to the strange loss of the starboard side of the main portion of the wreck, and to splitting the ship where she actually broke; it is striking that the DNC had always said that, *in extremis*, an explosion of the warheads of the inboard torpedoes would break the ship just about where it is broken.

'My sad conviction that *Hood* got nowhere near *Bismarck* with her gunnery has become the firmer the more I have thought about the possible scenarios of how *Hood* might have coped with the sudden demise of her control top while changing targets at the same time. It is a pity that Holland turned when he did, exposing his vulnerable sides, but I find it quite understandable that he would want to develop his full firepower as the combined salvoes of the two German ships crashed around him – and scored hits. To criticize him for this would be the worst of armchair tactics. But, at the same time, the German success should not be overestimated. Exercise *Rhein* was doomed as soon as Holland's Battle Cruiser Force successfully intercepted the German ships – a major and significant tactical success all on its own. Lütjens' instincts against action were absolutely right. He was bound to receive damage, which he did, damage that fatally compromised the operation. In that sense the Battle of the Denmark Strait was a British victory, albeit a tragically Pyrrhic one.

'In a final twist, the publicity given to the expedition has thrown up interesting new evidence that *Hood*'s magazine safety may have been compromised by over-eager crews. If so, new theories may be opened up. A magazine accident? Or perhaps more likely, a potentially dangerous shell hit converted into another 1916-like catastrophe? The ghosts of Jutland may after all still not have been finally exorcised by the time of the Battle of the Denmark Strait a quarter of a century later.

'We hoped the expedition would answer all our questions. It has answered some; but it has also created new ones. But, after all, history is "an argument without end" – and our arguments about the loss of *Hood* and *Bismarck* are now fundamentally better informed than they were before the *Northern Horizon* left Cork.'

For **Bill Jurens**, the technical challenges of what we found also constitute an 'argument without end': 'Our observations of *Hood* have – so far – turned up no single "smoking gun"' he writes. 'The exact position of the final penetration and the detailed mechanics of the first half-second or so of the subsequent burning will probably always remain a mystery. At best, only a few eyes could have ever known the truth of the first few split-seconds of the blast, eyes which were all forever shut half-a-heartbeat later. But, although the investigation could not provide conclusive evidence as to what *did* cause the fatal blast, it did enable us to exclude or discount some of the less likely hypotheses.

'It is, I think, important to make some effort to refute the hypothesis – solidified over the years into a "well-known fact" – that *Hood* was lost due to some sort of inadequacy of her deck armour; in other words, that she blew up just like her thin-decked near-sisters at Jutland. Although a deck penetration does remain a distinct possibility, it remains very far from being certainly the case. *Hood*'s deck armour was augmented quite substantially during the course of her construction, and although thinner than her designers would have liked – it's well to note that armour is always thinner than the designers would have liked – it remained at least reasonably appropriate for the duties to which she was assigned. Although it is true that changes during design and construction resulted in an armour suit that could be considered as somewhat of a hodge-podge, inefficiency is not the same thing as inadequacy.

'The expedition found no evidence whatsoever to suggest that the composition or quality of *Hood*'s steel was in any way substandard. If anything, my examination of the wreckage indicates the contrary. Speculations along these lines are most probably based on the fact that *Hood*'s theoretical stresses were greater than almost any other ship in the navy. Had *Hood* suffered any unusual damage or distortions in her hull or superstructure, local repairs and reinforcements would have undoubtedly been added, as they were on *Nelson* and *Rodney*. They were never done. They were never needed.

'Although *Hood*'s deck protection was indeed worse – but not a whole lot worse – than that of *Bismarck*, this was more due to the need to provide *Hood* with a very large engineering plant than to some oversight on the part of her designers. In the twenty-odd years that elapsed between the design of *Hood* and *Bismarck*, armour theory and technique had advanced only a little – but propulsion engineering had advanced a lot. This meant that *Bismarck* could obtain her 28-knot speed using a much smaller and lighter engineering plant than that required by *Hood*. And the weight savings went into armour.

'I must part company with my friend and colleague Eric Grove on the issue of the torpedo warheads. We did find half of the body of one torpedo on the bottom, and it's possible that it is the remnant of the weapon, left after its warhead exploded. But my preliminary visual observations lead me to think this unlikely – leaving us, I feel, with no significant evidence that an explosion of the above water torpedo tubes contributed to the loss of *Hood*. Again, it will take months or even years of detailed study of the undersea videotapes to settle the matter.

'*Hood* was a good ship. There was little wrong with her design, and nothing wrong with her steel. The more one looks at the detailed records, for example the huge drawings of the ship in the Admiralty files stored at the National Maritime Museum, the more one is impressed with the sheer skill and creativity of those who conceived, delineated, and built her.

'As for *Bismarck*, and the loss of her steering – the single factor that led most directly to her destruction – there has long been speculation about whether some way could have been found to restore steerage, or to repair the damage. Most of this, one might almost say all of it, is entirely unrealistic. Although in good weather some ships can indeed be steered – at least roughly – with engines alone, this usually requires that the rudder be locked fore and aft or be missing entirely. When the speed is low, or when the weather is bad, then meaningful steering with engines usually becomes impossible. This is the norm, not the exception. As far as freeing the rudder goes, few individuals who have not been in the rudder room of a battleship (as I have) can truly appreciate just how massive the operating equipment is, and how difficult it can be to gain the necessary access to conduct repairs – even in a dry dock.

'After great contemplation, I remain unconvinced that the standard justifications regarding British activities during the final action are technically believable. The usual reason given for Tovey's rejection of an torpedo-plane attack to finish off *Bismarck* revolves around his apparent fear that the British aircraft would accidentally attack one of the British ships in the vicinity. But if those concerns were justified, assuming that gunfire really was the most effective weapon to employ against the *Bismarck*, Tovey should have known that *Bismarck* would have been much more vulnerable to long range plunging gunfire – from, say, 27,000 yards – than close-in pounding. At that range, hits would have been relatively few, but those that did hit would have been deadly.

'One of the reasons we visited the *Hood* was to try to determine why she was lost. But marine forensics remains an embryonic science, and the marine forensics specialist is very often faced with a site which is – to say the least – highly inhospitable and inaccessible. There is no chance of recovering sufficient artefacts to reassemble the wreck – a procedure which air crash investigators consider routine – and the wreckage is often overgrown with decades of rust and marine growth. There is no aircraft-style black box. In many cases the technical observer feels more like an archaeologist than an engineer.

'Does this mean that marine forensics is a waste of time? The answer is no. Today, it lacks optimum efficiency primarily because, as a science, it is so new. We are a little like the original physicians who began to conduct autopsies during the Renaissance. Their early efforts, almost laughably crude and ineffective by current standards, nonetheless laid the foundations of work to come. The scientific method properly applied may seem slow, ponderous, and inefficient, but it is, given enough time and evidence, inexorable. Time – and videotape – are our tools.

'Some fifteen years ago, in *The Loss of HMS* Hood: *A Re-examination*, I wrote that it was now possible that before long, we might gaze again on the wreck of HMS *Hood* – and that only then would it be possible to write the final chapter in her life. That final chapter still remains to be written because though for many, work on this project is done, for me the work has just begun. Data acquisition must now give way to the more complex and, it must be admitted, considerably less exciting, job of data analysis.

'Papers must, and will, be written. Other experts, many with considerably greater expertise than mine in specific areas such as metallurgy, explosives, ship construction, naval tactics and weapons effects, will be consulted to clear up hundreds of mysteries which remain, or which have been discovered anew.

'Amongst all of this, we must remember that *Hood* was populated by men: men who imbued her solid steel framing with a sort of soul – the kind of soul only an aviator or a sailor can understand. Her men are gone now, but *Hood* herself remains. She lies alone, in quiet dignity, on the bottom, cradling her dead in a silent, still-impregnable tomb. It must, at times, have seemed that no one would ever come to visit her again. But finally we did.

'As we approached her wreck with the first light she had seen in more than sixty years, I silently mouthed the phrase:

'See, old girl, the world hasn't forgotten you after all…it just took us a while to get here.'

Rob White writes: Why do we seek to remember? The human body and mind tend to grow away from pain – the passage of time heals by the blessing of forgetting, physical and emotional hurt fading so they can't be recalled as they were felt at the moment of injury. Usually, that is. In the treatment of post-traumatic stress disorder, understanding is growing that trauma can disrupt or destroy that merciful capacity to "leave behind". But still, reviving memories of great human disasters like the battles that destroyed both *Hood* and *Bismarck*, must risk the re-awakening of the sense of pain and suffering that we normally, sensibly, avoid.

Why then seek as we have done in three television films, a website, news reports and a book, to recover the sounds and images of a terrible battle in which three and a half thousand men lost their lives? At first sight, surely such a cataclysm, with its agonizing consequences and the deaths of so many, would be better left in its moment in history.

But even to say this is to begin to understand the need to go back. Firstly, because of the drive to redeem – to redeem some of the horror and the suffering and the sadness by better understanding of what actually happened – in short, to humanize it. We feel that the more we know, the better we can deal with a disaster that has befallen human beings like ourselves. We can order it so that the pity and terror which it is so natural to feel, finds a framework of understanding. That framework can only be built out of knowledge; and new technology, particularly in the world of deepsea search, is enabling us to acquire more and more knowledge – if there is the will to go and find it.

Secondly, it is in the very nature of the deepsea search itself that we find another impetus to go back, to re-encounter tragedy.

Until very recently, neither *Hood* nor *Bismarck* could bear witness for themselves. Today, thanks to the skill and resolve of explorers like David Mearns, we have the enormous advantage of insight derived from actual historical location – the basis of all archaeology, and much of history. The implacable sea has, until now, placed a full stop after stories like that of *Hood* and *Bismarck*. Now that full stop is itself history, and we can wrest something back from the greatest force of nature on earth. Truly, 'the sea shall not have them.'

Finally, there is no doubt that the story of HMS *Hood* and the *Bismarck* is one of the great epics of naval warfare, in its confrontation of one of the most famous ships in naval history with one of the most powerful battleships ever produced by a European nation. The three days that began with the catastrophic sinking of *Hood* and ended in the cataclysmic destruction of *Bismarck*, go beyond being major historical event to tell us something about ourselves – who we think we are and what we want to become, as individuals and as nations. It is a great story, and it requires – and deserves – a great telling, especially to a new generation wondering how it might fare when put to such a test.

Arching over all this is the need and the duty to honour those who died. It was a clash between freedom and tyranny, part of a long struggle in which freedom was finally the victor. But the adversaries in this battle had at least one thing in common: they were striving to do their duty by their countries, even unto death.

And as we witness the humanity and modesty of HMS *Hood*'s sole survivor and his 'opposite numbers' from *Bismarck*, we can allow ourselves the hope that they hold on to: 'Never again.'

David Mearns concludes: As Rob White and I began writing this book, one key thought was very much in our minds: when thousands and thousands of words – and so many learned books – have been written about *Hood* and *Bismarck*, would it be possible to shed any new light on their story? More to the point, would

people today really be interested in the retelling of a story dating back sixty years, when the world was such a different place, and most of them were not even alive?

These are two very good questions to which I had no answers when I first set out to look for HMS *Hood*. There were two simple ideas behind the expedition: to tell the human story of *Hood* through the experiences of those who sailed on her, and to find out what actually happened to her on that tragic morning in the Denmark Strait by a visual investigation of the wreck. The addition of *Bismarck* to the expedition, inspired by Sarah Marris of Channel 4 Television, was a bonus that gave us the rare opportunity to look at the common history of these two great ships from both sides of their conflict. But would the results of the expedition justify its great cost and the possible reopening of old wounds?

The answer to both questions I hope will be a resounding 'Yes!' I say 'will be' because although much new information has already been revealed and the immediate public feedback has been overwhelmingly supportive, the true measure of our work will not be known for years. We have returned from the North Atlantic with an enormous amount of data for naval architects and historians to sift through. Hopefully, this forensic information will lead to a variety of technical publications that will help form the definitive story of *Hood* and *Bismarck*'s final moments. The conclusions in this book are preliminary, and I have no doubt they will be added to and improved by others with far more knowledge and expertise than mine. I hope what we have done will encourage that.

Since returning from the expedition, I have spoken to and read the letters of many who lost relatives on board *Hood*. Their most common sentiment was expressed to me in person by Alexander Kerr Manning, a former lieutenant-commander in the Royal Navy, who lost his uncle (and namesake) in *Hood* – Alexander Kerr, an Engine Room Artificer. Alex was initially unsure about the expedition and admitted that

he would have been happy if I had not found the wreck, as my failure could be taken as a sign that the *Hood* was not meant to be found. When he saw the first underwater pictures of *Hood* shown during Channel 4's *Hunt for the* Hood documentary, however, his reaction was not what he had expected. He said to me: 'A lump came to my throat the size of a house brick. I had no idea I would feel this way, but I was filled with a great feeling of happiness. Happy because now I finally knew where my uncle was. He was there.'

And as evidence that a new generation could indeed be touched by this story, I received the following note posted on the Channel 4 expedition website a few hours after the documentary had been aired. It read: 'My interest in HMS *Hood* and naval history in general started some thirty-two years ago, when, as a very young boy, my grandfather (who had served on HMS *Courageous*, some little while before she was sunk) introduced me to the story. One late night, when my parents were out and I was supposed to be in bed, we watched the film *Sink the* Bismarck! together and from that night onwards naval history has captivated me. It was an outstanding experience to sit with my sixteen-year old son and watch your webcast. It was something that I never dreamed would happen. I also have passed on the passion, in turn, to my son who watched just as avidly by my side.

Thank you for your achievement and the great delicacy and respect with which the matter has been handled. I will never forget the experience.'

My final thought about the wrecks of *Hood* and *Bismarck* concerns their status as war graves. The governments of Great Britain and Germany gave us their respective permissions to film these sacred sites on the basis that we would look, but not touch or disturb the wrecks in any way. Throughout our expedition I was very conscious that we were visiting the graves of 3,546 men, and that every step of the way had to be taken with the utmost sensitivity both for their memory and for their surviving relatives. For me, the most important thing we did was to place the memorial plaques on the sites so the sacrifice of each and every man was properly recognized. While there are no human remains to be seen or disturbed on either wreck, it is the memory of the men that must be protected. The wreckage, whether it be *Bismarck*'s hull or *Hood*'s bell, is all that remains, and by extension to the memory of the men, must also be fully protected from unauthorized disturbance. At a time when legislation in the UK is being reconsidered with a view to increasing the protection for maritime war graves, my sincere hope is that the great amount of interest this expedition has raised will stimulate action in that direction. We all owe the men of *Hood* and *Bismarck* that, at the very least.

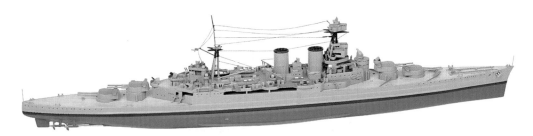

The 1:400 scale models of Hood *and* Bismarck *(top) that Colin Vass made especially for our expedition.*

DRAWING THE THREADS TOGETHER

NOTE

For a long time the official figure for those who died on *Hood* was 1,418, which is the figure that Ted Briggs MBE relies on. However, the hmshood website, having conducted exhaustive researches, now concludes that the true figure is 1,415. The best information the *Bismarck* association has is that 2,131 men were lost on *Bismarck*. There were three survivors from *Hood* and 115 from *Bismarck*. One German sailor rescued by *Dorsetshire* died the following day from his injuries and is included in the list of 2,131. After initially reporting the number of dead on *Hood* to be 1,418, the Admiralty later revised the number to 1,416. Unfortunately, this number has also proved to be incorrect because it included seventeen-year-old Norman Johnstone, a boy signalman who was killed along with thirteen others on the compass platform of the *Prince of Wales* when it was hit by a shell from *Bismarck* immediately after *Hood* sank. Somehow, Johnstone's name had mistakenly found its way onto the list for *Hood*.

SOURCES & BIBLIOGRAPHY

(Chapters 2, 4, 6, 8, 9)

Primary Sources

Bismarck

ADM 1/19999 Actions with the enemy: Sinking of German battleship *Bismarck*

ADM 199/1187 Pursuit & Destruction of German battleship *Bismarck*

ADM 199/1188 Pursuit & Destruction of German battleship *Bismarck*

ADM 234/321 No. 5: chase & sinking of German battleship *Bismarck* 23–27 May 1941

ADM 234/322 No. 5: chase & sinking of German battleship *Bismarck* 23–27 May 1941

ADM 234/509 Sinking of the *Bismarck* 27 May 1941: official dispatches

ADM 234/510 Sinking of the *Bismarck* 27 May 1941: plans

ADM 267/137 Notes on sinking of *Bismarck*

AIR 15/204 Sinking of the German Battleship *Bismarck*

AIR 20/1329 *Bismarck*: reports on sinking

CAB 106/333 Despatch on the sinking of the German battleship *Bismarck*, 27 May 1941, by Admiral Sir John C. Tovey, Commander-in-Chief, Home Fleet (Supplement to *London Gazette*)

War Diary of the Battleship *Bismarck*

Hood

HMS *Dorsetshire*: ADM 53/114133 Ships Log, May 1941

HMS *Norfolk*: ADM 53/114810 Ships Log, May 1941

HMS *King George V*: ADM 53/114504 Ships Log, May 1941

HMS *Rodney*: ADM 1/11817 Action with German battleship *Bismarck*: gunnery report of HMS *Rodney* & ADM 1/11818 Action with German battleship *Bismarck*: gunnery report of HMS *Rodney*

ADM 53/115028 Ships Log, May 1941

General

ADM 199/1942 Daily Ops Report, First Sea Lord, 1941

ADM 199/2227 War Diary Summary, May 1941

ADM 199/1933 First Lord's Records, April–June, 1941

HW1 1940–1945 P.M. Selected Signals

Führer Conferences on Naval Affairs 1939–1945 (Greenhill, London, 1990)

Sinking of Bismarck (Greenhill Books, London, 1990)

(Chapters 1, 3, 5, 7 & 10)

Bradford, Ernle, *The Mighty* Hood (White Lion Publishers, London & New York, 1974)

Coles, Alan & Briggs, Ted, *Flagship* Hood*: The Fate of Britain's Mightiest*

Warship (Robert Hale, London, 1985)

Hoyt, Edwin P., *Sunk by the* Bismarck: *The Life and Death of HMS* Hood (Military Heritage Press, New York, 1977)

Johnston, Ian & McAuley, Rob, *The Battleships* (Channel 4 Books, Macmillan, London, 2000)

Kemp, Paul J., Bismarck *and* Hood: *Great Naval Adversaries* (Arms & Armour Press, London, 1991)

Kennedy, Ludovic, *Pursuit: The Chase and Sinking of the* Bismarck (Collins, London, 1974)

Le Bailly, Sir Louis, *The Man Around the Engine: Life below the Waterline* (Emsworth, Mason, 1990)

Mullenheim-Rechberg, Baron Burkard von, *Battleship* Bismarck (The Bodley Head, Maryland, US, 1980)

Rhys-Jones, Graham, *The Loss of the* Bismarck: *An Avoidable Disaster* (Cassell, London, 1999)

Roberts, John, *The Battlecruiser* Hood (Conway Maritime Press, London, 1982)

Taverner, Nixie, *A Torch Among Tapers* (Bernard Durnford Publishing, West Sussex, UK, 2000)

Transcripts from interviews in 'Sunk by The *Bismarck*'/'The Mighty *Hood*', The Discovery Channel 1997.

ACKNOWLEDGEMENTS

Many people have contributed to making the *Hood / Bismarck* expedition a success. First and foremost I would like to thank the members of the HMS *Hood* Association and Kameradschaft Schlachtschiff *Bismarck*. Without their active support this project would not have been possible. In particular, Dieter Heitmann was very helpful in organising our meeting with the *Bismarck* survivors and with design of the memorial plaque. Specifically, I would like to thank Ted Briggs, Hans-Georg Stiegler, Heinz Steeg, Willi Treinies, and Rudi Romer. They graciously opened up a difficult period in their lives to be examined and for that I am eternally grateful. Above all, there has to be a special mention for Ted and Claire Briggs, who have given more of their time to this project than we could have reasonably expected.

Sarah Marris, of Channel 4, championed the idea of the expedition and it was her energy and enthusiasm that made it a reality. Julian Ware, of ITN Factual, worked alongside Sarah from the very beginning and steered the making of the documentaries to their successful conclusion. My thanks also to Sarah Ramsden and Tim Gardam of Channel 4 for entrusting us with their backing on such an ambitious project.

For their assistance in managing the project I would like to thank my colleagues at Blue Water Recoveries: Carole Menzies, Bob Hudson, Mark Cliff and Jim Mercer, who also created the wonderful mosaics in the book.

To Verity Willcocks and Emma Tait at Channel 4 Books for their patience and efforts in producing this book under the pressure of an extremely tight deadline.

My thanks to the representatives of the UK and German governments who worked to gain permission for us to dive on the two war grave sites: Captain Chris Palmer, Lt. Cmdr. Jonathan Hodgkins and Marion McQuaide of the UK Ministry of Defence; Hans Jorg Neumann of the German Foreign Office.

I would like to acknowledge and thank the following individuals and companies for their work behind the scenes in supporting the expedition: John Cannon, Steve Spivey, Brian Pulleyn and Simon Keane of MARR Vessel Management; John Kreider, Richard Fiske and Craig Bagley of Oceaneering Technologies; Tom Olkowski of Insite Tritech; Bill Donaldson and Clive Anderson of Thales Geosolutions; Pascal Cahalane of Clyde Shipping; Cork Dockyard; Gordon Mackie of Metworks; Tony Holland of IMC Superhub; Kristjan Tomasson; Stan Moroney and Alan Cameron of GSE Rentals; Joe Burge, Dick Bower, Malcolm Smith, Marilyn Bennett, Sophy Walker, Melissa Clive, Sophie Martin, Diana Hill, Jonathan Groves, and Kate Mayne of ITN Factual; Mathew Robinson, Jill Westbury, Rebecca Jeanes and Tim Bichara of Channel 4 Television; Dermot Blackburn; Patricia Martin of Holman, Fenwick & Willan; Martin Wicks and Danny Toull of Stackhouse Poland; Bruce Donald of Houlder Insurance Services; Yves Devillers; Peter Cope; Sebastian Remus; Chris Payne; Colin Vass; Sally Hersh and Tony Brooks; Frank Allen and Paul Bevand of the HMS *Hood* website.

To the entire *Hood / Bismarck* expedition team whose collective skill and hard work resulted in the location of both wrecks and the stunning images seen in this book. These are the people who were there, did it, and got the T-shirt: Jim Mercer of BWR; Captain Keith Herron and the crew of M/V *Northern Horizon*; Ron Schmidt, Andy Sherrel, Troy Launay, Dave Warford, Richard Dailey, Neil Corliss, Chuck Hohing, and Mick Schick of Oceaneering Technologies; Chris Jones of Thales Geosolutions; Will Handley of BFS Engineering; Rob White, Gary Johnstone, Emily Roe, Mike Robinson, Bob Newton, Kathy Taylor, Donald Begg, and Rob Gould of ITN Factual; Lindsay Taylor of *Channel 4 News*; Jean Louis of Devillers; Dr Eric Groves of the University of Hull; and Bill Jurens of Warship International.

Finally, I thank my wife, Sarah, for her love, support and advice, and for her understanding while I was away at sea and in the office on too many late nights.

David Mearns

I would like warmly to add my voice in thanking all those that David has mentioned – especially Ted Briggs. I have greatly benefited from his friendship, and his and Alan Coles' excellent book *Flagship Hood*. I am also most grateful to Baron Burkard von Mullenheim-Rechberg for permission to use extracts from his book *Battleship Bismarck*.

The wise counsel and firm support of Captain Bob McQueen CBE of the Royal Naval Association and Jonathan Powell of the Royal British Legion were invaluable throughout. Bill Jurens' profound technical understanding and extraordinary good humour have played a key role in the writing of this book. And I owe a special thank you to Dr Eric Grove of the University of Hull. His generous enthusiasm, inexhaustible knowledge, and eagle eye for new insights were also absolutely vital to the whole project.

I am fortunate too to have enjoyed such strong and creative support from the Editor-in-Chief of ITN, Richard Tait, in this as in many other projects. I am, as always, in his debt.

Finally, the love and support of my wife, Sue, has been the firm foundation on which all has rested. Over the last six years, going well beyond the call of duty has become routine for her, from coping solo with a lively family to proof-reading and greatly improving this book. I can only hope she won't agree too quickly when I say I really don't deserve her!

Rob White

PICTURE ACKNOWLEDGEMENTS

While every effort has been made to trace copyright holders for photographs and illustrations featured in this book, the publishers will be glad to make proper acknowledgements in future editions in the event that any regrettable omissions have occurred at the time of going to press.

Blohm & Voss: 2–3 (bottom), 33 (both), 35 (bottom), 56–7 & 63, 65; Dermot Blackburn: 75, 76, 88, 89; Courtesy of Ted Briggs: 68; Bundesarchiv: 35 (top), 59, 60; John Bush: 19; Central Press: 97; Discovery Channel: 36–7 & 52–3; GEBCO: 46; H. Holderness: 11 (bottom); IWM: 6–7, 20 (& 22–3), 31, 32, 64, 66, 67, 69, 98, 128, 142, 147, 148, 153; IWM/John Hamilton Copyright Mrs Betty Hamilton LD7415: 92–3 & 102–3; *Lloyd's List* : 39; Marr Vessel Management: 70 –1 & 72; Military Gallery, Bath, UK: 10, 124–5 & 137, 140; ML Design: 94, 114, 170 (top), 187, 200 (top); Musée de la Marine, Paris: 29; National Archives of Scotland: 9; National Maritime Museum: 50; Public Record Office, Kew: 109, 110, 111, 117, 119, 194; Supplied by RNAS, Yeovilton./Crown copyright: 131; Royal Naval Museum: 2–3 (top), 11 (top), 26; Courtesy of Sellick's, Plymouth: 13; Courtesy of Nixie Taverner: 24, 196; *The Times*: 40; Courtesy Frau Ute Urbahns-Junker: 34; Painting from autograph album courtesy of Mrs Yvonne J. Watts: 58.

The remainder of the images appearing between pages 36–55, 70–91, 104–123 & 154–220 supplied by David Mearns/Blue Water Recoveries.

INDEX